MW01093500

KANT ON REFLECTION AND VIRTUE

There can be no doubt that Kant thought we should be reflective: we ought to care to make up our own minds about how things are and what is worth doing. Philosophical objections to the Kantian reflective ideal have centred on concerns about the excessive control that the reflective person is supposed to exert over her own mental life, and Kantians who feel the force of these objections have recently drawn attention to Kant's conception of moral virtue as it is developed in his later work, chiefly the *Metaphysics of Morals*. Melissa Merritt's book is a distinctive contribution to this recent turn to virtue in Kant scholarship. Merritt argues that we need a clearer and textually more comprehensive account of what *reflection* is in order not only to understand Kant's account of virtue, but also to appreciate how it effectively rebuts longstanding objections to the Kantian reflective ideal.

MELISSA MERRITT is Senior Lecturer in Philosophy at the University of New South Wales. She has published widely on Kant's theoretical and practical philosophy in journals including *Philosophical Quarterly*, *European Journal of Philosophy*, *Southern Journal of Philosophy*, *British Journal for the History of Philosophy* and *Kantian Review*.

KANT ON REFLECTION
AND VIRTUE

MELISSA MERRITT

University of New South Wales, Sydney

CAMBRIDGE
UNIVERSITY PRESS

University Printing House, Cambridge CB2 8BS, United Kingdom

One Liberty Plaza, 20th Floor, New York, NY 10006, USA

477 Williamstown Road, Port Melbourne, VIC 3207, Australia

314–321, 3rd Floor, Plot 3, Splendor Forum, Jasola District Centre, New Delhi - 110025, India

79 Anson Road, #06-04/06, Singapore 079906

Cambridge University Press is part of the University of Cambridge.

It furthers the University's mission by disseminating knowledge in the pursuit of
education, learning, and research at the highest international levels of excellence.

www.cambridge.org
Information on this title: www.cambridge.org/9781108424714
DOI: 10.1017/9781108344005

First published 2018

Printed in the United Kingdom by Clays, St Ives plc

A catalogue record for this publication is available from the British Library

ISBN 978-1-108-42471-4 Hardback

To Markos and Eirene

Considered in its complete perfection, virtue is therefore represented not as if a human being possesses virtue but rather as if virtue possesses him; for in the former case it would look as if he still had a choice (for which he would need yet another virtue in order to select virtue before any of the other wares on offer).

Metaphysics of Morals (6:406)

Contents

Tables

Acknowledgements

Research on this project was supported by a grant from the Australian Research Council (DP 130100172). This financial support has been wonderful. I would like to thank Anne Engel and Sally Pearson for administrative help with the grant, and Harriet Levenston and Toshiro Osawa for research and editorial assistance. I would also like to thank my colleagues in philosophy at the University of New South Wales (UNSW) for their friendship and support.

Rachel Zuckert was extraordinarily kind to organise a workshop on the first draft of this manuscript, which took place at Northwestern University in May 2015. The discussion was helpful in many ways, and I would like to thank the participants for their acumen and generosity: Mark Alznauer, Jochen Bojanowski, Bill Bristow, Bridget Clarke, Andrew Cutrofello, Janelle DeWitt, Guy Elgat, Avery Goldman, Rafeeq Hasan, Sasha Newton, Stefan Schick, David Sussman, Helga Varden, Stephen White and Rachel Zuckert. I also benefitted from challenging discussion in a separate session with Chicago-area graduate students Abby Bruxwoort, Reza Hadisi, Morganna Lambeth and Hao Liang.

Some of this material was initially presented in talks, and I am grateful to the organisers and audiences on each occasion. Discussion of my earlier work on reflection at the University of Leipzig in 2013 helped me map out the discussion in Chapter 1, and I am grateful particularly to comments then from Andrea Kern, Matthias Haase and Sasha Newton. An early version of Chapter 1 was presented at David Macarthur's seminar series at the University of Sydney in 2014. Material from Chapter 3 was presented at philosophy colloquia at the University of Adelaide and Dartmouth College in 2015. Parts of Chapter 5 were presented at the Society for German Idealism and Romanticism session at the 2017 Pacific Division meeting of the American Philosophical Association. Parts of Chapter 6 were presented at the conference 'Nature and Culture in German Romanticism and

Idealism' (UNSW and the University of Sydney, 2015), the 2015 Pacific Division meeting of the American Philosophical Association, the 12th International Kant Congress (University of Vienna, 2015) and the workshop 'Conceptions of Practical Reason' (UNSW, 2015).

Some parts of this book overlap with work I have published elsewhere. Some of the material in Chapter 1 is drawn from my 'Varieties of Reflection in Kant's Logic', *British Journal for the History of Philosophy* 23 (2015): 478–501, copyright © British Society for the History of Philosophy (BSHP), parts of which are reprinted by permission of Taylor & Francis Ltd, www.tandfonline.com, on behalf of the BSHP. After writing the first draft of the manuscript, I developed the discussion of attention from Chapter 3 together with my colleague Markos Valaris; as a result, there is some overlap between my discussion of Kant's remarks on attention in the *Anthropology* and our discussion of the same passages in our co-authored paper, 'Attention and Synthesis in Kant's Conception of Experience', *Philosophical Quarterly* 67/267 (2017): 571–92, parts of which are reproduced here by permission of Oxford University Press and the Scots Philosophical Association.

I would like to thank Elizabeth Harrower and Text Publishing Australia for permission to quote from two of Harrower's novels for the epigraphs of Parts I and II of this book. The first epigraph is © Elizabeth Harrower, from *The Watch Tower*, published by The Text Publishing Company Australia, 1966, 2012; the second is © Elizabeth Harrower, from *In Certain Circles*, published by The Text Publishing Company Australia, 2014.

I would also like to thank Hilary Gaskin and the staff at Cambridge University Press for their guidance, and two anonymous readers for the Press for their helpful comments.

I have often been struck in the course of the twelve years or so since I completed my PhD at the University of Pittsburgh by the enormity of my intellectual debts to the people who advised and supported me during my time there: above all, to Steve Engstrom, who advised my dissertation on Kant with kindness and wisdom; and to John McDowell, whose work on virtue has influenced me here in surprisingly deep-seated ways.

I am very lucky to share my life with so kind and generous a soul as Markos Valaris. He is also an excellent philosopher. I enjoy and learn so much from our discussions about philosophy. I don't tend to enjoy his criticisms of my work, but I always benefit greatly from them. He found time to provide extremely helpful comments on two complete drafts of this manuscript, and talked me through several difficult patches along the way. And while our young daughter, Eirene, has certainly not read or commented on anything that I have written here, she has nevertheless weighed in on it all, by so thoroughly transforming my view of what does and does not matter.

Abbreviations and Conventions for Citing Kant's Works

1 Kant's Texts in German

References to the works of Kant, with the exception of the *Critique of Pure Reason*, follow volume and page of the German Academy edition: *Kants Gesammelte Schriften*, edited by the Königlich Preußischen Akademie der Wissenschaften, later the Deutschen Akademie der Wissenschaften zu Berlin (Walter de Gruyter (and predecessors), 1902–). I have used both the complete print edition and the electronic edition, which comprises only volumes 1–23 (Berlin: Karsten Worm, 1998) and is available in the Past Masters humanities texts database (Charlottesville, VA: InteLex).

References to the *Critique of Pure Reason* follow the Academy edition, but are cited according to the pagination of the first ('A') and second ('B') editions of 1781 and 1787, respectively. If the cited passage is included in both editions, the citation includes both A and B page references.

When context makes it obvious which text I am referring to, I drop the abbreviation of the title and cite just the Academy volume and page (or A/B pagination in the case of the first *Critique*). I have typically rendered all points of emphasis in Kant's texts with italics, ignoring the difference between bold and *Sperrdruck* as two distinct modes of emphasis found in the Academy edition. Generally, I explicitly remark on emphasis only if I have *altered* Kant's beyond this, so it may be taken for granted that any emphasis in my quotation tracks an emphasis in the original German.

My abbreviations of Kant's works track the German titles, as follows:

A Works Published During Kant's Lifetime

Anth *Anthropologie in pragmatischer Hinsicht = Anthropology from a Pragmatic Point of View* (1798) – Ak. 7

Aufklärung	'Beantwortung der Frage: Was ist Aufklärung?' = 'An Answer to the Question: What is Enlightenment?' (1784) – Ak. 8
Beo	*Beobachtungen über das Gefühl des Schönen und Erhabenen = Observations on the Feeling of the Beautiful and the Sublime* (1764) – Ak. 2
G	*Grundlegung zur Metaphysik der Sitten = Groundwork for the Metaphysics of Morals* (1785) – Ak. 4
KpV	*Kritik der praktischen Venunft = Critique of Practical Reason* (1788) – Ak. 5
KrV	*Kritik der reinen Vernunft = Critique of Pure Reason* (1781/1787) – Ak. 3/Ak.4
KU	*Kritik der Urteilskraft = Critique of the Power of Judgment* (1790) – Ak. 5
MAM	*Muthmaßlicher Anfang der Menschengeschichte = Conjectural Beginning of Human History* (1786) – Ak. 8
MS	*Die Metaphysik der Sitten = Metaphysics of Morals* (1797) – Ak. 6
Rel	*Die Religion innerhalb der Grenzen der bloßen Vernunft = Religion within the Boundaries of Mere Reason* (1793) – Ak. 6
LJ	*Logik Jäsche* = Kant's lectures on logic, edited by G. B. Jäsche (1800) – Ak. 9
Orientiren	'Was heißt: Sich im Denken orientiren?' = 'What is Orientation in Thinking?' (1786) – Ak. 8
Prol	*Prolegomena zu einer jeden künftigen Metaphysik, die als Wissenschaft wird auftreten können = Prolegomena to Any Future Metaphysics* (1783) – Ak. 4
Päd	*Immanuel Kant über Pädagogik* = Kant's lectures on pedagogy, edited by Theodor Rink (1803) – Ak. 9
VKK	*Versuch über die Krankheiten des Kopfes* – Ak. 2

B   Nachlass

*Notes and Fragments (*Reflexionen*)*
References to Kant's *Reflexionen* have three elements: first, the abbreviated title and reflection number (e.g. RL-2564); second, the estimated date of the remark, in square brackets (according to the suggestions of Adickes noted in the front matter to Ak. 14); and third, the citation according to volume and page in the Academy edition.

RA   *Reflexionen zur Anthropologie* = Kant's handwritten notes on anthropology – Ak. 15

RL   *Reflexionen zur Logik* = Kant's handwritten notes on logic – Ak. 16

RMet   *Reflexionen zur Metaphysik* = Kant's handwritten notes on metaphysics – Ak. 17–18

RMor   *Reflexionen zur Moralphilosophie* = Kant's handwritten notes on moral philosophy – Ak. 19

Unpublished Manuscripts

EE   *Erste Einleitung in die Kritik der Urtheilskraft* = the first introduction to the *Critique of the Power of Judgment*, unpublished in Kant's lifetime – Ak. 20

H   *Handschrift* = handwritten manuscript of the *Anthropology*, which includes marginal notes and crossed-out passages not in the published text – Ak. 7

Records of Kant's Lectures
On logic (Ak. 24):

LB   *Logik Blomberg* (early 1770s)
LBu   *Logik Busolt* (c. 1789)
LD-W   *Logik Dohna-Wundlacken* (c. 1792)
LPh   *Logik Philippi* (1772)
LPö   *Logik Pölitz* (c. 1780)
WL   *Wiener Logik* (c. 1780)

On anthropology (Ak. 25):

ABu   *Anthropologie Busolt* (1788–89?)
AColl   *Anthropologie Collins* (1772–73)
AMr   *Anthropologie Mrongovius* (1784–85)
AParow   *Anthropologie Parow* (1772–73)
Menschenkunde   *Anthropologie Menschenkunde* (1781–82)

On moral philosophy (Ak. 27):

MC   *Moralphilosophie Collins* (c. mid 1770s; see Naragon 2006)
MV   *Moralphilosophie Vigilantius* (early 1790s)

On metaphysics (Ak. 29):

MetMrong   *Metaphysik Mrongovius* (early 1780s)

2 Kant's Texts in Translation

For the most part, translations from Kant's texts are my own, although I consult the translations in the *Cambridge Edition of the Works of Immanuel Kant* (abbreviated CEWIK) when available (and, in the case of the *Critique of Pure Reason*, the Norman Kemp Smith translation as well). The series editors of the CEWIK, published by Cambridge University Press, are Paul Guyer and Allen Wood; the editors and translators of given volumes vary. Where I discuss or dispute a point of translation in the text, I indicate the translator in question. However, I do not make a note of every point of departure from the CEWIK translations.

The following editions of Kant's work in English translation were consulted:

Kant, Immanuel. 1992. *Lectures on Logic*, edited by J. Michael Young. Cambridge: Cambridge University Press.
Kant, Immanuel. 1996. *Practical Philosophy*, edited by Mary J. Gregor. Cambridge: Cambridge University Press.
Kant, Immanuel. 1996. *Religion and Rational Theology*, edited by Allen W. Wood and George di Giovanni. Cambridge: Cambridge University Press.
Kant, Immanuel. 1998. *Critique of Pure Reason*, edited by Paul Guyer and Allen Wood. Cambridge: Cambridge University Press.
Kant, Immanuel. 2002. *Critique of the Power of Judgment*, edited by Paul Guyer. Cambridge: Cambridge University Press.
Kant, Immanuel. 2002. *Theoretical Philosophy after 1781*, edited by Henry Allison and Peter Heath. Cambridge: Cambridge University Press.
Kant, Immanuel. 2003 (1929). *Critique of Pure Reason*, translated by Norman Kemp Smith. Basingstoke: Palgrave Macmillan.
Kant, Immanuel. 2005. *Notes and Fragments*, edited by Paul Guyer. Cambridge: Cambridge University Press.
Kant, Immanuel. 2007. *Anthropology, History, and Education*, edited by Günter Zöller and Robert B. Louden. Cambridge: Cambridge University Press.

Introduction
Rethinking the Kantian Reflective Ideal

0.1 The Importance of Reflection

There can be no doubt that Kant thought we should be reflective: we ought to care to make up our own minds about how things are and what is worth doing. The reflective person is not blindly driven on by habitual patterns of thought and desire, by the exigencies of tradition and external authority. She is able to 'step back' from all of this and assert herself as the master of her own thought. This is a commonplace Enlightenment ideal: Kant was by no means the first to insist on the importance of thinking for oneself, questioning epistemic authority and standing guard against the insidious power of prejudice.[1]

But in Kant, this ideal takes root in a metaphysics that distinguishes the mechanical operations of nature from whatever can be won in the expression of self-determined human reason. Kant understands the great bulk of prejudices (although not, as we will see, the entirety of them) as a tendency towards cognitive passivity, glossing them as the '*inclination . . . towards the mechanism of reason rather than towards its spontaneity under laws*' (LJ 9:76; tracking RL-2527 [early 1770s], 16:406; see also LD-W 24:738).[2] To make oneself into a properly self-determined cognitive agent – and ultimately into a properly self-determined human being – is an achievement of some kind. When and how is this won? Kant seems to tell us that we must aim for it on the occasion of every judgment. He repeatedly claims that 'all

---

[1] Kant and others debated the question of 'What is enlightenment?' in the *Berlinische Monatsschrift* and other venues in the 1780s (see Schmidt 1996 and Ciafardone 1990, 321–75 for texts). The topic of enlightenment also figures widely in Kant's writings, from ethics to anthropology to logic. One of the main sources of his conception of enlightenment is the discussion of prejudice that figured in eighteenth-century logic texts, including G. F. Meier's (1752) *Auszug aus der Vernunftlehre*, from which Kant lectured over the course of several decades. For historical discussion of enlightenment and the theory of prejudice in the Enlightenment era, see Schneiders (1983); for a focused account of these issues as they figure in Meier and bear on Meier's influence on Kant, see Pozzo (2005).

[2] On the methodological issues surrounding working with the record of student notes from Kant's lectures, and regarding *Logik Jäsche* in particular, see §0.4 of this Introduction.

judgments . . . require a *reflection* – if not before the judgment, then 'at
least following critically after it' (A260–1/B316–7). He speaks even of some
such reflection as a matter of 'duty' (A263/B319).[3] With this, we can begin
to make out that the Kantian reflective ideal might stand in an uncertain
relation to moral requirement and virtue.

Many will be inclined to suppose, in light of remarks such as these, that
the Kantian reflective ideal is precious, hyper-deliberate and repugnantly
moralistic. Versions of this Kantian caricature abound in exegetical and
non-exegetical philosophical work, and likewise across work that is both
sanguine and sceptical about Kantianism. An example from sceptical quarters provides an apt illustration: '[T]here . . . seems to be something wrong
with Kant's ideal of the rational person. This person is always in control.
Reason is always holding onto the reins of the soul, ensuring that mental
processes are in accord with rational requirements . . . But there is more in
life. Being rationally reflective and being rational are not supremely valuable modes of thought and being, but forms of thought and being among
others' (Zangwill 2012, 357).

It is no exaggeration to claim that Kant accords supreme value to being
rationally reflective. The error does not lie there. But just what this means,
and what the ideally reflective person looks like by Kantian lights has been
poorly understood. My overarching aim in this book is to show why the
supreme value that Kant accords to being reflective does not yield the common caricature, and to develop an alternative account of the Kantian reflective ideal.

0.2   Modelling a Solution

Why has Kant's conception of reflection been poorly understood? One
problem is the complexity of the textual record on reflection, which I can-
vas in Chapter 1: there are various notions of reflection invoked in a range
of different contexts, of varying degrees of technical specificity. I am going
to set those complications entirely to one side for now, to focus just on the
idea that reflection is a kind of 'stepping back' from the immediacy of judgment and action in order to inquire into, and critically assess, its sources or
operative principles. There are certain ways of running with this idea that
lead to obvious problems.

---

[3] In the Amphiboly, Kant says that anyone who wants to judge about things a priori is subject
to a 'duty' of 'transcendental reflection'; I give an account of transcendental reflection in Merritt
(2015).

Take Kant's claim that all judgments require reflection. If the relevant notion of reflection is some deliberate consideration of the source of one's taking things to be a certain way – and an assessment of whether that source entitles one to judge accordingly – then the requirement seems overly demanding and out of step with what we generally have in mind when we think of what it is for a cognitive state to be justified. As Andrew Chignell puts it, 'Typically . . . the sort of justification we're interested in is a state rather than an activity. A subject's belief that *p* can *be justified*, even if the subject doesn't *do* anything to determine that it is' (2007, 328). Indeed, it is perhaps owing to its apparent implausibility that Kant's claim that *all judgments require reflection* has scarcely figured in the interpretive literature on reflection; and where it is noted (as in Chignell 2007), there seems to be some readiness to pass it off as a slip of the pen.

But Kant's claim is not one-off. It appears not only as cited in both editions of the *Critique of Pure Reason*, but also throughout the various records of Kant's lectures on logic, in his handwritten Nachlass and in *Logik Jäsche*.[4] It also figures (albeit obliquely) in the *Anthropology*, where Kant claims that 'reflection . . . is required' for any cognition – including sensible experience – because cognitions, one and all, 'rest on judgments' (Anth 7:141). Of course, what Kant might have meant when he claimed that *all judgments require reflection* is a difficult question. The aim of Part I of this book is to address that question in full acknowledgement of the problem just raised. By my lights, the seriousness of the problem comes down to this: if we take the claim that *all judgments require reflection* to lie at the heart of Kant's account of reflection, and if we suppose this reflection to be a deliberately undertaken activity of some kind, then we will be hard pressed to accommodate modes of cognitive activity – modes of knowing – that are perfectly well justified, and quite possibly the expression of a certain cognitive excellence, but that are not deliberate in any direct or interesting way, like sensible experience.[5]

Consider next how a similar set of problems might arise for practical judgment, which in Kant's view is itself a determination of the will, and so properly expresses itself in action. Presumably, most of us act unreflectively much of the time: we just carry on and do what it occurs to us to do. We do

---

[4] See also LJ 9:76 ('we cannot and may not judge about anything without *reflecting*') and LB 24:161 (reflection is 'necessary for any judgment'). These claims are complemented by an overarching conception of prejudice as 'judgment without reflection' that figures widely in the lectures and hand-written Nachlass: see LB (24:168 (twice), also 165, 167), LPh (24:547), WL (24:863), RL-2519 [1760s] (16:403), RL-2534 and RL-2536 [both c. 1776–78], where prejudice is judgment that 'precedes reflection' (16:408). Further discussion of these claims follows in Chapter 1.
[5] McDowell (1994, 2009) is concerned with a problem along these lines.

not step back from the default views that we have about what to do, to consider in each case what its underlying principle is and whether that principle meets some legitimating standard. But this is what the reflective person of Kantian ethics is imagined as doing. This person is widely supposed to have some particular skill at identifying the 'subjective principles' – or *maxims* – on which he proposes to act; and he is supposed to be resolute about submitting those principles to the appropriate test. Kantian maxims are commonly interpreted as subjective principles of action specifying, in the first person, to do action of type A in circumstances of type C for end E.[6] To consider the maxim, the agent not only needs consider what he proposes to himself to do; he must also regard the proposed action as an instance of some action-type, which is linked both to some general description of the circumstances in which actions of that type are warranted or permissible or required, as well as to some general characterisation of the end for which such actions may or ought to be performed. So, our reflective moral agent must recognise himself as being in such circumstances and having adopted such ends as warrant the action in question. Necessary (although not sufficient) warrant for an action lies in its moral permissibility. The special test is supposed to check for precisely that – whether the action, determined as the action that it is in light of its maxim, accords with the requirements of morality. The ideally reflective agent is envisaged as someone who most assiduously tests whether he proposes to act on a maxim whose universal adoption he can coherently will.[7]

There are many problems with this picture of the reflective moral agent. First, it is not clear that one's maxims can be readily identified, as Kant himself points out on occasion.[8] Second, the proper scope of this reflective activity is unclear. Surely (common sense protests) I can act well – my

---

[6] Kant calls a maxim a 'subjective principle of action' (G 4:421n), but what exactly he means by this and how general such a principle must be in order to count as a maxim has been debated and remains a subject of consternation for Kant's commentators; among the best recent studies of the difficulties of interpreting Kant on maxims is Kitcher (2003). If one takes it that universalisation tests (the so-called 'CI-procedure') form the foundation of moral normativity by Kant's lights, then one will in turn need to commit to a particular view about what the general form of a maxim is. However, I do not assume this view about the foundation of moral normativity in my arguments about Kant on the importance of being reflective. I take maxims to be general practical commitments about what is a reason for doing what; I take it that, for Kant, these commitments are endorsed when we act (whether we step back and explicitly formulate and assess these commitments or not). The maxims that will particularly concern me in the central arguments of this book are the three maxims of healthy understanding, which Kant claims properly govern cognitive conduct.

[7] Brewer (2000, 2002) queries this picture of the reflective moral agent, and considers whether Kant offers the resources to reject it; however, his conclusions are ambivalent.

[8] O'Neill (1998) emphasises this, citing a memorable remark from *Religion*: 'we cannot observe maxims, we cannot do so unproblematically even in ourselves' (6:20). The lesson she (rightly, in my view) aims to draw from this is that the cultivation of virtue doesn't rest chiefly on introspection and

actions can be perfectly well warranted, and quite possibly even morally *good* – without going through all of this. Third, there is generally no time to cogitate in this way – to step back from the immediacy of action to identify one's maxim and perform an assessment of its universalisability. Further, in many situations, surely the *right* action, the morally worthy action, will be one that issues as an immediate response to one's simply seeing one's situation in a certain way. These are familiar objections to what is presumed to be the Kantian reflective ideal in ethics. Critics of Kant who lodge these objections very often embrace some form of virtue ethics, and contemporary Kantians who acknowledge the force of these objections have argued that the resources to address them can be drawn from later developments in Kant's ethics, particularly his account of virtue in the *Metaphysics of Morals*.[9]

The turn to virtue among Kantians is part of a larger philosophical trend. In the past half-century or so, there has been a resurgence of interest in the concept of virtue in ethics and epistemology.[10] In both cases, the movement can be described as a broadening of view from isolated episodes of action or belief to the character of the agent who acts or takes things to be a certain way. This broadened view calls for us to recognise that a comprehensive range of capacities and dispositions – including capacities of attention, perception, feeling and desire – is integral to a general outlook oriented towards the relevant moral or epistemic goods. Now, there are many reasons why philosophers have found inquiry along these lines worth pursuing. But within broadly rationalist quarters – where what makes character good or virtuous is that it is appropriately governed by rational principle – making virtue central conceivably provides a kind of buffer against the caricature, at least in its moral guise.

This is because the entire range of capacities and dispositions proper to virtue will be conceived as shaped – or made what they are – by reason. Reason infuses the whole package, which includes capacities that are passive in their operation, such as perception and feeling. The exercise of such

the self-ascription of maxims. Cf. Grenberg (2005, 49–51, 62–64, 97–103), who argues that O'Neill overstates the opacity point, and suggests that moral reflection centrally involves attentiveness to one's own inner life. While many of Grenberg's criticisms of O'Neill are apt, I argue in this book that reflection – and hence, in turn, specifically *moral* reflection – cannot chiefly be an introspective activity understood along such lines.

9   This approach to Kantian ethics has gathered considerable steam in recent years; consider e.g. two recent edited collections devoted to the issue (Betzler 2008; Jost and Wuerth 2011).

10 In ethics, the seminal text is Anscombe (1958). Attention to virtue in epistemology came considerably later – beginning with some of the papers collected in Sosa (1991). Not until Montmarquet (1993) and Zagzebski (1996) was virtue epistemology pursued from cues borrowed from virtue ethics, however.

capacities can be recognised as proper to virtue and, as such, no less an expression of the self-determination proper to a rational being than overt efforts of deliberation and inquiry. The virtuous person will not be pictured as excessively deliberate about meeting moral requirement, because it will be recognised that much of the moral work will already be done simply by seeing one's situation in the right light.[11]

I am sanguine about taking a virtue-focused approach to Kant, as my work in this book will attest. But the approach comes with certain risks – not least the danger of making Kant's critical philosophy, arguably the high-water mark of the Enlightenment ethos, into something that it is not. Much contemporary work on virtue draws on Aristotle, but there is little reason to think that Kant thought especially long or hard about him; in fact, Kant's conception of virtue draws more from the Socratic tradition developed by the Stoics, which has exerted relatively little influence over contemporary discussion of virtue.[12] So, we need to be careful about the philosophical assumptions driving any virtue-focused approach to Kant.

Further, while the recent focus of scholarly attention on Kant's conception of moral virtue might help to dismiss the caricature of the reflective moral agent, it is not clear whether (or how) it can address the problems ensuing from the *general* importance that Kant places on being reflective. Consider again Kant's claim that 'all judgments require reflection'. How

---

[11] This broadly rationalist tradition of virtue ethics draws typically from Aristotle; an important example is McDowell (1979). Herman (1993, 2007) develops a compelling Kantian account of virtue along these (broadly Aristotelian) lines. It should be noted that the development of broadly rationalist virtue ethics has not been uniformly neo-Aristotelian. Murdoch (1971, 36) argues that 'the exercise of our freedom is a small piecemeal business which goes on all the time' through the exercise of attending properly to persons; she presents her position as Platonic in spirit (and, it should be noted, McDowell 1979 suggests it as an influence). Although Murdoch's essays in that volume attack then-contemporary (i.e., mid-twentieth century) Kantianism, she is consistently careful to distinguish her target from Kant himself; indeed, despite superficial appearances otherwise, her own variety of moral rationalism is not so far from Kant by my lights (see Merritt 2017b). Reading Murdoch has influenced my project here to some extent, although I have not attempted to work with Murdoch's writings directly in what follows, and I won't make an explicit case for the closeness that I find. Grenberg (2013, 292) also notes Murdoch as an influence on her work on Kant's conception of virtue, but takes the *attention* required to live well to be directed at the goings-on of one's own inner life (2013, 24 and 159–86), which I think misses the spirit of Murdoch's distinctive notion of attention – although I cannot argue this point here.

[12] Grenberg (2005, 49–51) notes some of the distorting effects of taking cues from Aristotle when interpreting Kant's conception of virtue. While I agree with her remarks that some of the key differences between Kant and the Stoics on virtue turn on differing views of human nature (see Grenberg, 2005, 20–2), I also think that Kant draws more from Stoic ethics than she realises. See Sherman (1997, 99–120) for the beginnings of an account of the relevance of the Stoics for Kant's conception of virtue – although ultimately, she takes Kant to be more deeply allied with Aristotle. I do not track the influence of the Stoics on Kant in this book, but aim to develop this line of inquiry in future work.

might the common complaint that this requirement is overly demanding play out in the practical case? We can find an example in a recent debate between Martin Sticker (2015) and Ido Geiger (2015). For Sticker, universalisation tests are the foundation of moral normativity, and implicitly the fundamental exercise of moral reflection by Kant's lights. Sticker considers the worry that Kant may have an overly demanding view of moral reflection, which he aims to assuage with the suggestion that we need run the test on a maxim only once – after that, we can simply act on the maxim without again stepping back in this way (2015, 982). Geiger replies that Sticker's proposal effectively waives the requirement to be reflective, at least for the most part; what we should do instead, Geiger suggests, is 'make reflection less demanding' (2015, 993–4).

The spirit of Geiger's rejoinder may simply be to point out that by Kant's lights, a life that is lived well can only be reflective through and through – and not solely when we submit maxims to universalisation tests. That, I would endorse. But I cannot accept the assumption that such a picture of a reflective life should show reflection to be less demanding than the maxim-universalising view. For if we interpret Kant's claim that *all judgments require reflection* as calling for stepping back on the occasion of every judgment, and then baulk at the implausibility of this, we will have already conceded too much to a picture of the Kantian reflective ideal that I aim to reject: we will assume that the requirement is overly demanding, when we should worry that the interpretation of the demand has gone awry.[13] There is important foundational work to be done on what Kant takes *reflection* to be – in general terms – so that we might, down the road, arrive at a more stable and compelling account of its role in moral life. My arguments in this book follow that trajectory.

0.3   Précis

In Chapter 1, I begin by drawing a distinction between constitutive and normative requirements to reflect. It is partly constitutive of what it is to possess a rational mind that one has an at least tacit handle on oneself as the source of a point of view on how things are or what is worth doing. We cannot think at all without this; this self-consciousness – or *reflection*, I argue – is a constitutive requirement on thought. Reflection in this sense needs to be distinguished from the consideration of whether one has reason to take it that p or to φ: such questions can be settled in judgment, but there

---

[13] I thank Bridget Clarke for pressing me to clarify my point along these lines.

is a subjective orientation to such thinking that consists in taking a certain interest in oneself as the one who settles the question. I argue that this is the sense of reflection Kant has in mind when he claims that *all judgments require reflection*. As we learn through close examination of Kant's views on prejudice, his idea is not that it is impossible to make use of one's cognitive capacities at all without this reflection, but only that it is impossible to do so *well*. That is why reflection, in this sense, is a normative requirement on judgment.

However, the account I offer of the normative requirement to reflect in Chapter 1 is only preliminary, as it does not provide ready resources to meet the objection, already raised in this Introduction, that it is overly demanding (or, rather, makes the wrong demands). In Chapter 2, I suggest that Kant offers a more nuanced account of the requirement in question when he formulates three 'maxims' of 'healthy human understanding' in some of his later work. One of my aims is to show that the requirement issued in the claim that *all judgments require reflection* is both normative (we cannot make *good use* of our cognitive capacities without it) and yet need not be conceived as a deliberately undertaken activity of some kind. To that end, I argue that reflection, in this sense, is internal to sound judgment: it is nothing separate from considering the objective cognitive question *in the right spirit*, or *with the right frame of mind*. This is how I argue that the requirement to reflect in this sense lodges at the level of character, rather than piecemeal on the occasion of each and every act of judgment.

In Chapter 3, I take on questions about the relation between the constitutive and normative requirements to reflect, arguing that as soon as the first is met (and thus, there is genuine thought), the latter must be met *to some degree* as well. My aim here is to clarify what is basic to cognitive agency by Kant's lights. I do this by looking into Kant's remarks about perception, attention and experience in the *Anthropology* and in related passages of the *Critique of Pure Reason*. I argue that experience requires attention by Kant's lights; this in turn allows us to understand how the enjoyment of experience is an engagement of cognitive agency, despite its putatively passive character. From this, we can begin to understand how, by Kant's lights, sensible experience is in principle no less the expression of our rational self-determination than overt efforts of deliberation and the like. This concludes Part I, which focuses on the interpretation of Kant on reflection.

The account of the normative requirement to reflect in Part I raises questions about the relation between cognitive and moral character. In Part II, I argue for the thesis that moral virtue is a specification of general cognitive virtue, and that general cognitive virtue is nothing other than the notion of healthy understanding discussed in Chapter 2: I call this the *specification thesis*.[14] The specification thesis presupposes a certain conception of reason: namely, that reason is at bottom a cognitive capacity, albeit one admitting of distinct theoretical and practical employments. However, some Kantians think that only the theoretical exercise of reason is genuinely cognitive, and assume that when Kant speaks of 'practical cognition' – as he often does – the cognition in question does not share anything basic, qua cognition, with theoretical cognition. I disagree: the textual evidence, as I see it, over-whelmingly supports the ascription of the former view to Kant. Since this remains a contested issue among Kantians, and since the specification the-sis might seem to some to run afoul of Kant's remarks about the 'primacy of practical reason', Chapter 4 adduces the textual evidence for the con-ception of reason I attribute to Kant, and explains why my thesis does not get into trouble over the 'primacy of practical reason'. This sets the stage for Chapter 5, which argues for the specification thesis. There, I argue that healthy understanding is a conception of good cognitive *character*, which I then locate in relation to good moral character through the account of virtue in the *Metaphysics of Morals*. This work underwrites the project that occupies me for the final two chapters, which is to elaborate on the cogni-tive basis of moral virtue by Kant's lights.

In Chapter 6, I examine Kant's qualified endorsement of the idea that moral virtue may be a certain sort of skill (*Metaphysics of Morals* 6:383–4). Exploring the historical context of this remark, and carefully working out its philosophical implications, allows me to begin to make clearer and more determinate sense of the cognitive basis of moral virtue. This is also where my alternative sketch of the Kantian reflective ideal begins to take shape, firmly planted at considerable distance from its widely peddled caricature. Chapter 7 elaborates on the cognitivist implications of the skill model of

---

[14] 'Cognitive virtue' is not a term Kant himself used, and so I should set out with at least a rough and ready account of what I do and do not mean by it. I have chosen not to use the terms most widely in use in contemporary virtue epistemology: 'intellectual virtue' and 'epistemic virtue'. What is meant by these of course varies from theory to theory, but there are two assumptions that may be explicitly or implicitly bound up with their use – or interpretation – in contemporary circles. One is the common assumption that knowing is essentially or exclusively theoretical (i.e. concerns natural or historical facts); the other is the somewhat less common assumption that knowledge is essentially realised only in the explicit grasp of claims and principles. Kant himself assumed neither. As to the first, see Chapter 4. As to the second, we will see that Kant considers at some length modes of knowledge that are possible without explicit grasp of the principles that makes the knowledge in question possible (Chapters 2 and 6). So, I have chosen to speak of 'cognitive' virtue to distance myself from either assumption, regardless of the extent to which they may or may not be operative in any given contemporary conception of intellectual or epistemic virtue.

moral virtue, and demonstrates how this model plays out at greater length in the Doctrine of Virtue of the *Metaphysics of Morals*.

0.4   Comments on Methodology

One of my motivations for working on Kant's conception of reflection is to reconstruct Kantian commitments about mental agency. There is a tendency among commentators, when giving an account of the core arguments of Kant's critical philosophy – above all in the *Critique of Pure Reason* – to craft explanations of cognitive activity in terms of what faculty contributes what to the production of knowledge. But it seems to me that we should never lose sight of the fact that it is a *person* who knows, believes, perceives, is inclined to think one thing, judges another. Although there is a place for considering how Kant assigns various cognitive tasks to various cognitive faculties, in my view the core arguments of Kant's critical philosophy should be interpreted in a manner that tethers these arguments to a ground-level view of our cognitive lives, and the nature and scope of the agency that we have in them. In this book, I am mostly interested in the ground-level view; and to maintain some kind of focus on it, it will be necessary to take the results of the core arguments of the critical philosophy more or less for granted. Thus, I will have little or nothing to say about how Kant arrives at the particular set of principles he claims are constitutive of human reason in its theoretical employment, nor about how he stands to claim that the categorical imperative is constitutive of human reason in its practical employment. I am interested, rather, in what follows about the agency of creatures who are so constituted, in some sense, by nature.

Much of my work in this book connects the dots between claims Kant made in various places and in disparate contexts in order to work out his commitments on the topics of interest: reflection and cognitive virtue. This interpretive work takes place where various lines of philosophical inquiry converge – particularly in Kant's ethics, anthropology and logic. While my discussion has roots in Kant's critical-period works, it is mostly in his later works – chiefly the *Metaphysics of Morals* (1797) and *Anthropology from a Pragmatic Point of View* (1798) – where the key ideas that I am concerned with are developed. I have also found Kant's handwritten Nachlass and the records of notes from his lectures on these subjects to be helpful in this reconstructive work. My principles in working with such materials are as follows. First, while there are a few places where I consider at some length this or that remark from the handwritten Nachlass, my intention is that this should only corroborate a picture that rests on an interpretation of the texts Kant wrote and prepared for publication himself. Second, since the handwritten notes – collected in volumes 15 through 19 of the Academy edition as *Reflexionen* on various topics (anthropology, logic, metaphysics and moral philosophy, respectively) – came from Kant's own pen, I tend to accord them a somewhat higher status, as a source for working out Kant's views on a given matter, than the student notes from his lectures on these topics. For we in fact know relatively little about how the lecture notes originated; and in many cases, the notes were likely taken by professional note-takers who may not themselves have had any first-hand understanding of the topics being discussed.[15] This is not to say that the lecture notes cannot inform an interpretation of Kant, only that we should be careful about how we put them to use: they need to fill out and corroborate a picture that is formed by close study of the works that Kant wrote himself, and ideally also saw to publication.

Special concerns hold for the *Jäsche Logic*, which (perhaps owing to its placement in the subset of volumes in the Academy edition devoted to works published in Kant's lifetime) is often treated by commentators as if it were on par with works Kant wrote himself and saw to publication. Towards the end of his life, Kant commissioned Gottlob Benjamin Jäsche to draw up a text of his logic lectures; to this end, he provided Jäsche with his own heavily annotated copy of the logic textbook from which he had lectured over many decades, Georg Friedrich Meier's *Auszug aus der Vernunftlehre*. Kant's notes were written in the margins and between the lines of the text itself, and on interleaving pieces of paper; they are collected as *Reflexionen zur Logik* in volume 16 of the Academy edition. To generate his text, Jäsche can only have interpolated from those notes, and probably also from copies of lecture notes in circulation in Königsberg at the time. There is, further, no evidence that Kant approved the text that Jäsche came up with.[16] So even though Kant commissioned the *Jäsche Logic*, and even though it was published in his lifetime, we have good reason to handle it cautiously. When working with it, I typically begin by checking to see if the remark that I am interested in can be traced directly to Kant's handwritten notes, and cite both in conjunction when such correspondence can be found (noting that the relevant passage in *Jäsche* 'tracks' a given *Reflexion*). Then, at least, I know that the remark is not merely Jäsche's interpolation.

---

[15] For documentation of some of these issues, see Naragon (2006) and Boswell (1988). For a proposal on how to work with the lecture notes on logic, see Lu-Adler (2015).

[16] As Young (1992, xvi–xviii) and Naragon (2006) both point out. Something similar holds for Friedrich Theodor Rink's compilation of Kant's *Lectures on Pedagogy* (Päd) – although in that case, we know even less, since we don't have the handwritten notes that Kant supplied to Rink.

PART I

Reflection

Like most people, she naturally believed that what she had not experienced was either non-existent or of no importance. Who ever heard an egoist admit to ignorance?

Zoe, in Elizabeth Harrower's *In Certain Circles*
(Harrower 2014, 166)

CHAPTER I

Kant on the Requirement to Reflect

1.1 Preliminaries

My aim in this chapter is to show that Kant distinguishes between constitutive and normative requirements to reflect. This distinction has not been much noted in the interpretive literature on Kant. This is because the constitutive requirement that I have in mind principally goes under another name (pure apperception), and the normative requirement that I have in mind has been overlooked altogether. Prima facie grounds for pursuing my thesis can be found in Kant's distinctive, and well known, version of the cogito: 'The *I think* must be *able* to accompany all of my representations' (B131–2). Intuitively, this is a claim about the basic nature of a rational mind: namely, that a rational mind, or rather the possessor of such a mind, is necessarily capable of stepping back from its own representations in order to recognise them *as* its own. What it doesn't tell us is when and how this reflective capacity is to be engaged, and to what end. We uncover a normative requirement to reflect when we consider those issues. Kant's account of a normative requirement to reflect can be found where the concerns of epistemology, logic, ethics and anthropology intersect in his later work. My aim in the next two chapters is to uncover that account, and to situate it within an extended family of conceptions of reflection.

Let me first give some indication of the complexity of the textual record on reflection (*Überlegung, Reflexion*).[1] Kant sometimes speaks of reflection as (a) the activity of thinking quite generally,[2] or as (b) the self-consciousness that is internal to the activity of thinking or that makes it 'possible'. This, as I will argue, is the notion of reflection as partly constitutive of the rational mind. To reflect in this sense is to have some (typically

---

[1] Kant consistently glosses the German *Überlegung* (and cognates) either with the Latin *reflexio* or the Latinate *Reflexion*: see e.g. A260/B316, LJ 9:94, Anth 7:139 and 141, RA-650 [1769–70] (15:287) – strongly suggesting that he regards the two terms as interchangeable. According to Liedtke (1966, 208), the translation of the Latin *reflexio* with the German *Überlegung* can be traced to Baumgarten.

[2] See RA-425 [1776–78] (15:171), and implicitly Prol (4:288). This usage is rare.

tacit) handle on oneself as the source of a point of view on how things are or what is worth doing. We can't think at all without this; and, thus, reflection in this sense is partly constitutive of rational thought. More widely discussed among Kant scholars is his suggestion that reflection might be (c) some mental operation by which concepts, or general representations, are possible. I will argue that this conception of reflection is only notionally distinguishable from reflection in sense (b), and indeed that senses (a)–(c) are all variants of the constitutive notion of reflection. Now, as I noted in the Introduction, Kant repeatedly claims that (d) *all judgments require reflection*: and here, as I will explain, reflection figures as a normative requirement on judgment, since it is a requirement that one must meet if one is to make *good use* of one's cognitive capacities. My task in this chapter is to distinguish the constitutive requirement to reflect as it figures in (a)–(c) from the normative requirement to reflect that figures in (d).[3]

1.2 Drawing the Distinction: Two Notions of Reflection

Although the distinction between constitutive and normative requirements to reflect is largely overlooked by Kant's exegetical commentators, it figures in recent neo-Kantian work in philosophy of action and mind, particularly that of Christine Korsgaard. Since I think Korsgaard gets something deeply right about Kant's conception of reflection – something that exegetical commentators tend to miss – I want to begin by setting that out, before bringing out her work's potentially instructive ambiguities. Go back, then, to the Kantian cogito: 'The *I think* must be *able* to accompany all of my representations.'[4] The remark might be read as simply saying that a rational intelligence is necessarily capable of representing with some awareness that it is doing so. While that may be true, such a rendering fails to take

---

[3] This does not exhaust the ways in which Kant appeals to reflection. In the ethical works, reflection figures in cognates, where it suggests (e) a considered endorsement of practical principles and ends. This appeal to reflection is obscured in standard English translations, which, for understandable reasons, have Kant speaking of 'considered' (rather than 'reflected' or 'reflected upon') maxims and principles (*überlegte Maximen*, KpV 5:118; *überlegte Grundsätze*, MS 6:383–4), and of virtue as resting on a 'considered' resolution of some kind (*überlegter Vorsatz*, MS 6:380; *überlegte Entschließung*, MS 6:409). I will mostly consider these remarks in Chapters 6 and 7, but I will have something to say in passing here about KpV 5:118.

There are also, of course, (f) the special 'reflective' judgments at issue in the *Critique of Judgment*. I will not attempt to consider how such judgments might figure in the map of reflection provided here; but, prima facie, I see no reason to assume that these judgments can be *identified* with reflection, as is widely assumed (Allison 2001 is representative of this tendency). I would rather take it that these judgments somehow render thematic the essentially reflective nature of the rational mind, but I won't argue the point here.

[4] Explicitly invoked by Korsgaard (2009, 18).

the full measure of the principle's formulation in the first-person singular. When we take this duly into account, Korsgaard has suggested, we will be able to appreciate the broadly practical significance of Kant's principle. It can be admitted as a plain fact about how a rational intelligence *is*, that it can stand at some distance from its own representations. But this fact gives rise to a problem – the inherently first-personal problem of needing reasons to believe and to act – and, it seems, an imperative to address that problem. 'The reflective mind cannot settle for perception and desire, not just as such. It needs a *reason*. Otherwise, at least as long as it reflects, it cannot commit itself or go forward' (Korsgaard 1996, 93). Reflective distance allows us to view our representations as mere proposals about how things are and what to do – and, viewing them thus, to endorse or reject them accordingly.

Let me make clear what I find insightful about this. Korsgaard suggests that there is a master inference at work, that a fact about the reflective structure of the rational mind has broadly practical implications. Further, she suggests that reflection is internal to judgment. In other words, the objective orientation of thought is always implicitly subjective as well: what to make of one's own cognitive and conative constitution remains a live question, one that is determined, continually, by what one admits as reasons for belief and for action.[5]

Yet, the account is vague about the nature and scope of the requirement to reflect. Consider Korsgaard's ambiguous proviso that a rational mind 'cannot commit itself or move forward' without endorsing some of its perceptions and desires as *reasons* for belief and action, 'at least as long as it reflects' (1996, 93). It is in virtue of the reflective nature of our minds that we are *such as can reflect*; but that tells us nothing about when (how long, how often) we must reflect. The answer to that question, moreover, is not neatly separable from what we might say about the nature of that 'must'. If the answer were that we could not judge or act at all without reflecting, then we would be reflecting as long as we were judging and acting, and reflection would be partly constitutive of those activities. But if the answer

---

[5] Does Korsgaard suppose that reflective endorsement answers the 'need' of a rational mind for reasons by *giving* it reasons that it (or its possessor) would not otherwise have? Or is reflective endorsement, in her view, a matter of *recognising* the reasons that one has anyway, regardless of whether one appreciates these reasons and endorses them? It is widely supposed that Korsgaard is a voluntarist about reflective endorsement, and thus takes the first view (see e.g. Larmore 2008, 112–22 and Wood 2008, 106–22). I think this may be an interpretive mistake (but if it is, it is one which Korsgaard seems to invite); however, that is an issue for Korsgaard exegesis, which I will not take on here. I mention it because it is relevant to the question of what to make of the Kantian reflective ideal: whether the self-determination at issue rests on a voluntarist foundation or whether it is to be won through knowing, broadly construed. I will be arguing for the latter.

were that we could judge and act without reflecting, only we could not do so *well*, then the requirement to reflect would be normative in some sense. These sorts of answers about the nature of the requirement again do not swing independently of the question about the scope of the requirement, because they entail conclusions about when reflection is either (out of sheer necessity) going on or ought to be going on.

Now, the idea that the requirement to reflect might be *constitutive* of judging and acting seems to be blocked by the apparent fact that we can judge and act without ever putting ourselves, or finding ourselves, at the sort of reflective distance that Korsgaard has in mind. If we commit ourselves directly in judging and acting, then reflection might not be even partly constitutive of those activities, since reflecting will not be what commits us to a view about how things are or what is worth doing. We're already committed. The Kantian idea that Korsgaard draws upon here is that any analysis of what it is to commit oneself through judging or acting directly always uncovers some *implicit endorsement* of a view about what one has reason to believe or to do. Suppose my five-year-old daughter, Eirene, is struggling to tie her shoes. As long as she is trying to tie her shoes, even if she can't quite, then we say (à la Korsgaard) that she is endorsing an impulse or a desire of some kind: she allows the impulse to tie her shoes to be operative in her, which commits her to the view that tying her shoes is worth doing.

Before we complain that this grossly distorts the reflective capacities of young children, let's propose a distinction. Suppose that there is one sense of reflection that, as it were, goes on by default whenever anyone does anything – or has a view about how things are – at all. One 'reflects' in this sense simply by having some tacit handle on oneself as the source of a point of view. Call this **reflection-c** – since, as we will see, on Kant's view it is constitutive of the thinking of a rational being. It may need to be distinguished from – and complemented by – some souped-up variety of reflection that does not obtain by default, and which the ordinary five-year-old seems only barely capable of. This is the reflection that Eirene would go in for if, in the midst of her efforts, she were to stop and ask herself: 'Why bother?' Reflection in this sense belongs to the *deliberate consideration* of whether one has reason to φ or to take it that *p*. The objective question here is whether *p* or whether it is good, or would be good, to φ; the subjective orientation of such thinking consists in recognising that one addresses the question to oneself. It is not a merely tacit recognition of oneself as the source of a point of view on how things are or ought to be, but rather involves caring about how one's point of view is constituted. If we ought to care how that point of view is constituted – even though it will be constituted in some way or another regardless of whether or not we care – then we will have identified a normative requirement to reflect. Call it **reflection-n**. My next task is to demonstrate Kant's commitment to this distinction between reflection-c and reflection-n.

Let me outline how I will proceed. In §1.3, I present a puzzle about reflection that arises in Kant's discussion of affect and passion as distinct modes of reflective failure. Prima facie, any resolution to the puzzle would call for there to be two senses of reflection in play – reflection-c and reflection-n. In order for us to resolve it, we will need to understand how Kant distinguishes reflection-c and reflection-n; as we will see in §1.4, his distinction in this regard maps on to the distinction that he draws between 'pure' and 'applied' modes of logic: pure logic has reflection-c in its sights, while applied logic has reflection-n. What we learn about the distinction between reflection-c and reflection-n in this context will then be brought back to bear on the interpretive puzzle about affect and passion as distinct modes of reflective failure in §1.5. Although this approach will have us switching between two considerably different corners of Kant's corpus, it stands to reveal that Kant has a unified and coherent conception of reflection – or, at least, that a close family of ideas is at work across a wide range of contexts.

1.3   A Puzzle about Reflection

Kant discusses affect and passion at length in the *Anthropology* (7:251ff.), and makes many of the same points in his discussion of the self-mastery required for virtue in the *Metaphysics of Morals* (6:407–9) and of the sublime in the *Critique of Judgment* (5:272–5). I will draw on all three of these sources here, although my focus will be on the *Anthropology* account.[6] Many commentators who have addressed these passages have taken note of Kant's remarks about reflection in this context; however, there has been little attempt to work out what account of reflection is implied in these remarks, or to assess its relation to Kant's remarks on reflection in other contexts, chiefly in logic.[7] Such an approach has therefore done little to advance our understanding of what reflection is by Kant's lights. With that

---

[6] I examine the MS account of affect more closely in Chapter 7. On affect and passion, see also the following stretches of the student notes on Kant's lectures on anthropology from the critical period: Menschenkunde (25:1115–25), AMr (25:1353–6), ABu (25:1519–27).

[7] See e.g. Denis (2000), Frierson (2003), Formosa (2011) and Hare (2011) – where there is little effort to explain just what the 'reflection' is that is missing. Frierson (2014) does, however, provide an account: he effectively takes reflection to be deliberation, and holds that affect suspends the capacity to deliberate entirely (although momentarily), whereas passion involves deliberation or practical thinking but

in mind, I shall begin not by turning immediately to the logic – where *reflection* plainly figures as a technical term of sorts – but by looking at what Kant suggests about the role of reflection in the emotional and desiderative life of a human being when he points to affect and passion as distinct modes of reflective failure.

In this context, Kant presents reflection (*Überlegung*) as 'the rational representation [Vernunftvorstellung] of whether one should give oneself up' to a certain feeling, or instead 'refuse it' (Anth 7:251). He then attempts to illustrate this, at least indirectly, with an example of a rich man who is thrown into an 'affected state' when his servant clumsily breaks a precious crystal goblet. What distinguishes *affect* from other modes of feeling, Kant explains, is not so much its qualitative intensity – although affects do indeed tend to be 'stormy' (Anth 7:265, KU 5:272n; cf. MS 6:408) – but rather 'the lack of reflection' involved (Anth 7:254). To suffer an affect is to be thrown into a state of mind in which one is momentarily unable to reflect (Anth 7:251; MS 6:407; KU 5:272). As we will see, what Kant evidently has in mind here is reflection-c: affect involves losing even that self-consciousness that is implicit inasmuch as one judges or acts intentionally at all.[8] If so, then Kant already says too much when he claims that his unreflecting rich man 'gives himself over completely to this one feeling of pain' (Anth 7:254). For if affect momentarily suspends the capacity to reflect-c, it should not leave the rich man the resources to *give himself* over in one way or another at all: rather, it must be that he *so finds himself.*

How is affect different from passion? The first thing to note is Kant's claim that passion is compatible with 'the calmest reflection' (Anth 7:265).[9] The second is that the difference can be tracked by locating affect with our capacity for *feeling*, and passion with the 'faculty of desire' (KU 5:272n; Anth 7:252; MS 6:408–09). Passion is therefore an expression of a person's views about what is worth having, or going for, or doing – or, for that matter, rejecting or avoiding. 'The calm with which one gives oneself up [to passion] permits reflection and allows the mind to form principles on it' (MS 6:408; see also Anth 7:265). This is why Kant goes on to claim that passion 'always presupposes a maxim on the part of the subject' (Anth

---

without a consideration of the value of the maxims on which one acts from prudential and moral points of view (2014, 231). While there is something right in this (affect does suspend, among other things, the capacity to deliberate), I object to Frierson's assumption that reflection (of any sort) *is* deliberation. One of my overarching aims in this book is naturally to present an alternative account.

[8] By extension, it must also suspend the capacity to reflect-n; but Kant's *point*, when he says that affect lacks reflection, is that it lacks even reflection-c.

[9] Kant also says that affects are 'stormy and unpremeditated' whereas passions are sustained and considered [überlegt]' (KU 5:272n).

7:266): to be driven by a passion is to be committed to a view of what is worth doing, on what grounds, and for what end.

So there is some sense in which affect lacks reflection, and passion involves – indeed, as some of the preceding remarks seem to suggest, even *requires* – reflection. However, at the same time, Kant suggests that both are modes of reflective failure. For it is a striking feature of the *Anthropology* account that affect and passion are presented, each in its turn, as a kind of *blindness* (7:253, 7:266). I will examine these remarks in full once we learn more about how Kant distinguishes reflection-c and reflection-n in logic. At this point, we can assume that Kant is speaking metaphorically: someone who succumbs to affect, or is caught up in the throes of passion, does not literally lose visual capacity. The idea is rather that these are states where one fails to notice something one ought to notice. Someone who is blind in this metaphorical way needs to look again, consider a situation – or perhaps an entire past history – in a new light. And this means, in a common-sense way, that such a person ought to *reflect*. Now, ultimately I will provide more of an interpretation of Kant's claims about the blindness of affect and passion, as the blindness is not quite the same in each case. But the common-sense connection between metaphorical blindness and reflective failure provides enough to go on to see that there is a puzzle here: If affect and passion are both modes of reflective failure, then how can Kant say that affect lacks reflection, while passion is compatible with – and may even require – reflection? The solution must be that Kant draws on different notions of reflection. Affect lacks reflection altogether: it is a momentary madness, whereby one loses one's grip on oneself as the source of a point of view on how things are and what is worth doing. Affect lacks reflection-c, and a fortiori lacks reflection-n. But passion involves reflection-c: a passionate person takes a point of view on how things are and what is worth doing. Yet, affect and passion are alike modes of reflective failure, since they render one blind to what one needs to pay attention to in order to see one's situation aright. And this, ultimately, needs to be understood in terms of the normative requirement to reflect.

1.4 Constitutive and Normative Requirements to Reflect as Distinguished in Logic

The distinction that I have been sketching between constitutive and normative requirements to reflect is clearly demarcated in Kant's logic: for, this distinction tracks the distinction that Kant draws between 'pure' and 'applied' logic. So, I will begin with a few words about Kant's conception of logic, focusing on how he draws that division (§1.4.1). I will then identify the conception of reflection that figures in pure general logic, showing it to be a constitutive requirement on thought (§1.4.2). The normative requirement to reflect is expressed in Kant's repeated claim that *all judgments require reflection*: I will explain how this counts as a normative requirement on judgment, and provide a preliminary interpretation of this claim (§1.4.3).[10]

1.4.1 Logic: Pure and Applied, Domain-Independent and Domain-Relative

Kant elaborates on his conception of logic when he introduces his readers to the project of 'transcendental logic' that will occupy him for the vast bulk of the *Critique of Pure Reason*. Logic is 'the science of the rules of the understanding in general' (A52/B76); it is concerned with the necessary rules of thought. Kant first points out that logic can be distinguished depending on whether it is concerned with 'the general, or the special, employment of the understanding' (A52/B76). General logic is concerned with the necessary rules of thought as such, and so it abstracts from any consideration of what our thought might be about (A52/B76–7; cf. G 4:387). General logic is, as I will say, *domain-independent*. 'The logic of the special employment of the understanding' does not make this abstraction; it 'contains the rules for thinking correctly about a certain kind of objects' (A52/B76). With this, Kant points to *domain-relative* logic. The transcendental logic that Kant aims to pursue in the *Critique of Pure Reason* is domain-relative: it is chiefly concerned with the necessary rules for thought about phenomenal objects, or objects in the domain of nature.[11] Kant also distinguishes between pure and applied logic. Thus, he maps logical inquiry along two axes: a logic can be either pure or applied, and either general or domain-relative. (Table 1 shows these two axes.)

In principle, this yields four modes of logical inquiry: pure general logic, pure domain-relative logic, applied general logic and applied domain-relative logic. I will be mostly concerned with the division between pure and applied logic here, since that is what enables us to pick out distinct constitutive and normative requirements to reflect. To distinguish pure from applied logic, Kant says that pure logic abstracts entirely

---

[10] The discussion in §1.4 is drawn from Merritt (2015), 'Varieties of Reflection in Kant's Logic', *British Journal for the History of Philosophy* copyright © BSHP, reprinted by permission of Taylor & Francis Ltd, www.tandfonline.com on behalf of BSHP.

[11] Cf. Tolley (2012) for a contrasting (and, I think, far more controversial) position denying the domain-relative status of transcendental logic.

from all empirical conditions under which our understanding is exercised [ausgeübt], e.g. from the influence of the senses, the play of imagination, the force of habit and inclination, etc., and so from all sources of prejudice. (A53/B77)

By abstracting entirely from all empirical conditions under which our cognitive capacities are put to use, pure logic sets to one side certain facts about human psychology that make us liable not to make good use of our cognitive capacities. Thus, applied logic deals with the broadly practical *problem* of how to make good use of our cognitive capacities: I will consider it in §1.4.3. Pure logic sets this problem entirely to one side. Pure logic deals with *constitutive* requirements on thought: that without which there could be no employment of the understanding – no thinking – at all. Thus, Kant remarks that *pure* general logic 'contains the absolutely necessary rules of thought, without which there could be no employment of the understanding' (A52/B76).[12] By contrast, applied logic is concerned with *normative* requirements on thought, or with what is necessary to make good use of our cognitive capacities.[13]

Kant continues by likening the division between pure and applied logic to the division between 'pure ethics' and a 'doctrine of virtue'. Pure ethics

---

[12] This remark is one half of a sentence in which Kant accounts for what pure general logic is. Kant, I am arguing, maps logical inquiry along two axes: pure versus applied, and general versus domain-relative. Pure general logic is plotted along both: it is pure and it is general. The remark I have just quoted in the main texts glosses its *purity*; Kant continues, glossing its *generality*: 'it treats of understanding without any regard for the difference of the objects to which the understanding may be directed' (A52/B76). Here, we are concerned just with the distinction between pure and applied logic – the horizontal axis of Table 1. That is why I have relegated this complication to a footnote. I provide a more extensive account of Kant's mapping logical inquiry along these two axes in Merritt (2015).

[13] Tolley (2006) argues against the prevailing view that Kant takes logic to be a 'normative' science – a view that he notes is based almost entirely on LJ (9:13–16) and argues is at odds with a range of Kant's other views. (I would add that I have been unable to trace LJ (9:13–16) to Kant's handwritten notes on logic, which might place it under further suspicion.) Tolley does not draw attention to the distinction between pure and applied general logic: his remarks mostly assume that logic is pure, not applied. On Tolley's terms, a being that is subject to a normative law 'must both be able to succeed *and be able to fail* to act (or be) in accordance with the law' (2006, 375). What I would add to this is that such a possibility comes into view with *applied* logic.

But surely there is some sense in which pure logic should be deemed 'normative': after all, Kant speaks of logic (evidently meaning pure general logic) as a 'canon' for the 'correct use' of cognitive capacities (A796/B824; RL-1571 [early to middle 1750s] 16:8; RL-1579 [1760s] 16:18; RL-2173 [late 1770s] 16:258; cf. A132/B171). What does it mean to say that logic is a canon for correct use? Consider that there is something like a canon (a set of rules) for permissible moves in chess; someone who makes a canon-violating move is doing *something else* with the pieces – something other than playing chess. Something similar might be said of one who violates a rule in the canon of pure general logic: he is not, in this instance, (e.g.) inferring at all. So we might say that a canon is 'normative' because it regulates practice by ruling things out of bounds, as non-thought and non-chess; but this is not the sense I have in mind here, which aligns with Tolley (2006) as well.

provides an account of the principles constitutive of any determination of the good, whereas a doctrine of virtue 'considers these laws under the hindrances of the feelings, inclinations, and passions to which human beings are more or less subject' (A55/B79; see also G 4:410n). Where this comparison breaks down, of course, is that ethics is a domain-relative inquiry, and *general* logic is not.[14] But no matter: for, at present, we are concerned just with Kant's distinction between pure and applied logic. Pure logic is concerned with the constitutive requirements on thought; and pure ethics is likewise concerned with the constitutive requirements on practical thought about the good. Applied logic is concerned with the normative requirements on making good use of our cognitive capacities, taking full account of the human liability not to do so; and a 'doctrine of virtue', as Kant sketches it here, is similarly concerned with the determination of the good in the face of the normal human liability not to move sure-footedly on this.[15]

Having distinguished between pure and applied logic, my next aim is to identify senses of reflection proper to each. In §1.4.2, I will argue that pure logic is concerned with reflection-c, which is most basically pure apperception. In §1.4.3, I will show that applied logic is concerned with reflection-n, and in that context will offer a provisional interpretation of the claim that *all judgments require reflection*.

1.4.2   Reflection-c in Pure Logic

Pure logic deals with constitutively necessary principles and sources of thought; so, to identify the reflection that belongs under the scope of pure logic, we will need to begin by considering what thought is. Kant says that some animals can compare and associate representations, but they do not think.[16] Kant generally speaks of thinking as the activity of the intellect or understanding (broadly construed); and he takes this activity to involve

---

[14] That ethics and logic differ in this way is made quite explicit at G (4:387).

[15] Note that the transition from pure ethics to the doctrine of virtue, and likewise from pure to applied logic, does not amount to a change of subject: it is not as if the moral law becomes irrelevant in the doctrine of virtue, or the law of non-contradiction irrelevant in applied logic. The 'applied' inquiries consider the same principles, only with certain facts about the human condition now brought clearly into view. Yet, *for that very reason*, additional principles that have no place on the left will become special foci of concern in the 'applied' inquiries – the three maxims of healthy understanding will provide an example of this later. Thanks to Mark Alznauer for prompting this clarification.

[16] Anth §1 (7:127); LJ (9:64–5); LD-W (24:702); MetMrong (29:888).

general representations – concepts, fundamentally.[17] Thus, we think whenever we conceive a general representation (a concept), and in turn whenever we employ a concept as the determination of some other representation (i.e. judge), and finally whenever we consider the entailment and exclusion relations among given judgments (i.e. infer). So, all thinking, it seems, depends on concepts.

Is there any claim in the offing that concepts depend on some activity or operation of the mind that could be called 'reflection'? If so, then that would be a conception of reflection that naturally figures within the ambit of pure general logic. Most recent accounts of Kant on reflection are anchored in a passage from *Logik Jäsche* that claims that the source of concepts 'as to their form' – i.e. as to their mere generality, irrespective of content – consists in three 'logical acts of understanding [logische Verstandes-Actus]':

(1) *comparison* [*Comparation*], i.e. the comparison [Vergleichung] of representations among one another in relation to the unity of consciousness;

(2) *reflection* [*Reflexion*], i.e. the reflection as to how various representations can be conceived in one consciousness .[Überlegung . . . wie verschiedene Vorstellungen in Einem Bewußtsein begriffen sein können]; and finally

(3) *abstraction* [*Abstraction*], or the separation [Absonderung] of everything else in which the given representations differ (LJ 9:94).

The passage is billed as an account of the 'logical origin' of concepts. Since this account belongs under the banner of *general* logic, it abstracts entirely from what thought might be about. There can be nothing left for such an account to concern except the mental activity in virtue of which it is possible to represent with the form of generality at all. That is why the text indicates that general logic can consider concepts 'only *subjectively*' (LJ 9:94): it claims that concepts are possible through a certain mental activity.[18] These three mental operations, the text claims, 'constitute [ausmachen] a concept' (LJ 9:93).

---

[17] An exception might be the aesthetic judgment of reflection, a non-cognitive mode of judgment that nevertheless exercises the 'faculty of concepts' but without employing any particular concept. However, as already noted, I am bracketing this type of judgment for present purposes.

[18] Longuenesse (1998, 5–6) and Smit (1999, 209–10) both note that while we today tend to assume that talk of mental operations has no place in pure logic, early modern logicians did not.

Let me pause to acknowledge the received view about what reflection is for Kant. Most commentators focus on this passage about the three mental acts (comparison, reflection, abstraction), together with the example that Jäsche appended about looking at a spruce, a willow and a linden and forming the concept *tree* (LJ 9:94–95). Many have taken note of the circularity of this account; I argue at length elsewhere (Merritt 2015) that we should be wary of supposing that Kant means to put on offer an account of the generation of concepts from non-conceptual materials, and that the spruce–willow–linden example (which cannot be traced to Kant's handwritten notes) should not have canonical status in our interpretation of what Kant means by 'reflection'. By contrast, the 'three mental acts' passage just quoted, with the attendant suggestion that they are the mental operations required to represent with the form of generality at all, can be traced nearly verbatim to RL-2876 [c. 1776–78 or c. 1778–83] (16:555). Now, it would distract from the present line of thought to rehearse my arguments against the widespread view that reflection for Kant *just is* some mental operation involved in the *generation* of concepts from non-conceptual materials. What I will take on board here is rather the idea that *one* sense of reflection, for Kant, is a certain mental operation required to *grasp* a concept – i.e., to represent with the form of generality at all. My immediate aim now is to show why this counts as a mode of reflection-c.[19]

The 'three mental acts' passage points to a kind of reflection that figures as a constitutive requirement on thinking. But what exactly is this requirement? The passage glosses reflection as the recognition of some basis for unifying mental contents into a single thought. This activity presupposes some comparison of representations, disregarding features in which they differ. To recognise both that the book is green and that the cup is as well is to represent them both through one and the same rule – even though, in

---

[19] Like most commentators, Frierson (2014, 103–4) takes it that the reflection mentioned in the three mental acts passage (LJ 9:93–4) is a certain mental operation involved in the *generation* of concepts from non-conceptual materials, and accordingly draws on the spruce–willow–linden example that follows in Jäsche's compilation. However, he departs from the received view in taking this notion of reflection to point to a *normative* requirement on concept formation. Kant, on Frierson's reading, is not there making a claim about 'how people in fact arrive at concepts, but how one *should* arrive at concepts' (2014, 104). But it is puzzling how this suggestion could accord with Kant's claim that the three mental acts *constitute* what it is to represent with the form of generality at all. Thus, even if one's concepts are badly formed – although Frierson doesn't spell out how to think about this – thinking them at all should still involve the three mental acts, according to Kant. (By my lights, the background problem here is that Frierson does not take account of Kant's distinction between pure and applied logic; so, when he goes on to suggest that the normative ideal of concept formation is nothing other than 'healthy understanding', he has crossed from pure logic, which deals with constitutive requirements on thought, to applied logic, which deals with normative requirements on judgment – without clearly appreciating the difference.)

their particularity, they might be quite different shades of green. To do this is to grasp a rule that can govern the determination of indefinitely many other representations. If the same thing is thought in all of these determinations, then there is a sense in which one and the same 'consciousness' unifies them. Representations, moreover, are unified only in thinking them; they are not unified, as it were, under their own steam. Therefore, the appreciation of how various representations can be grasped in one and the same consciousness (to 'reflect', as it is put here) entails, as part of this, the thinking subject's at least tacit handle on himself as the source of this unity.

At the outset of this chapter, I briefly took account of the complexity of Kant's textual record on reflection. I noted that Kant sometimes speaks of reflection as (a) the activity of thinking generally, and sometimes (b) as the self-consciousness that is internal to the activity of thinking or that makes it 'possible'. Further, there is the bit of the textual record that we have just considered here where reflection is (c) some mental operation by which concepts are possible. Under (a), the activity of the intellect is conceived in the highly general terms by which it is distinguished from sensibility. We see this when Kant claims that the intellect, viewed in distinction from sensibility, 'only reflects' (Prol 4:288): that is, it does not receive representations, but only unifies them to some determinate content, such as can figure in judgment. That is tantamount to how I have just presented reflection as it figures under (c).

That leaves item (b), that reflection can refer to the self-consciousness that is internal to thinking. Reflection, in this sense, would be nothing other than pure apperception. The textual evidence for this claim comes from the *Anthropology* (7:134n). Kant speaks there of an 'inner activity' by which 'a concept (a thought) becomes possible' and calls that 'reflection' – which straightforwardly accords with sense (c). He also claims there that pure apperception is the self-consciousness 'of reflection [der Reflexion]': it is the consciousness of 'the "I" as *subject* of thinking (in logic)' (7:134n). This remark does not unambiguously entail an identity between reflection and pure apperception: it arguably leaves open the possibility that Kant means to distinguish between the mental activity of reflection and the thinking subject's (separate) consciousness of this mental activity; on this reading, he would be calling the latter 'pure apperception' and distinguishing it from the former, which would remain 'reflection'. But this reading fails to recognise the implications of the account of reflection reported in the 'three mental acts' passage: namely, that 'reflection' as to how various representations can be unified in a single consciousness must always involve the possibility of recognising that *one's own thinking* is the source of this unity. Therefore, Kant must mean either to identify reflection with pure apperception in this remark (Anth 7:134n) or at least to take the two to be so closely linked that only a notional distinction between them can be drawn.

The result is that items (a) through (c) of the textual record all belong together as remarks about a constitutive requirement to reflect: a reflection that is always going on, by sheer default, inasmuch as one manages to think at all.[20] This notion of reflection belongs to pure logic, which is concerned with the constitutive requirements on thought. It is also the reflection-c that I identified in §1.2, and glossed as the typically tacit handle that one has on oneself as the source of a point of view on how things are or what is worth doing. Putting it in those terms, however, acknowledges that ground-level thinking typically concerns objects: *phenomenal* objects in the case of theoretical thinking, and *action* (or the good) in the case of practical thinking. Pure *general* logic abstracts from the content of thought; and so its reflection-c is strictly only the typically tacit grasp one has of oneself as the source of one's own thoughts. However, the conception of reflection as a constitutive requirement of thought at issue in pure general logic should be subject to inflection by a pure *domain-relative* logic such as Kant's transcendental logic. For this very reason, Kant argues in the first *Critique*'s Transcendental Logic that the self-consciousness internal to thought as such is a 'synthetic unity' according to certain a priori principles where that thought concerns objects in the domain of nature. (See again Table 1.) This is how we arrive at the idea of reflection-c as the (typically) tacit handle that one has on oneself as the source of *a point of view on how things are.*

1.4.3   Reflection-n in Applied Logic

At the beginning of this chapter, I set out four ways Kant speaks of reflection in the textual record; in the previous subsection, I grouped three of them – (a) through (c) – as various ways of referring to reflection as partly constitutive of thought. That leaves (d), the claim that all judgments require reflection. This claim appears across a range of texts, including the

---

[20] An anonymous reader asks why I take reflection in this sense to be 'a requirement rather than a fact'. Calling it a requirement registers its modal force. And the requirement is *constitutive* because there can be no thinking without it. Calling something a requirement does not, simply as such, entail the possibility of failure. Calling something a *normative* requirement – as I have been spelling out that idea in this chapter – does.

discussion of reflection in the Amphiboly chapter of the *Critique of Pure Reason*. Interpreters of the Amphiboly have almost uniformly neglected to take account of the clear allusions that Kant makes there to the project of applied logic, and thus have failed to appreciate the conception of reflection in play therein.[21] Applied logic is concerned with the problem of how to make good use of our cognitive capacities, having in full view our congenital tendencies to do otherwise. Arguably, its central tenet is the claim that *all judgments require reflection*. My aim now is to provide an account of this normative requirement to reflect, drawing from the Amphiboly and the logic lectures.

Kant claims that *all judgments require reflection*;[22] he also consistently presents prejudice as *judgment without reflection*.[23] This tells us that the first statement points to a normative requirement to reflect – *normative*, since we can judge without reflecting in this way, only we cannot do so well. Therefore, we can account for what reflection-n is by first considering the status of prejudice as judgment where the normative requirement to reflect is not met.

One clue to Kant's account of prejudice is the remarkable consistency with which he identifies three sources of prejudice: habit or custom (*Gewohnheit*), inclination (*Neigung*) and imitation (*Nachahmung*).[24] These are mechanical principles for the association of representations. I underscore that the sources of prejudice are not themselves prejudices:[25] they are just unavoidable facts about how the human mind works. They are nothing for which one can be praised or blamed, or otherwise held to account. Kant points out, for example, that we could not learn anything

---

[21] However, Kohl (2015, 309–10) may perhaps recognise something *like* the distinction I am drawing between reflection-c and reflection-n when he remarks that apperceptive self-consciousness is a more basic kind of reflection than 'the reflective act of making a conceptually determinate judgment of experience' (309, n. 18) – although he does not elaborate on what he has in mind, so the comparison cannot be assessed further here.

[22] As noted in the Introduction (§§0.1 and 0.2). In the KrV Amphiboly, Kant says that 'all judgments . . . require a *reflection*' (A260–1/B316–7). See also LJ 9:76 ('we cannot and may not judge about anything without *reflecting*') and LB 24:161 (reflection is 'necessary for any judgment').

[23] Prejudice glossed as 'judgment without reflection' figures widely in the lectures and handwritten Nachlass, as noted in the Introduction (§0.2). The passages include: LB (24:168 (twice); also 165, 167); LPh (24:547); WL (24:863); RL-2519 [1760s] (16:403); see also RL-2534 and RL-2536 [both c. 1776–78], where prejudice is judgment that 'precedes reflection' (16:408).

[24] The three sources of prejudice are clearly not meant to be mutually exclusive; Kant's logic lectures catalogue a wide variety of particular types of prejudice, many of which could only arise from the conjoint operation of at least two of these sources (e.g. the prejudices of prestige from all three conjointly). For citations, see LJ (9:76), tracking RL-2519 [1760s] (16:403); see also LB (24:167,187 and passim); WL (24:865 and cf. 791); LD-W (24:738); LPh (24:426); LPö (24:548). The sources of prejudice are also mentioned obliquely at A53/B77 and A260–1/B316.

[25] This is a mistake that Sandel (2014, 1ff.) makes in his passing interpretation of Kant on prejudice.

without imitation;[26] and he seems prepared to grant that Hume made a perfectly sound psychological point about custom.[27] Consider as well that non-rational animals and human babies clearly have habitual desires for things (inclinations), but they do not have prejudices. Having an inclination is not the same thing as having a view about how things are or what it would be good to do. Prejudice requires a capacity to have such views: like passion, it involves reflection-c. So, when Kant says that inclination always gets 'the first word' in representations dependent on the faculty of desire (KpV 5:146–7), his remark is already restricted to human beings who have come into the use of their reason – creatures on whom the inclinations make some kind of *claim* about what it would be good to do. Inclination is a source of prejudice owing to the reflective structure of the rational mind, where there is some possibility of further considerations entering in, something beyond the 'first word' – and so it is with creatures who face some problem of determining which considerations to accept as reasons for belief or action. There is a presupposition of agency behind the notion of prejudice, even if prejudice itself is a kind of failed agency.[28]

Consider now this remark from the main discussion of reflection in the first *Critique*, in a chapter called the Amphiboly of the Concepts of Reflection:[29]

> Many a judgment is accepted out of custom, or connected through inclination; but since no reflection precedes it, or at least critically follows it, it is taken as one that has its source in the understanding.

[26] KU 5:308; Anth 7:225; cf. Päd 9:447.

[27] Kant's usage of the term 'habit' (*Gewohnheit*) very often alludes to a Humean notion of custom as a 'subjective necessity' (B5, B20, B127, A760/B788, A765/B793; Prol 4:258, 272; KpV 5:12–13, 51; MS 6:340; Anth 7:147).

[28] Cf. Frierson (2014, 190), who claims that 'prejudices are faulty principles connecting cognitions' – and thereby takes prejudices to be principles for making faulty *inferences*. He goes on to suggest that when prejudices underwrite faulty inferences, the higher cognitive faculties 'are not *absent*; they are simply not efficacious. Just as the various inclinations or commitments of character can be "living" or "dead", so too for basic cognitive powers' (2014, 192). In Chapter 5, I will argue that there are commitments proper to the basic use of cognitive powers; so, in that respect, my account might be consonant with his. The passages that Frierson cites as evidence are from the record of Kant's lectures (Metaphysik L₂ 28:565 and Metaphysik K₃ 28:824); but – interesting as those remarks are – they are not, in their given context, immediately relevant to the discussion of prejudice without further reconstructive argument on Frierson's part. Frierson's interpretation also overlooks more obvious textual sources for Kant's account of prejudice: above all, it does not take account of the three sources of prejudice (imitation, inclination and custom) that crop up in nearly every discussion of prejudice in Kant's corpus. Finally, the idea that prejudices are principles for faulty *inferences* is also too narrow: surely, things can just *strike* one as being a certain way through the force of prejudice.

[29] In Merritt (2015), I offer a more comprehensive reading of the Amphiboly's claims about reflection, including Kant's remarks about 'logical' and 'transcendental' modes of reflection. I set those details aside for present purposes. The present passage fills out Kant's claim in the Amphiboly that 'all judgments . . . require a *reflection*' (A260–1/B316–7), quoted in the Introduction (§0.1, ¶2).

Manches Urtheil wird aus Gewohnheit angenommen oder durch Neigung geknüpft; weil aber keine Überlegung vorhergeht, oder wenigstens kri-
tisch darauf folgt, so gilt es für ein solches, das im Verstande seinen Ursprung
erhalten hat. (A260–1/B316)

Kant alludes here to the problem of prejudice by mentioning our readiness
to 'accept' judgments out of custom, or to 'connect' them through inclination – that is, he points to two of the three standard *sources* of prejudice –
and then claims that *without reflection* our default position is to take such
judgments to have their source in the understanding. Reflection, he thereby
implies, is a matter of calling this default presumption into question. Writ
large, prejudice is the default presumption that one knows, when one may
be in no position to know. To understand Kant's conception of prejudice,
we should consider not only why he thinks this default position obtains,
but also why it can be an epistemic liability.

Kant never gives a direct answer to my first question, on why the cognitive default is to take oneself to know. But that this should be the case can
hardly be surprising. Kant appears to endorse some version of Aristotle's
famous claim that we all desire by nature to know.[30] Some evidence for
this supposition includes Kant's mention of a 'natural drive . . . to enlarge
our cognition', listed not only alongside a natural (and likewise distinctively
human) drive for honour, but also alongside natural drives for food, sex and
movement that are proper to rational and non-rational animals alike (MS
6:215).[31] But we can also trace this cognitive default to the Kantian account
of reflection-c, which I have been glossing as the (typically tacit) awareness
one has of oneself as the source of a point of view on how things are. This
is internal to rational thinking, whether such thinking is cognitively sound
or not: it is with us all the time. The package of claims, then, is this: the
engagement of our cognitive capacities is extremely basic to living a human
life – indeed, it is a more or less continuous aspect of it; we have a natural
drive to know that is likewise engaged more or less continuously when we
are awake (although it may, because of this, scarcely register as an explicit
item in one's mental life); and, thus, we tend to take it as given that we
do know. When this is admitted without warrant, Kant seems to say, we
have prejudice in its most general terms. The following remark from the

---

[30] Aristotle (1984, 1552), properly cited as *Metaphysics* A.1, 980a26. For illuminating scholarly discussion
of this famous remark, and its relation to various conceptions of knowledge in Aristotle, see Cambiano (2012). For a recent endorsement of the Aristotelian claim, and observations on its unfashionableness in epistemology today, see Zagzebski (2012, 33–5).

[31] Related to this is Kant's taking the appropriate cultivation of our cognitive capacities to be 'our
original vocation [Bestimmung]' (Aufklärung 8:39) and 'essential end' (KU 5:294n). I discuss this
further in Chapter 5.

lectures hints at this package of claims: 'a prejudice is indeed nothing other than the mere desire to want to judge, but without the proper acuity or reflection' (LB 24:187).[32]

This brings us to *reflection*, which Kant seems to think is required in order to issue the general epistemic warrant at stake. In the Amphiboly, Kant presents reflection as an attempt to settle a question about the source of one's taking things to be a certain way:

> The first question before all further treatment of our representations is this: In which cognitive faculty do they belong together? Is it the understanding, or is it the senses, before which they are connected [verknüpft] or compared? (A260/B316)

Notice what is taken as given: some *connection* of representations.[33] This, we might say, is what is reflected *upon*. To reflect, Kant here implies, is to consider the source of the given connection of representations. The connection is 'given' because this is how things strike one as being. Therefore, the reflection that is at issue in this remark cannot be reflection-c, the subject's tacit handle on herself as the source of a point of view on how things are. For that is already presupposed, and there is nothing to *do* in reflecting in that way. What is at issue seems instead to be something that one is called upon to do – and something that one could perfectly well fail to do, while still being committed to a view about how things are (thus still reflecting-c). So, it must be a normative requirement to reflect that is at issue: reflection-n.

What exactly is it, though, to reflect-n? The passage just quoted is echoed in *Jäsche*, which – after reiterating the claim that 'we cannot and may not

---

[32] It may be helpful to consider Kant's claims about prejudice writ large in connection with the interesting discussion of epistemic self-trust in Zagzebski (2012). Zagzebski includes epistemic self-trust among our 'pre-reflective' cognitive endowments, on a par with the natural desire for truth. Following work on trust by Annette Baier and Karen Jones, Zagzebski takes epistemic self-trust to be 'a hybrid of epistemic, affective, and behavioural components' – e.g. *believing* in the reliability of one's cognitive capacities, *feeling* trusting of them and *treating* them as trustworthy (2012, 37 and 45), although the three aspects need not always be operational at once. Baseline epistemic self-trust and a natural desire to understand might be given cognitive resources that call, by dint of our rational nature, for development and perfection along certain lines. That, at any rate, is the view that I will attribute to Kant, and it has some similarities to Zagzebski's Aristotelian account. But what, prima facie, should we make of Kant's suggestion that prejudice writ large is essentially unwarranted epistemic self-trust? Perhaps the answer is just that the prejudiced person is inadequately committed to considering the grounds that he has for this baseline self-trust.

[33] Thus, it becomes clear that, if the reflective question is not to be entirely trivial, the 'given representations' at issue in the Amphiboly account cannot be *sensible* representations (which is what Kant sometimes means by such a phrase). It would be silly to consider, of a certain sensation of taste or pain or colour, whether or not it arises from sensibility or understanding; I note this in Merritt (2009).

judge about anything without *reflecting* – goes on to gloss reflection as a matter of 'comparing' a 'cognition with the cognitive power from which it is supposed to arise (sensibility or understanding)' (LJ 9:76). (See Table 2 for further references.) Both passages have us suppose that the reflective person inquires into the specific source of that given connection of representations. In both cases, the reflective person is presented as considering whether they are connected by way of 'the senses' or 'the understanding'.[34] Presumably, these labels serve to distinguish two different ways in which one can arrive at a view about how things are: namely, owing to contingencies in how one is, and has been, affected by things (sensibility), or by some active exercise of one's capacity to determine how things are (understanding). So, the reflective person is presented as querying some given connection of representations – one by which she has a view on how things are – in order to consider, as it were, how this point of view is forged. We are invited to suppose that if the reflective person recognises that the given mental state is forged by contingencies in how she is or has been affected by things (sensibility), she will duly back off from claiming epistemic warrant on its basis; but if the given mental state is forged by some active exercise of her capacity to determine how things are (understanding), then the cognitive claim is at least potentially well warranted.[35]

Now, there are obvious problems with this picture of the reflective person. Perhaps the greatest difficulty is that it presents reflection as if it were an introspective affair – a matter of attending to the given mental state as some occurrent arising in one's mental life, in an effort to determine its aetiology. This could only be a highly sophisticated cognitive skill of some kind, and hardly the sort of thing that could be required with each and every judgment. I will return to this difficulty at the end of the chapter, when we will be better positioned to see our way forward to a solution.

1.5   Affect and Passion as Modes of Reflective Failure

Now that we have an account of Kant's distinction between reflection-c and reflection-n, we can return to the puzzle about affect and passion. The puzzle is that Kant intuitively presents affect and passion as modes of reflective failure, while at the same time claiming that affect lacks reflection, whereas

---

[34] See A260–1/B316–7; LJ 9:76; LPö 24:547; WL 24:862–3. See Table 2 for comprehensive citations.

[35] This interpretation of the activity of reflection is corroborated by the following remark from critical-period logic lectures: 'A prejudice is a *principium* for judging based on subjective causes that are regarded as objective. Subjective causes all lie in sensibility. Objective grounds lie in the understanding' (WL 24:863).

passion involves reflection. The solution, as I have indicated, is that there are two types of reflection at issue. We are now in a better position to understand what Kant is saying about reflection in his discussion of affect and passion; and in the process of working out those matters, we can further develop the account of reflection gleaned from Kant's logic.

1.5.1   What is Reflection?: Inferences from the Anthropology's Rich Man

Let us return, then, to our rich man who is in an 'affected state'. What exactly is the reflection that he is missing? Kant seems to give two different accounts of it. One account can be drawn from Kant's general gloss on reflection in this context, as already noted: reflection is the rational assessment of whether one should accept or refuse a given feeling (Anth 7:251). There is something to clarify here, since surely the feeling itself is a given fact. The servant has broken the rich man's precious goblet and he is upset: so he cannot refuse the painful feeling inasmuch as it is already an item in his mental life. What he might be in a position to refuse or accept, could he reflect, is how it engages a point of view on what matters and what is worth doing. If our rich man turned reflective, he might feel no less pain; he might only refuse to be carried by the pain into yelling at the servant.[36]

Yet, we seem to find a somewhat different account of the missing reflection in Kant's presentation of the example itself. The rich man in the grip of affect, Kant claims, is unable to *compare* the given mental state – the particular painful feeling over the broken goblet – with some broader view of the pleasures that his life stands to afford him:

> The rich person, whose servant clumsily breaks a beautiful and rare crystal goblet while carrying it around, would think nothing of this accident if, at the same moment, he were to compare this loss of *one* pleasure with the multitude of *all* the pleasures that his fortunate position as a rich man offers

[36] David Sussman suggested to me (in conversation) that the goblet example illustrates a complex state that has an affective element (rather than 'pure affect'). The rich man, after all, seems to take a point of view on how things are: Kant (as we are about to see) suggests that 'he feels as if his entire happiness were lost' (7:254), which would surely require having a grip on himself as the source of a point of view on how things are (and hence reflection-c). Moreover, my own embroidery on the example, which imagines the rich man being carried by his affect into yelling at the servant, certainly points to something that he *does*, and is responsible for doing, and so should likewise minimally involve reflection-c. I accept the complexity of the example, and the subsequent difficulty of working with it. However, if affect lacks reflection-c in Kant's view, then for its duration one lacks so much as a point of view on how things are: affect is a kind of momentary madness. This is compatible with recognising the lingering aftereffects of affect, which may drive one to do certain things (e.g. yell at the servant), and so to take a certain point of view on how things are and what is worth doing (which involves reflection-c).

him. However, if he now gives himself over completely to this one feeling of pain (without quickly making that calculation in thought), then it is no wonder that, as a result, he feels as if his entire happiness were lost. (Anth 7:254)

This seems to make reflection out to be a matter of putting things into perspective: if our rich man reflected, he would make that comparison, and could recognise that *one broken goblet is nothing in the scheme of all this*. Thus, Kant, in the *Anthropology*, seems to present us with two very different views about what reflection is. First, he presents it as the consideration of whether to accept or reject a given feeling in light of some kind of commitment to a broader whole. Reflecting, as he first presents it, is how one lives up to that broader whole, as it were. But then his actual sketch of what it would have been for the rich man *to reflect* seems to suggest that reflection is simply a matter of making a comparison, the force of which is basically descriptive: the reflecting rich man, we are told, would have compared his present pain to the totality of pleasures in his life. And while recognising the relative insignificance of the present pain against that background might have the beneficial effect of calming him down, the comparison does not itself seem to have prescriptive or proscriptive force.

To make progress, let us try to distinguish various things going on under the umbrella of 'reflection' in these remarks from the *Anthropology*. First, there is the activity of 'comparison', which nearly always crops up in Kant's remarks on what reflection is.[37] What is it to compare two things? If I said to you, 'Compare this sheet of paper with your right pinkie finger', you would need to have some basis on which to compare the two. It is not possible to compare X and Y without having in mind some feature in virtue of which they are to be compared, or can be regarded as comparable.[38] Kant

---

[37] Recall the account of reflection-n from applied logic: it involves comparing a given 'connection' of representations with (as Kant says) 'sensibility or understanding' (see Table 2 for references, and variants). The reflective person considers the source of that connection – and thus whether she is warranted in taking herself to judge how things are. There are problems with the applied-logic account of reflection-n, to which I will return. At any rate, some commentators fail to distinguish between comparison and reflection altogether, presumably because the two are so closely associated in Kant's account; for example, Longuenesse (1998, 113, 114 and 123) conflates them, presumably on the basis of Kant's claim that 'one could . . . say that *logical reflection* is a mere comparison' (A262/B318). In Merritt (2015), I suggest that this remark about 'logical reflection' concerns the comparison of concepts in order to set them into a systematic whole, and I argue that Kant, in the remark, is drawing on a received rationalist conception of reflection (i.e. one having roots in Leibniz and developed by Meier, the author of the logic textbook from which he lectured over many decades). That is to say: I don't think that this remark about 'logical reflection' is indicative of Kant's considered and core view on reflection.

[38] If I tell you to compare X and Y but don't tell you on what basis, then (assuming that you are willing to go along with my command) you will need to cast about for applicable standards of

typically speaks of reflection as involving a comparison between a given
mental state and some broader whole. Reflection involves, but is not to be
identified with, some such comparison. Reflection would rather be a matter
of accepting or rejecting one of the elements of comparison, typically the
given mental state (the painful feeling, in our example). To reflect, Kant
suggests, is to reject whatever does not accord with a commitment to the
whole, and accept whatever does accord with it, and in this way to live up
to one's commitment to the whole. The activity of reflection should then
be guided by that commitment, which brings with it its own principle. In
overview, this is the proposal:

(1)   Kant typically speaks of reflection as involving comparison between a
      given mental state and some broader whole. Comparison and reflec-
      tion should be distinguished.
(2)   Any act of comparison requires a rule or standard of comparison (that
      in virtue of which two given things figure as comparable at all).
(3)   Kant implies that reflection itself is a matter of accepting or rejecting
      one of the elements of a comparison, typically the given mental state.
(4)   This acceptance or rejection must be governed by something other
      than the rule of comparison, since it has prescriptive or proscriptive
      force (to accept or reject one of the elements). A rule of comparison
      does not (just by itself) have prescriptive or proscriptive force.
(5)   Therefore, reflection will need a guiding principle.

I will map this account of reflection back onto the account from applied
logic in §1.6. For now, let us bring these points to bear on the example of
the rich man. Kant presents him in the grip of affect, and then invites us to
consider what it would have been for him *to reflect*. He imagines that the
reflecting rich man would compare the present pain with the sum total of
pleasures of his life, presumably regarding them as quantities of feeling on
some kind of pain–pleasure scale. But the reflective question is whether he
should endorse or reject the given mental state (the present pain) in light
of that comparison. The comparison does not itself mandate an answer to
the reflective question. Reflection needs a governing principle. What is it
that he cares to preserve, or realise, through his acceptance or rejection? He
might make his calculation for hedonic ends: then, his acceptance or rejection of the given mental state would answer to his calculation of whether

comparison. My point is just that the activity of comparison requires some such standard: you
aren't yet *comparing* the two until you are comparing them in light of some particular feature or
standard of comparison.

it would maximise or detract from the sum total of pleasures with which he compares it. (This principle of reflection does not obviously mandate rejecting the given pain: it might well profit that aggregate if he allowed the pain to drive him to yell at the servant.) Alternatively, the rich man might reflect with an (only arguably) more high-minded principle in mind: he might accept or reject the given feeling as he compared it with some broader view of the various pleasures he regards as proper to the life he means to lead – a view that might be informed, say, by a conception of himself as equally the benevolent master and the great collector and connoisseur. The point is that the comparison at issue must be guided by some underlying normative commitment, if there is to be any *reflection* – at least as Kant presents it in this context.

At the same time, nothing we have considered so far in Kant's account of the rich man's reflective failure entails that reflection requires any *particular* governing principle. By that passage alone, we might surmise that a reflective person should only be committed to his own consistency. This follows from the reflective person's being poised to accept whatever given mental state accords with the broader whole, and to reject whatever does not: the reflective person has some sort of investment in the broader whole (although this investment can of course be called into question). If a normative commitment to consistency is all that reflection essentially requires, then a *voluntarist* interpretation of Kant's account of reflection will be perfectly adequate. To illustrate this, consider again the reflective rich man. He has a painful feeling, and he faces a question about whether to accept or reject this feeling. Cleaving to principle (whatever principle) requires a certain way of settling the reflective question. If his acceptance of the hedonist principle is fixed, then it is not open to him whether to accept or reject the given feeling (assuming, at least, that the hedonist principle yields an unambiguous answer about pleasure maximisation). But he could always abandon his commitment to the hedonist principle. He might choose to commit himself to some other governing principle, and all the while care about his own consistency. So, if the mark of a reflective person is simply a concern for one's own consistency, then reflection will not obviously require anything other than a voluntarist conception of endorsement.

But this is not Kant's view – at any rate, it is not what Kant principally has in mind when he celebrates the reflective person. To explain this point, we will need to understand how affect and passion both count as modes of reflective failure: that is, we will need to account for the blindness metaphor. As we will see, passion is effectively a form of prejudice by Kant's lights. This will enable us to draw a further lesson from Kant's account of prejudice that will rule out the viability of a voluntarist account of reflective endorsement. Kant, as we will see, conceives of reflective endorsement in resolutely cognitivist terms: the governing commitment of a reflective person, for Kant, is always (and most generally) to knowing.

1.5.2   The Blindness of Affect and Passion

Although Kant distinguishes affect from passion – saying that the one lacks reflection altogether, while the other is 'compatible with the calmest reflection' and always involves 'maxims on the part of the subject' (§1.3) – he also claims that affect and passion are alike forms of blindness. My aim in this subsection is to account for this blindness, showing that this is what accounts for affect and passion as modes of reflective failure.

Let's begin, then, with Kant's claim that 'affect makes us (more or less) blind' (Anth 7:253; cf. KU 5:272). It is not hard to explain his point through the example of the rich man. If the rich man were able to reflect, Kant supposes, he would 'think nothing of this accident' – which presumably means that he would regard it as *not mattering*, as not particularly worth his attention. This implies that reflection might make available some capacity for discrimination, some ability to have a view on what does and does not matter. Yet, it cannot quite be the case that the rich man in the grip of affect has no view on what matters. To the contrary, it seems to *matter very much* to him that his precious goblet is broken. Indeed, as long as he is in the grip of affect, this may well be all that matters to him: his entire world has momentarily shrunk down to the pain associated with the loss of his precious goblet. And that, intuitively, is the source of his blindness. Notice that there is no likely shortage of introspective vividness: the feeling is forceful. All there is, for the rich man, is an overwhelming feeling: he cannot, for the moment, so much as survey the situation, and consider what does and does not matter within it. To do that, he would have to have some handle on himself as the source of the point of view in question. But that is precisely what he has lost, inasmuch as he has succumbed to affect. This is what Kant means when he claims that affect lacks reflection:[39] it lacks reflection-c.[40]

---

[39] Anth 7:251, 254; MS 6:407; KU 5:272.
[40] Kant's remark on affect in the *Metaphysics of Morals* brings this point out. After noting that affect makes reflection 'impossible or more difficult', Kant elaborates that for this reason an affect is said to be '*sudden* or *abrupt* [*jäh* oder *jach*]' – *assaulting*, we might say – 'and reason says, through the concept of virtue, that one should *get hold of* oneself' (MS 6:407–8). See also Frierson, who remarks that 'there is no 'practical perspective' on actions from affect' (2014, 250).

Passion differs from affect on precisely this point. Consider Kant's example of the '*passionately* ambitious person', again from the *Anthropology* (7:266). He consistently acts with an eye to what he takes as a reason for doing what, inasmuch as he consistently takes it that whatever promises to put him in position to be honoured by others is what ought to be done. Passion involves *taking* a view of what matters and what is worth doing. This is why it is compatible with – indeed, even requires – reflection-c: it requires having some tacit handle on oneself as the source of the point of view in question.[41] But does the passionate person exercise a capacity to discriminate between what does and does not matter? Yes, but a faulty one. To understand why, we need to consider the blindness of passion; and to do that, we need to introduce another detail of Kant's account.

Kant says that passion is a certain sort of *inclination*. We know from §1.4.3 that inclination is one of the three sources of prejudice; I will return to this. First, we need to understand more clearly what 'inclination' (*Neigung*) means. Kant regularly defines 'inclination' as 'habitual desire' (see e.g. Anth 7:251, 265; MS 6:212; Rel 6:28). An inclination must therefore be more than an impulse to do (or not do) something. Rather, it is desire that has become entrenched to some degree through habit, and its habitual character gives it a force of its own. Passion, Kant sometimes seems to suggest, is just an inclination that has become *especially* entrenched: '[a] passion is a sensible desire that has become a *lasting* inclination' (MS 6:408; emphasis altered). On this account, inclination and passion would seem to be the same in nature, and to differ only in degree.

But that gloss is unsound, because it does not accommodate Kant's view that passion is culpable – whereas inclination, simply as such, cannot be. Kant's point is not simply that passion is an inclination that is supported by an especially durable habit; rather, it is that passion is an inclination that has been adopted as a policy of some kind. It is 'an *illness*' (Anth 7:266), but, curiously, one for which its sufferer is to be *blamed*: 'passions are not, like affects, merely *unfortunate* states of mind pregnant with many ills [mit viel Übeln schwanger], but are without exception *evil* [*böse*] as well' (Anth 7:267; see also MS 6:408). Although Kant is often mistakenly assumed to think otherwise, by his lights there can be nothing culpable about inclination or habit per se.[42] It is a given psychological fact about us, and other animals, that patterns of pleasure and pain naturally work themselves up

---

[41] '[P]assion (as a state of mind belonging to the faculty of desire) takes its time and reflects, no matter how fierce it may be, in order to reach its end' (Anth 7:252).

[42] Carlisle (2014, 94–104) provides an example of the standard misreading of Kant on the issue of habit, and on this point in particular.

into inclinations to pursue or avoid. We could not coherently aspire to free
ourselves from inclination. We cannot make ourselves into creatures that
encounter the world always perfectly afresh, without anticipatory dispositions and habitual desiderative orientation.[43] This is true generally of the
sources of prejudice, as I have noted: the three sources of prejudice are facts
of human psychology. Human thought irremediably involves mechanisms
of habit, inclination and imitation. We cannot change this about ourselves.
Yet, if passions are 'evil' – and prejudice, more generally, *is* culpable – then
surely we must be under some obligation to free ourselves from them. And
if we are so obligated, we must also be, at least in principle, so capable.

The only thing that could account for the culpability of passion is its
relation to the will.[44] Inclination is an expression of the faculty of desire;
but it is not, simply as such, an expression of the will. Only when a person
allows himself to act on the direction of some inclination does it figure in
the exercise of the will. A passion is therefore not simply an inclination that
has become especially settled through habit; what makes an inclination a
passion is that one has endorsed, unreflectively through habitual action, a
certain principle of action. Here, the contrast with affect might help: affect
is a sudden and sharp feeling that, as it were, *comes over* one, assaulting one
from without – whereas passion is an orientation of mind that is continually sustained from within, by the gradual accretion of how one commits
oneself directly in action. Kant likens the power of affect to 'water that
breaks through a dam', and passion to 'a river that digs itself deeper and
deeper into its bed' (Anth 7:252). The passionate person takes a view of
what matters and what is worth doing that moves over and over the same

---

[43] Kant does admittedly take the seemingly extreme view that, '[a]s a rule, all habit [Angewohnheit]
is reprehensible' (Anth 7:149); so, if inclination is 'habitual desire [habituelle Begierde]', then it
might seem that inclination must be, simply as such, 'reprehensible' too. However, this is a place
where standard English translations obscure distinctions that Kant draws in German and Latinate
German. The main distinction is between *Angewohnheit* and *Gewohnheit*: the latter is a more neutral
term for 'habit' or 'custom' (see also Bacin 2010, 210, n. 24). *Logik Pölitz* has Kant remarking that
'*Gewohnheit* is a facility to do something and it is good', whereas '*Angewohnheit* . . . is the necessity
to do something thus, as one has done it a while ago' (24:548). *Angewohnheit*, in Kant's usage,
consistently implies physical necessitation through the force of habit, which is, as such, at odds with
freedom. Compare this with Kant's view that passion enslaves a person: 'the unhappy man groans in
his chains, which he nevertheless cannot break away from because they have grown together with his
limbs' (Anth 7:267); the habit involved in passion must be *Angewohnheit*, not *Gewohnheit*. And it is
Angewohnheit that is, simply as such, reprehensible, not *Gewohnheit*. Finally, Kant's gloss on habitual
disposition (*habituelle Disposition*) as a disposition that is 'incurred through habit [Gewohnheit]'
(Anth 7:286) suggests that the Latinate *habituel* in Kant's account of inclination tracks the German
Gewohnheit, not *Angewohnheit*. This all provides ancillary textual support for my claim that it would
make no *sense* for Kant to hold that inclinations, simply as such, are reprehensible.

[44] This conclusion can be drawn from the combined force of the remark about passion just quoted
(Anth 7:267) and Kant's discussion of the distinction between *Übel* and *Böse* (KpV 5:60).

terrain, etching ever deeper and more fixed tracks for the movement of thought, ultimately overwhelming his resources to take an appropriately discerning view on what matters and why.[45]

The reflective failure of passion should therefore also be conceived as resulting in a certain form of blindness. Our passionately ambitious person, we might suppose, also cares about having friends and being a loving father. Yet, his passion pushes his thoughts along tracks that render him 'blind to these ends, though his inclinations still summon him to them' (Anth 7:266). If a new acquaintance calls to invite him for dinner, he feels a pull of some kind; if his son asks for help with his homework, he feels a pull of some kind. Thus, he is summoned. But then his thoughts turn compulsively to his work – which, let us suppose, is the vehicle through which he compulsively seeks honour – and he declines the invitation; or his attention turns mechanically to his email, and he listens with half an ear to his son. The invitation to dinner, and the request for help, do not figure as fully salient for him. They figure instead as nagging distractions from a driving train of thought.

Kant also remarks on the blindness of sympathy, which in a pre-critical work he presents as a passion (Beo 2:215–16), and then later, in the second *Critique*, as an inclination (KpV 5:118). But the spirit of both passages is remarkably similar: Kant is taking aim at sympathy as an unreflective response to the struggle or suffering of others. Now, it is surely often the case that awareness of another person's struggling provides one with a reason to go over and help. Recently, I was among a handful of people left at the end of a child's birthday party. The child's great-grandmother, in a walker, was struggling to pick up a cup that someone had left on the ground. Noticing this, several of us clearly felt some impulse to go over and pick up the cup for her. But this impulse would be misleading if this were a situation in which the most helpful thing to do involved leaving the struggling person alone – if, for example, it would only have been condescending to pick up the cup for her. (Much surely rests on *how* one helps her pick up the cup, if one does.)

Whether or not it was such a situation, I leave open. My point is that *inclination* surely does not, simply as such, prevent one from seeing what one needs to see in order to act well. Kant's view seems rather to be that

---

[45] Kant consistently says that passion is more dangerous, and more culpable, than affect. Susceptibility to affect is merely 'childish': it involves a mere 'weakness in the use of one's understanding coupled with the strength of one's emotions' – implying that passion, by contrast, involves the active misdirection of one's capacities (MS 6:408). See also KU (5:272n), where Kant suggests that affect only momentarily hampers freedom of mind, whereas passion is its self-incurred forfeiture.

inclination renders one 'blind' only if it compels one to act before one manages to consider whether one has good reason to act as the inclination bids. Sympathy only compromises one's capacity to take a discriminating view of what one has reason to do, Kant suggests, when it 'precedes reflection [Überlegung] on what is duty' and in turn *determines* one's view of what duty requires (KpV 5:118). But this does not exclude the possibility that sympathy might need to be fully integrated into a capacity to take an appropriately discriminating view of what matters and why, in the light of moral requirement. Indeed, this is what Kant goes on to propose, in his later account of virtue, where the cultivation of sympathy as a disposition of *feeling* – neither as inclination nor as passion – is a duty of virtue (MS 6:452, 456–7).[46] And this suggests two things: first, that there is more to our emotional life, by Kant's lights, than affect and passion; second, that Kant evidently takes there to be 'healthy' emotions that contribute to sound judgment,[47] inasmuch as the cultivation of sympathetic disposition is a duty of virtue. Sympathy, on that condition, would not render one blind: it would instead contribute to one's being appropriately sighted.

1.5.3   *Passion and Prejudice: A Lesson from the Logical Egoist*

I will return to this last point later in the book, since it belongs to the account of virtue which I am not yet in position to provide.[48] My immediate concern is to clarify the status of passion as reflective failure. We have learned that the passionate person reflects-c, because he commits himself directly in action; but he fails to meet some normative requirement of reflection – he fails to reflect-n. How are we to understand that failure? Kant seems to chalk the problem up to the passionate person's failure to take the appropriate interest in his own consistency: he 'makes *part* of [his] end the *whole*', violating 'the formal principle of reason itself' (Anth 7:266). But this remark is undercut by a ready counterexample. Suppose that our passionately ambitious man did not care about being loved: suppose, that is, that his relentless drive for honour did not leave him 'to please one

---

[46] The dating of Kant's remarks about sympathy is indicative of an evolution in his thinking on the matter – i.e. from sympathy as a *passion* in the 1764 *Observations* (Beo 2:215–16), to sympathy as an *inclination* in the 1788 *Critique of Practical Judgment* (KpV 5:118), to this claim that the cultivation of sympathetic *feeling* is a duty of virtue in the 1797 *Metaphysics of Morals*. It lies outside of the scope of this book to defend a theory about the evolution of Kant's views on sympathy, but I will have more to say about the Doctrine of Virtue account in Chapter 7.

[47] To suppose otherwise is to subscribe to a *really* tired caricature of Kant – and one roundly dismissed by much work of the past couple of decades (for a relevant recent collection, see Cohen 2014a).

[48] See Chapter 7, §7.3.1.

inclination by placing all the rest in the shade or in a dark corner' (Anth 7:266). Suppose that he suffered no inclination that summoned him in any direction contrary to this one end. If we take reflection-n to involve nothing more than a normative commitment to consistency, we cannot make out his failure.

The possibility of a consistent passionately ambitious person suggests that we need another account of the reflective failure of passion. The connection that I have begun to trace between reflection and clear-sightedness – and likewise between reflective failure and blindness – may suggest another angle. What it suggests, at least prima facie, is that the mark of a passionate person consists in his failure to take an appropriate interest in his capacity to discern what matters and why. But we need to be careful here. For Kant's passionately ambitious man might be quite discerning, quite skilfully attentive, to whatever it is in his circumstances that answers to his commitment to securing honour for himself. He might have all of that in spades. The problem is rather that the aetiology of passion has left him with a grip on what matters that he cannot readily shake off, or gain any critical distance on. And this has likely robbed him of an adequate openness to how things are. He compulsively seeks honour; and he has forged this commitment unreflectively, by habitually gratifying some honour-seeking drive, so he is not readily able to step back from this commitment and evaluate it. As a result, he is able to appreciate saliences along only one track – a track on which he seems to be more or less stuck. And because of this, he fails to recognise all that ought to matter to him.

What I am saying is this: Kant claims that the passionately ambitious person will be *inconsistent*, and I counter that this is not necessarily so. The lesson I draw from this is that the reflective failure of passion cannot be chalked up to a failure to meet a formal requirement of consistency. Such a failure may be involved, but it does not get to the heart of the matter. Therefore, the mark of a reflective person must be something more than a concern for his own consistency: when he accepts or rejects a given mental state, he must do so on some grounds other than its mere compatibility with his identification with some broader whole (e.g. to live a life of honour), where that identification is chosen at will. The alternative is to recognise that there is some substantive normative commitment that the reflective person, simply as such, must have.

But what is that normative commitment? The answer, I think, likes in recognising that passion must effectively be a form of prejudice. We have already seen that Kant takes there to be three sources of prejudice – inclination, habit and imitation – and that he specifically takes inclination to be the source of passion. (He cannot, as I have already explained, mean to *identify* inclination with passion.) Another reason to suppose that passion is a mode of prejudice is, again, its *blindness*: a passionate person fails to attend properly to what ought to matter to him. And what ought to matter in practical thought is not simply what answers to some internally consistent set of practical commitments, in Kant's view. Let me elaborate a bit more on Kant's account of prejudice to support these claims.

Recall the passage about reflection from the first *Critique*'s Amphiboly (A260–1/B316) quoted in §1.4.3: from it, we learned that an unreflective person will presume – apparently by default – that any given view he has about how things are 'has its source in the understanding'. Now, to be precise, Kant speaks there of judgments that are 'accepted', rather than of individuals who *judge*. It is a potentially disquieting difference, because it suggests that the person who 'accepts' a judgment might do so without exercising full agency in determining how things are. And thus, we might draw the conclusion that prejudice is a failure of cognitive agency, whereas the reflective person cares to assert herself as the master of her own thought in the face of the fact that inclination, custom and imitation will normally exert pressure on her to take things to be a certain way. These interpretive conclusions are correct, as far as they go, but it is all too easy to be misled by them. One immediate clarification is in order: Kant's considered view is that one exercises cognitive agency badly in prejudice, but not that one fails to exercise cognitive agency altogether. Taking things to be a certain way is an exercise of cognitive agency, even if we don't deliberately reflect on the soundness of those views and the principles on which they rest.

To further clarify the point that prejudice is a failure of cognitive agency, we need to consider another crucial point of Kant's account of prejudice. Prejudice comes in two broad classes: prejudices of cognitive passivity and prejudices of logical egoism. If we simply say that a reflective person cares to assert herself as the master of her own thought, we mark a suitable contrast against the prejudices of cognitive passivity, which Kant glosses as the '*tendency towards passive use of reason*, or *towards the mechanism of reason rather than towards its spontaneity under laws*' (LJ 9:76, emphasis in the original; tracks RL-2527 [c. early 1770s] 16:406).[49] But, as I just argued, there is a sense in which a passionately ambitious person cares to assert himself as the master of his own thought; and that the 'reflection' of such a person will require nothing other than a commitment to consistency. And such a figure – i.e. the *consistent* passionately ambitious person – will make a poor

[49] This remark was quoted in the Introduction, §0.1, ¶2.

contrast against the other broad class of prejudice, that '*based on self-love* [*Eigenliebe*] or *logical egoism*' (LJ 9:80).[50] Kant consistently claims that the prejudices of logical egoism stem from a readiness to treat the agreement of one's judgments with those of others as a dispensable criterion of truth:[51] 'The *logical egoist* considers it unnecessary . . . to test his judgment on the understanding of others' (Anth 7:128). In *Jäsche*, we have the addition that the mark of such prejudices is a tendency to treat as true whatever is 'the product of one's own understanding, e.g. one's own system' (LJ 9:80).[52] The logical egoist will tend to admit as true whatever readily fits into, and thereby reinforces, his internally consistent view of things. The logical egoist is also prone to reject as false whatever he happens to lack insight into (RL-2553 [c. mid-1750s], 16:413), and to that extent is unable to absorb into his 'system'. Logical egoism therefore involves a normative commitment to one's own consistency, and the logical egoist apparently cares very much to assert himself as the master of his own thought. He prides himself, we might even suppose, on his capacity to take a discriminating view of what does and does not matter, what is and is not a reason for doing and believing what.

It is precisely because the logical egoist mimics the reflective person that he allows us to correct for how we might otherwise be led astray by our first inferences about reflection.[53] We would be forced to conclude that the logical egoist is very reflective if we took reflection-n to involve nothing more than an active commitment to consistency. Such a conception of reflection-n does not require anything other than a voluntarist notion of reflective endorsement – one that secures the possibility of taking *or* leaving any given view about how things are, since the governing principle of reflection is itself adopted at will. The logical egoist is likewise the arbiter of her own system. The example of the logical egoist shows that Kant rejects a voluntarist conception of reflective endorsement. And the passionately ambitious person is a kind of logical egoist, whose blindness therefore should be understood in cognitivist terms. The possibility of a *consistent* passionately ambitious person tells us that the failure of passion

---

[50] Logical egoism is a recurring topic in the record of his logic lectures (see also LB 24:151, 178–9, 187; LPh 24:427; LBu 24:643; WL 24:874; LPö 24:549; LD-W 24:740), as it had its roots in Meier (on this, see Pozzo 2005).

[51] LJ 9:80; LPh 24:428; LBu 24:643; LD-W 24:740; RL-2563 [c. 1760–early 1770s] (16:418); RL-2564 [c. 1764–69] (16:418).

[52] This remark cannot be traced to the handwritten Nachlass; but we do find there a closely related remark associating the 'prejudice of unity' with logical egoism (attached as a 'later addition' to RL-2564 (16:418)).

[53] See the remark at LB 24:187 to the effect that logical egoism seems 'initially to be allowed', but 'on closer investigation' must be recognised as a prejudice, and thus as a form of reflective failure.

cannot simply be chalked up to a failure to appreciate all of one's own ends. The passionate person fails to register adequately what in his situation is salient to his acting well, where *acting well* must admit of some standard of correctness beyond his own internal consistency.

We have been considering the implications about reflection in Kant's account of affect and passion. The distinguishing mark of affect is its lack of reflection. By that, Kant means that affect lacks reflection-c: that typically tacit handle that one has of being the source of one's own thoughts, or being the source of a point of view on how things are.[54] Affect is blind because it radically (although, fortunately, only momentarily) occludes genuine self-conscious thought: there is just searing, overwhelming feeling. A fortiori, affect lacks reflection-n as well: someone who succumbs to affect cannot so much as survey his situation and consider what he has reason to do. Passion involves taking a point of view on how things are and what is worth doing: passion requires reflection-c, just as all genuine thought does. But Kant says that the passionate person is blind. His habits of attention run along tracks that render him unable to consider his situation freely, or openly. So, he is blind to what he would need to attend to in order to act well. The possibility of an internally consistent passionately ambitious person teaches us that the passionate person cannot *simply* be making a mistake on his own terms. As a result, we can conclude that the normative requirement to reflect calls for more than a commitment to one's own consistency. The normative requirement to reflect calls, rather, for a commitment to *knowing*. To explain why I think this, let me show how the account of reflection-n from this section can be merged further with what we know about reflection-n from applied logic.

1.6   Reflection-n: Merging the Accounts

In §1.5, we drew inferences about reflection from Kant's account of affect and passion as modes of reflective failure. We learned there that reflection involves comparing a given mental state against some broader whole. The reflection itself, however, is a matter of accepting or rejecting that given

---

[54] My gloss on reflection-c as the *typically tacit* grip one has on oneself as the source of one's own thoughts is partly a nod to common sense: we are most often engaged in our thoughts without rendering thematic to ourselves that these thoughts are *our own*. Cf. Zagzebski's (2012, 29–30) related, but somewhat stronger, point about the 'effortless adjustments' we make to our thoughts – for example, to address an internal inconsistency between the belief that one has turned off a sprinkler system and the perception of hearing the sprinklers turning on – that do not obviously require any explicit recognition that these incompatible thoughts are our own.

mental state depending upon its compatibility with that whole, or whether it realises or in some sense 'lives up to' that whole. I argued that reflection must involve some kind of commitment to a governing principle. This governing principle stakes an interest in the idea of the whole: for, this is what one wants to realise or preserve when one accepts or rejects a given mental state.

The account of reflection-n from applied logic in §1.4 involves many of the same features. First, Kant indicates that comparison is involved in, or required for, reflection. Second, one of the elements of comparison is a given mental state. The citations on reflection-n collected in Table 2 indicate that the given mental state is sometimes characterised as a 'connection' of representations, sometimes as a 'cognition' and sometimes as a 'judgment'. There is no inconsistency in this, particularly if we bear in mind that Kant takes prejudice to be judgment that lacks reflection-n. In other words, 'judgment' and 'cognition' in these remarks are not success terms. Kant also underscores that the connection of representations at issue is *given*: things strike one as being a certain way, and the reflective person considers – and assesses – the source of this impression. Reflection, as Kant variously says in this context, is a matter of comparing a given view of how things are with the *cognitive faculties*,[55] or with *laws of understanding and of reason*[56] (see Table 2). This account of reflection-n is worrisome in several respects. First, it seems to present reflection as an introspective affair – a matter of attending to the given mental state as some occurrent arising in one's mental life, in an effort to determine its aetiology. Second, on such an interpretation, reflection-n looks to be a highly sophisticated cognitive skill of some kind, and hardly the sort of thing that could be required of anyone with each and every judgment.

However, an alternative interpretation comes into view if we recall some of the lessons about reflection drawn, via inference, from the *Anthropology* account of passion as a mode of reflective failure. In that account, reflection is a matter of comparing a given mental state against some broader whole that the subject in some sense *identifies with*, or has an *interest in*: the reflective person cares to realise or preserve that whole when she accepts or rejects the given mental state. Bring this to bear, now, on the account of reflection-n from applied logic and we get the following result. The greater whole with which the reflective person identifies would be the cognitive

---

[55] KrV (A260–1/B316–17); LJ (9:76); LPö (24:547); WL (24:862–3).

[56] LPh (24:424) and RL-2519 [c. 1760–70] (16:403) both say this; see also LB (24:161 and 165), LBu (24:641), RL-2536 [c. 1776–78] (16:408), LPh (24:424) and LD-W (24:737) for close variants.

capacity as it is exercised according to its necessary principles. The reflective person, on Kant's model, would then find herself with some default view about how things are, and would reflect-n by considering whether this point of view is connected in such a way as to hold only for herself, or whether instead it is connected in such a way that should hold for any other judging subject. Only then could the connection of representations be appropriately responsive to how things are independently of any particular judging subject – and so, potentially, to how things are *in the object*.

Thus, the greater whole that the reflective person, so conceived, cares to preserve or realise through this acceptance or rejection is the cognitive power as such. We might then be able to say that the requirement to reflect-n is met by taking the appropriate interest in one's own cognitive agency, where this need not be something that one *does* on this or that occasion, but can rather simply be a matter of *knowing how* to make good use of one's cognitive capacities at all. My aim in the next chapter is to develop this idea, and show how it allows us to address the lingering worries about the normative requirement to reflect.

1.7   Conclusion

In this chapter, I have argued that Kant distinguishes between constitutive and normative requirements of reflection. The first I have dubbed 'reflection-c', and have glossed as the typically tacit handle one has on oneself as the source of a point of view, both on how things are and on what is worth doing. Reflection-c, in other words, is a necessary condition of both theoretical and practical thought. It is itself a tacit grip on one's own agency as a thinker: my representations are not states of consciousness that are merely delivered to me, but rather are formed as I move about in the world and attend to this and ignore that, listen to this person and fail to see that one, work out an explanation of this phenomenon and daydream about something else. These thoughts, and this view on how things are and what matters, are mine. But I am not actively thinking, in the normal case, that these thoughts are mine. Hence, the stress Kant puts on his own version of the cogito, the apperception principle: 'The *I think* must be *able* to accompany all of my representations' (B131). There is necessarily a standing possibility of my actively thinking that these thoughts are mine, but I may not in fact actively think this all that often. Yet, the possibility of doing so is necessary: that is what makes me a thinker, rather than something to which states of consciousness can only be delivered. Thus, this constitutive

Table 1 *Two axes of logical inquiry*

	PURE outlines **constitutive requirements** on thought (including reflection-c)	APPLIED outlines **normative requirements** on judgment (including reflection-n)
GENERAL (domain-independent)	**Pure general logic** presents constitutive requirements on thought as such **Reflection = pure apperception,** the (typically tacit) self-consciousness of 'the "I" as *subject* of thinking (in logic)' (Anth 7:134n)	**Applied general logic** concerned with what is required to make good use of one's cognitive capacities **Reflection** figures in the maxim that 'we cannot and may not judge without reflecting' (LJ 9:76). Reflection is the antidote to prejudice
SPECIAL (domain-relative)	**Transcendental logic** pure, domain-relative logic. It presents constitutive requirements on thought about *phenomenal objects* **Reflection-c** here is the *synthetic* unity of apperception	Applied, domain-relative logic might deal with normative requirements on judgment in a particular domain of thought (e.g. speculative metaphysics) Merritt (2015) argues that the 'transcendental' reflection that Kant claims is a 'duty' for anyone who 'wants to judge something about things a priori' (A263/B319) draws from the conception of reflection proper to applied logic

reflection – the typically tacit grip on myself as the source of my own thoughts – is what makes reflection of a different sort possible: namely, reflection-n. It involves considering whether things really *are* as I take them to be, and whether this or that really *is* worth doing. This requires a commitment to some standards of correctness or objectivity. Reflection-n is, in a sense that remains to be clarified, something we need to actively do.

I began this chapter by raising questions about the nature and scope of any requirement to reflect. The nature of this requirement has been addressed by distinguishing the constitutive and normative principles at work. But the *scope* of the requirement remains unsettled. For the account of reflection-n from Kant's applied logic gives the impression that reflection-n is a deliberate activity to be performed on the occasion of each and every judgment – something that one must do, the story goes, in order

Table 2 *Reflection in applied logic*

Glosses on REFLECTION-N		Elements of comparison
Critique, Amphiboly (1781/87)	'the consciousness of the relation of given representations to our various sources of knowledge by means of which alone their relation under one another can be correctly determined' (A260/B316) 'All judgments, however, and indeed all comparisons, require *reflection*, i.e. distinction of the cognitive faculty to which the given concepts belong' (A261/B317)	'Sie ist das Bewußtsein des Verhältnisses gegebener Vorstellungen zu unseren verschiedenen Erkenntnißquellen, durch welches allein ihr Verhältniß unter einander richtig bestimmt warden kann' (A260/B316) 'Aber alle Urtheile, ja alle Vergleichungen bedürfen einer *Überlegung*, d.i. einer Unterscheidung der Erkenntnißkraft, wozu die gegebenen Begriffe gehören' (A261/B317)	**given representations/given concepts** *with* **sources of knowledge/ cognitive powers**
Jäsche Logic (1800)	'comparing a cognition with the cognitive power from which it is supposed to arise (sensibility or understanding)' (9:76)	*überlegen* = 'ein Erkenntniß mit der Erkenntnißkraft, woraus es entspringen soll, (der Sinnlichkeit oder dem Verstande) zu vergleichen' (9:76) **Identical glosses** in *Logik Pölitz* (c. 1780) (24:547) and *Wiener Logik* (c. 1780) (24:862–3)	**cognition** *with* **the cognitive power from which it should arise**

Nachlass sources

Dohna-Wundlacken Logic (c. 1792)	'I reflect on something when I compare it with the laws of understanding' (24:737)	'Ich überlege etwas, wenn ich es mit den Gesetzen des Verstandes vergleiche' (24:737)	[indeterminate] *with* **laws of understanding**
Busolt Logic (c. 1789)	'when we compare our judgment with the laws of understanding' (24:641)	'Reflexion oder Ueberlegung, wenn wir unser Urtheil mit den Gesetzen des Verstandes vergleichen' (24:641) **Cf. RL-2536** [c. 1776–78]: comparison with 'rules of understanding' (16:408)	**judgment** *with* **laws of understanding**
Philippi Logic (1772)	'to compare something with the laws of understanding and of reason' (24:424) **Identical gloss at RL-2519** [c. 1760–70] (16:403).	'Ueberlegung heißt etwas mit den Gesetzen des Verstandes und der Vernunft vergleichen. Wenn der Verstand seine Urtheile nicht mit seinen Gesetzen vergleicht; so nimmt er sie an ohne Ueberlegung' (24:424)	[indeterminate] *with* **laws of understanding and of reason**
Blomberg Logic (early 1770s)	'to compare something with the laws of understanding' (24:161) 'comparison of a cognition with the laws of the understanding and of reason' (24:165)	'*Überlegung* heißt etwas mit denen Verstandes Gesetzen vergleichen' (24:161) 'die Vergleichung einer Erkenntniß mit denen Gesetzen des Verstandes, und der Vernunft' (24:165)	**cognition** *with* **laws of understanding and of reason**

to secure epistemic warrant for any given view that one has about how things are. So conceived, the requirement to reflect-n seems to make the wrong demands on us, and to make them too much: it plays into a picture of the Kantian reflective ideal that should be dismissed as a tired caricature. But, as long as reflection-n is taken to be a deliberate 'stepping back' owed on the occasion of every judgment, we have not yet secured any entitlement to send it away.

In the remainder of this book, I will be arguing for a conception of reflection-n as embedded in appropriately developed cognitive capacities. My aim will be to show that reflection, by Kant's lights, *need not* be an essentially episodic and deliberate affair, a matter of 'stepping back' on the occasion of each and every judgment. As I make this case, I do not mean to run headlong into the opposing caricature, that there is no necessary place for 'stepping back' in a life that is lived well. Of course there is. But the picture that I am after is one where the quality of what one might be doing when one *does* deliberately consider and assess the grounds for one's taking things to be a certain way, and where one has *good reason* to do this, is itself conditioned by the quality of the resources that one has developed by taking an interest in one's cognitive agency, and thus by reflecting according to the model that I now set out to develop.[57]

---

[57] Thanks to Bridget Clarke for suggesting this clarification of my position on the 'stepping back' model of reflection-n. See Clarke (2010) for a clear account of why neo-Aristotelian virtue ethics does not embrace the opposing caricature at issue – i.e. that the virtuous person has no need to reflect in a deliberate and episodic way.

CHAPTER 2

Healthy Human Understanding

> I am an enthusiastic advocate of healthy human understanding.
>
> Kant, in preparatory notes for the *Prolegomena* (23:59)[1]

2.1 Introduction

My aim in the previous chapter was to distinguish between constitutive and normative requirements to reflect. This distinction, I argued, can be mapped on to Kant's distinction between pure and applied logic: the former abstracts from, as the latter does not, certain facts about the human condition that make it such that we are liable not to make good use of our cognitive capacities. Thus, the requirement to reflect at issue in applied logic – the requirement that figures in Kant's claim that 'all judgments require reflection' – is *normative*, because the claim is not that it is impossible to judge without reflecting in the relevant sense, but rather that it is impossible to judge *well*.

But our first-pass interpretation of the requirement to reflect-n failed to address the objection that the requirement is out of step with what we normally have in mind when we take a belief or a judgment to be justi-fied. This objection presupposes that reflection-n must be a deliberately undertaken activity of some kind, something required on the occasion of each and every judgment if one is to avoid falling prey to prejudice and the like. My strategy for addressing this objection is to provide an account of reflection-n that shows it to be internal to sound judgment, or simply part of what it is to make good use of one's cognitive capacities in judgment. The idea that reflection-n is internal to sound judgment allows for the pos-sibility that reflection-n is nothing other than considering how things are

---

[1] 'Ich bin ein enthusiastischer Vertheidiger des gesunden Menschenverstandes.' I discuss the motiva-tion and context of this remark at the end of §2.3.

as this is *carried out in the right spirit*, or with the right frame of mind.[2] On this picture, the basic activity is judging how things are, and the requirement to reflect-n bears on the frame of mind required to do that well.

I will make this case by arguing that Kant reconceives of the requirement to reflect-n in terms of a set of three maxims that he presents in various lights – but above all, perhaps, as maxims of 'healthy human understanding'. In the *Critique of Judgment*, he presents these maxims as the articulation of the frame of mind or 'way of thinking' – *Denkungsart* – required to make 'purposive use' of one's cognitive capacities (KU 5:295). To make *purposive* use of one's *cognitive* capacities can only be to put them to use in such a way as to have knowledge by means of them; to do this is to judge. Hence, the three maxims would concern the frame of mind required to make good use of one's cognitive capacities in judgment – so that the only activity at issue is that of determining, objectively, how things are. The requirement to reflect-n can then be met in the adverbial aspect, as it were, of judging in *the right frame of mind*.[3]

Thus, my aim in this chapter is to show that Kant offers a more nuanced articulation of the normative requirement to reflect through the three maxims of healthy human understanding. In this way, I aim to sketch an alternative to supposing that reflection-n must be a deliberately undertaken activity of some kind – something one must *do* on the occasion of each and every judgment, over and above the judging itself. I will begin with a basic presentation of the three maxims, identifying the various contexts in which they figure, and the prima facie reasons for supposing that the normative requirement to reflect is reiterated in terms of these maxims. In order to draw the connection between reflection-n and the three maxims, it will be necessary to examine closely Kant's conception of 'healthy human understanding' (*gesunder Menschenverstand*): this will occupy me throughout much of the chapter. I will next explain how the maxims concern the basic epistemic commitments that are required to make good use of one's cognitive capacities. Finally, I will consider why Kant presents the three maxims not only as a basic requirement of ordinary or common human understanding – where epistemic 'health' results from meeting this requirement – but also as maxims the adoption of which leads, he claims,

---

[2] While this can allow for reflection-n to be a matter of 'stepping back', it should not be *identified* with 'stepping back' on the interpretation that I am after, as I noted at the conclusion to Chapter 1. My aim in this chapter is to develop the alternative account of reflection-n that secures this.

[3] Moreover, in Kant's usage, *Denkungsart* is consistently associated with the idea of *character*, insofar as character depends on one's cognitive and volitional commitments. So, the picture towards which I am working is one in which the requirement to reflect-n is met through the development of cognitive or epistemic character: see Chapter 5.

to wisdom (Anth 7:200, 228). I will sketch how Kant plausibly moves from the one idea to the other; but, as we will see, the issue raises questions about the relation between moral and cognitive virtue that will provide the impetus for Chapter 5.

2.2 The Three Maxims

Kant presents the three maxims several times in his later published work (once in the 1790 *Critique of Judgment*, twice in the 1798 *Anthropology*), once in *Logik Jäsche* in remarks that can be traced directly to Kant's handwritten notes on logic (RL-2273 [1790s], 16:294), several times in implicit or partial statement in his popular essays from the critical period and once in a letter to Moses Mendelssohn. They also appear repeatedly in the various records of Kant's lectures in logic and anthropology. On the whole, the idea that our thinking ought to be governed by the three maxims gains steam from the later critical period onwards. Although there are some noteworthy variations in Kant's presentation of the three maxims across these contexts – above all, there are two versions of the second maxim – on the whole, his presentation of them is remarkably consistent. I lay them out here without the encumbrance of citations; for comprehensive references, see Table 3.

The first maxim: to think for oneself.
The second maxim: to think in the position of another; or: to think in the position of everyone else.
The third maxim: to think always consistently with oneself.

The three maxims are introduced first in the context of logic: the earliest statement of them that I have been able to find (which is partial: it has only the first two) can be traced, if the Academy edition's dating is correct, to the late 1760s (RL-2564 [16:419]). They are presented later in *Jäsche* as 'universal rules and conditions for the avoidance of error' (9:57; tracking RL-2273 [1790s], 16:294) – i.e. with the human susceptibility to error firmly in view. So, it should be noted first that they belong to *applied* general logic, since they are issued with the normal epistemic liabilities of the human condition in full view.

This brings us to one consideration, prima facie, for taking the three maxims to be a further articulation of the requirement to reflect-n. As we saw in Chapter 1, when Kant claims that 'all judgments require reflection' – reflection-n – he consistently has in mind our susceptibility to prejudice. Our susceptibility to prejudice is tacitly at issue whenever Kant introduces the three maxims, as well. The first maxim figures, explicitly, as the maxim of the 'enlightened' (LJ 9:57) or '*unprejudiced* way of thinking [Denkungsart]' (KU 5:294). But this must be true of all three of the maxims. For as we saw in Chapter 1, Kant distinguishes between two broad classes of prejudice: the prejudices of cognitive passivity and the prejudices of logical egoism. A logical egoist would presumably take the first maxim to heart, and with it the third: for, the prejudices of logical egoism 'express themselves in a certain preference for what is the product of one's own understanding, e.g., one's own system' (LJ 9:80). Adoption of the second maxim would, however, inhibit this predilection. So it seems that, roughly speaking, we need the first maxim to protect ourselves against the prejudices of cognitive passivity, while we need the second to protect ourselves against the prejudices of logical egoism. Thus, the three maxims, as a collective package, should outline the commitments of the unprejudiced way of thinking.

What I have done so far is simply to point to the thematic differences between the first and the second maxims, suggesting that something from each is required in order to think in a way that is genuinely 'prejudice-free'. This, however, raises an immediate question about the place of the third maxim in the package. To adopt the first maxim is to take an interest in being the source of one's own thoughts: it is concerned with the *originality* of thought, in that (minimal) sense. To adopt the second maxim is to take an interest in the mutual intelligibility of one's own point of view on how things are and that of others: it is concerned with the *communicability* or *publicity* of thought. The third maxim enjoins one to take an interest in being the *coherent* source of one's own thoughts – which sounds quite a bit like having a preference for whatever is the product of one's own system. Thematically, it returns to originality; and thus, it seems to be, if anything, only an antidote to the prejudices of cognitive passivity, and in itself perfectly compatible with the prejudices of logical egoism. But Kant claims that the third maxim is 'the most difficult to achieve', as it arises from a certain 'combination of the first two': it presupposes having acquired a certain skill (*Fertigkeit*) with the first two maxims through repeated observance of them (KU 5:295).[4] If that is the case, then the adoption of the third maxim must be the acquisition of just that frame of mind in which originality and communicability figure as mutually supporting aspects of a single frame of mind, one oriented towards making 'purposive' use of one's

---

[4] This translation is my own; the CEWIK translation entirely obscures this notion of skill. On some related problems with the CEWIK translation of this remark, see Merritt (2011b, 235, n. 20).

cognitive capacities (5:295). The purposive use of one's cognitive capacities is, surely, knowing by means of them.[5]

My point in this section is rather simple. I have drawn on the following results from Chapter 1: (a) Kant's claim that 'all judgments require reflection' points to a normative requirement on judgment; and (b) this requirement to reflect-n is properly raised in the context of applied general logic, which holds firmly in view certain facts about the human condition that make it such that we are liable not to make good use of our cognitive capacities. Reflection-n, in this context, is introduced as the antidote to prejudice. Here, I have simply observed that the three maxims seem to yield resources for a more nuanced rendering of this claim. Liability towards the prejudices of cognitive passivity would need to be redressed through the commitment to originality that is rendered thematic in the first maxim, whereas liability towards the prejudices of logical egoism would need to be redressed through the commitment to communicability that is rendered thematic in the second maxim. But the evidence that I have mustered so far for the interpretive thesis of this chapter is circumstantial, and therefore inconclusive. What I have relied upon in this section is simply the observation that the possibility of standing guard against prejudice seems to be at issue in both contexts – i.e. both when Kant claims that 'all judgments require reflection' and when he presents the three maxims. This could simply mean that both fall under the scope of applied general logic. Moreover, whatever circumstantial evidence I have mustered here may seem to be weakened by the fact that the requirement to reflect-n concerns *judgment*, whereas the three maxims are formulated in terms of how one ought *to think*: only the second maxim, it appears, is explicitly linked to the power of judgment (see e.g. KU 5:295 and RA-456 15:188). But this appearance is misleading, as I will conclude in the next section: the three maxims of 'common' or 'healthy' understanding – so designated – must collectively concern the exercise of judgment, and the account of this is the evidence on which my interpretive case will rest.

Before taking that up, let me draw one further preliminary lesson about the three maxims. I began in this section by drawing out the implications

---

[5] This paragraph rehearses some of Merritt (2009, 2011b). James Montmarquet suggests that epistemic virtues can be grouped into two broad classes of intellectual courage and impartiality; these align thematically, it seems to me, with Kant's first and second maxims, respectively. Montmarquet presents them as 'complementary' classes of intellectual virtue because they 'concern opposite, but it seems equally important, sides of the balanced intellectual personality: the [virtues of intellectual courage] comprising the "inner-directed" virtues of a person of high intellectual integrity; the [virtues of impartiality comprising] the "other-directed" virtues which are necessary to sustain an intellectual *community*' (Montmarquet 1987, 484).

of their figuring under the scope of *applied* general logic. But there is something further to learn, by focusing now on their figuring in applied *general* logic. Logic is 'general' inasmuch as it abstracts entirely from the content of thought. Under the scope of applied *general* logic, the three maxims should concern requirements on making good use of one's cognitive capacities (in full view of congenital tendencies to do otherwise) *regardless* of whether the engagement of thought is theoretical (and concerns objects in the domain of nature) or whether it is practical (and concerns the good to be brought about through action). The three maxims are general: they hold regardless of whether the cognitive engagement of thought is theoretical or practical.[6]

2.3   Common and Healthy Understanding

Kant consistently glosses common human understanding as the power to judge *in concreto* (see Table 4). He distinguishes it, variously, from (a) learned understanding; (b) scientific understanding; (c) speculative understanding; and (d) cultivated understanding.[7] The basic difference at issue concerns whether one's grasp of rules or principles is tacit or express. A person of common understanding may be highly discerning about how things are, but cannot necessarily articulate the rules that governs this knowledge. By contrast, a person of learned understanding grasps rules explicitly as rules, representing them as related to other rules in some kind of systematic order. Common understanding is also typically – but not entirely consistently or sharply – distinguished from *healthy* human understanding: the latter is common understanding that meets some standard of correctness.[8] These distinctions are succinctly brought out in this passage from the *Prolegomena*:

> For what is *healthy understanding*? It is *common understanding*, in so far as it judges correctly. And what now is common understanding? It is the power

---

[6] For the most part, commentators appear to assume, implicitly, that the three maxims concern only the *theoretical* use of our cognitive capacities; by contrast, Munzel (1999, 223) notes Kant's claim that the three maxims 'lead to wisdom' (at Anth 7:200 and 228), and infers therefrom that the three maxims concern only the way of thinking required for the *practical* employment of reason. My view is distinct on both counts: since the three maxims belong to applied *general* logic, they bear on the good use of cognitive capacities *generally* (i.e. be that use theoretical or practical).

[7] Although (a) through (d) are various points of contrast against *common* understanding, 'cultivated' understanding (d) provides the best general label for the contrast. I have set up Table 4 accordingly. As I am about to explain, Kant has something in particular in mind when he speaks of 'cultivated' understanding in this sense: it is not simply an understanding that is developed in some way or another.

[8] McAndrew (2014) runs common and healthy understanding together, which leads him to miss the normative significance of the latter.

of cognition and of the employment of rules *in concreto*, in distinction from the *speculative understanding*, which is a faculty of the cognition of rules *in abstracto*. (Prol 4:369)

This passage sets out the two distinctions indicated initially in this section, between (a) common and learned (here, specifically 'speculative') understanding and (b) common and healthy understanding. In this section, my aim is to clarify these distinctions as they are set out in Table 4. First, I will account for the distinction between common and learned understanding – i.e. the top horizontal row on Table 4. Later, I will account for the distinction between common and healthy understanding (the left vertical column on Table 4), considering specifically the sense of correctness at issue. Finally, I consider *what it is* to judge *in concreto*, and the value Kant places upon this.

The distinction between common and learned understanding has its roots in Meier's logic text, from which Kant lectured over many decades (see RL-1571[mid-1750s], 16:8). The earlier record of logic lectures shows Kant following Meier closely, so we hear quite a lot about the distinction between common and *learned* understanding throughout the early *Blomberg Logik*, whereas the later *Dohna-Wundlacken Logik* puts Kant on record as complaining that Meier speaks too much of 'learned' cognition and ought to have framed his point in terms of 'scientific' cognition instead (24:717). In the *Prolegomena*, as I just noted, Kant distinguishes common or healthy understanding from 'speculative' understanding. To some extent, these are merely terminological differences, for the distinction is consistently drawn between common understanding as the capacity to judge *in concreto* and the however-designated capacity to grasp rules *in abstracto*. The latter is what Kant broadly signals as 'cultivated' understanding when he remarks, in his discussion of the three maxims in the third *Critique*, that common understanding can be distinguished 'as merely healthy (not yet cultivated [noch nicht cultivirt]) understanding' (KU 5:293). So, the crucial distinction at work – the one that principally interests me here – is between common understanding as the power to judge *in concreto* versus the capacity to cognise *in abstracto*.

The framing of this distinction in the third *Critique* should also tell us that we have a distinction at work here, not an opposition:[9] a healthy understanding can be cultivated in a certain way in the acquisition of learned or scientific understanding – and the acquisition of the latter should not, at least in principle, undermine the robustness of the former.

---

[9] Just as the logic lectures state: 'They are *distinctae*, to be sure, but not *oppositae*' (LB 24:21).

But when Kant distinguishes common or healthy understanding from 'cultivated' understanding, we should not thereby assume that there is no sense in which the former is cultivated, if by that we just mean developed in some way. His point is simply that common understanding is developed through practice, *as opposed to* being cultivated through instruction. This is quite clear when Kant alludes to the distinction between common and learned understanding in the first *Critique*. The passage comes from the outset of the Analytic of Principles: at this point in the *Critique*, Kant has provided an account of the concepts constitutive of the understanding (the categories), and is now setting out to provide an account of the 'transcendental' power of judgment. He remarks here that general logic is unable to provide any rules for the power of judgment, by which he means rules for distinguishing whether or not some particular falls under a given rule: for, any general instructions would have to come by way of more rules. Whatever might be said to account for the capacity to recognise the relevance of a rule in the determination of given particulars would fall outside of the scope of general logic, which abstracts entirely from the content of thought, and so from any substantive requirements governing thought in any particular domain. At this point, though, Kant also makes a distinct point about the difference between understanding, conceived as 'the faculty of rules', and power of judgment (*Urtheilskraft*), conceived as 'the faculty of subsuming under rules' (A132/B171): namely, that the power of judgment develops directly through practice, not instruction.

> [T]hough the understanding is capable of being instructed [fähig . . . einer Belehrung] and equipped through rules, the power of judgment is a special talent which wants not to be instructed [belehrt], but rather only to be practised. (A133/B172)

Here, his point is simply that a person can acquire rules through instruction, without thereby acquiring any skill at putting those rules to use in the cognitive engagement with particulars. Indeed, as he goes on to remark, it is possible to acquire learned understanding to a considerable degree without having common understanding at all.

> A doctor . . . a judge or a statesman can have many fine pathological, juridical or political rules in his head, to the degree that he can even be a thorough teacher of them, but yet may nevertheless easily stumble in the application of these rules, either because he is lacking in the natural power of judgment (although not in understanding) and can indeed grasp the universal *in abstracto* but cannot determine whether a case *in concreto* belongs under

it, or also because he was not trained sufficiently in this judgment through examples and actual business. (A134 /B173)

Again, we see that common and learned understanding are distinct: they can come apart. The record of the logic lectures shows Kant to be far more derisive than he is here about such a scenario where a person has learnedness without common healthy understanding;[10] here, he allows that such a person could at least potentially be a thorough teacher of the rules. At any rate, it becomes quite clear that common understanding is developed through practice rather than some kind of explicit instruction in rules. That is why *Logik Blomberg* presents common understanding as '*gebildete*' understanding (24:21) – for it *is* an understanding that has been educated, formed and developed in some sense – and yet notes that 'healthy human understanding grows without instruction [wächst ohne Unterweisung]' (24:23).

By referring to *healthy* human understanding, Kant points to the realisation of a *natural* standard in some sense. In *Blomberg*, learning to think is likened to learning to walk, presumably because natural impulses engage us in ways that lead to our learning both:

> As a human being learns to walk, so does he also learn to think. This understanding so educated [gebildete] [is] *sens commun*. When it is correct, it is called healthy understanding, because the skill [Fertigkeit] of using it is subjected to a common use. The frequent use of our understanding among the objects of experience makes us finally fit to use it correctly. It can become correct, then, through mere practice and use. (LB 24:21)

A child will have a natural impulse to develop certain motor skills, among them walking; the capacity to walk will be acquired by engaging this impulse – attempting to walk, until she reaches the point where she can walk.[11] Hence, the capacity to walk is acquired through exercise and practice. But what about thinking? Kant clearly means thinking deployed for a cognitive end, not thinking merely as some state of consciousness or another. Indeed, if we are to take the comparison with walking at all seriously, then the idea should be that there are undeveloped movements of the mind that only gradually become *thoughts* inasmuch as they are 'subjected to a common use': and by that, presumably, he means something like a shared understanding of how things are.[12] (Likewise, there

---

[10] *Logik Blomberg* (24: 18ff., passim) in particular records Kant taking an especially mocking tone about such pedantry.

[11] I discuss this sort of example further in Chapter 6 (§6.3), in connection with Kant's discussion of skill.

[12] I develop this idea in Chapter 3.

are the undeveloped bodily movements of infants that gradually become, through some kind of effort and practice, particular motor skills, such as walking.)

Health, in its standard meaning, can be thought of as the robustness of the realisation of a form of life. It is a normative standard in the sense that a creature can be alive without being healthy. But to be healthy is, at least in some sense, to be what one properly ought to be as an instance of a certain life form. Now, Kant repeatedly points to healthy understanding as a basic requirement: 'the least that can be expected of one who makes claim to the name of a human being' (KU 5:293; cf. KU 5:265, LB 24:21). There are aspects of physical health that we think of in these terms, at least barring physical impediments – e.g. the capacity to walk. It would take a strange (and probably pathological) sort of wilfulness to fail to develop the capacity to walk, barring physical disability: it just comes as part of the normal course of things, and in that sense is not normally regarded as a particular achievement. It is just what is expected. But the same does not quite follow, apparently, for common human understanding – at least not inasmuch as it realises the standard of health. By 'common', Kant stresses, he does not mean 'the same as the vulgar [das vulgare], which is encountered everywhere': the common understanding, inasmuch as it realises this standard of health, is rather 'a merit [Verdienst] or an asset [Vorzug]' (KU 5:293) – suggesting that it is a good acquired through some kind of deliberate effort. Healthy human understanding is an achievement of some kind; we will examine that idea when we return to the three maxims in §2.4.

This standard of cognitive health is also conceived, perhaps not surprisingly, as a standard of correctness. As already noted, healthy understanding is simply common understanding that is correct (Prol 4:369; see also AParow 25:359, LB 24:22). But there is an ambiguity in this. Kant glosses healthy understanding (*gesunder Verstand*) as 'nothing other than' the 'correct use' of the power of judgment (KU 5:169). The idea might then be akin to the correct use of a tool: there is a certain way that one needs to hold a knife, and to manipulate it, if one is going to put it to purposeful use – say, to cut cleanly and efficiently with it. But there might also be further requirements or guidelines that come into play depending on what one is aiming to cut (leather or cake, say). What might lead to efficient cutting in one case (e.g. making little sawing movements) will not lead to efficient cutting in another (where a single downward pressure might work best). So, there might be general requirements on correct use – what obtains as long as one aims to make purposeful use of the tool or capacity in question – and further requirements on correct use that depend on the particular object on which one puts the tool or capacity to use. As I suggested in the previous section, and aim to defend further in the remainder of the chapter, the three maxims of healthy human understanding point to a *general* standard of correctness for the exercise of judgment *in concreto*. But Kant also often speaks of 'healthy' understanding, as formed through the engagement of the relevant substantive principles constitutively required for thought in a certain domain. Common understanding grasps these principles only tacitly: the comprehension of these principles is manifest directly in an appropriate engagement with the relevant particulars. It is distinguished from learned or scientific understanding, which grasps the principles *as* principles – expressed in the form of universality – and in this respect, at least, is clear where common understanding remains obscure (KU 5:238; Anth 7:139–40).

But the obscurity at issue concerns only the grasp of the rules themselves, as rules: a person with healthy understanding should be perfectly sharp-sighted about the particulars. That common understanding figures as 'obscure' at all is perhaps a relic of the German rationalist tradition – and Meier's logic – from which Kant's take on the idea of common versus learned understanding proceeds in the first place. Kant makes quite clear that, in his view, common understanding is lacking in nothing essential in many contexts. Consider this remark from Kant's account of the principle of the permanence of substance (the First Analogy) in the first *Critique*:

> I find that in all ages, not only philosophers, but even the common understanding, have presupposed this persistence as a substratum of all change in the appearances, and always also take it to be indubitable – it is only that the philosopher expresses himself on this point somewhat more determinately in saying that in all alterations in the world *substance* remains and only the *accidents* change. (A184/B227)

Common understanding and the philosopher alike grasp the principle of the permanence of substance – but each in a different way. Common understanding engages with particulars in such a way as to make manifest its grasp of the principle: there is an understanding of, and engagement with, the particulars that relies tacitly on the knowledge that there is something that endures through alterations in the phenomena, so that this something does not itself pop in and out of existence. But there is no explicit grasp of this principle in common understanding. Kant's remark here is actually part of a complaint: what philosophers typically add to this is simply the explicit representation of this principle in an ontology, without any account of its validity. Philosophers, Kant continues, have never yet attempted any 'proof of this obviously synthetic proposition' (A184/B227): to do that, presumably, requires not mere abstraction or learnedness, but science. Nevertheless, anyone who is capable of enjoying experience of an objective world must, in Kant's view, grasp this principle; we only require learnedness to formulate the principle, and science of some sort to justify it.[13]

In light of this, it is worth pointing out that Kant sometimes links healthy understanding to experience. One example comes from the continuation of the passage from *Blomberg*, where 'the skill [Fertigkeit]' of healthy understanding is

> subjected to a common use. The frequent use of our understanding among the objects of experience finally makes us fit to use it correctly. It can become correct, then, through mere practice and use . . . [T]he only instructor [Lehr Meister] of common understanding is experience. (LB 24:21)

These remarks reinforce the interpretation of the passage from the First Analogy just offered: common understanding is developed through concrete engagement with particulars, and thus through experience. The core idea here might just be that it is the concrete engagement with particulars that develops, or renders fit, one's understanding. Hence, Kant goes on record, in the passage just quoted, saying that experience is the sole instructor of common understanding: for it has knowledge through practice and use, knowledge which cannot (as such) be received through the communication of rules or principles. The relevant capacity can only be

---

[13] The experimental natural scientist portrayed in the *Critique*'s Preface, who puts nature to the question by framing 'experiments thought out in accordance with' certain principles – namely the principles 'according to which alone agreement among appearances can count as laws' (Bxiii), to wit: the principles of pure understanding – also presumably grasps these principles explicitly and *in abstracto*. However, the experimental natural scientist is presumably happy to rely on them to frame the experiments required to elucidate the phenomena, without taking up the fundamental ontological claims behind them and their justification.

Cf. G (4:389–90), where Kant contends that '[a] metaphysics of morals . . . is indispensably necessary', as its demonstration of the source of the moral law in a priori reason stands to ward against common corruptions in moral thinking (e.g. in taking ostensible moral requirements to hold only for the most part, so as to make an exception for oneself). However, this remark does not touch the crucial issue for us here. For, it is possible for a person's moral thinking to be perfectly sound and her judgment perfectly sharp-sighted without her having any *explicit* grasp of the metaphysics of morals (indeed, even including an explicit grasp of the moral law in a formula). After all, one of Kant's characteristic claims is that metaphysics is not strictly a learned endeavour: we grasp basic metaphysics (whether that of nature, or of morals) tacitly simply in being able to make good use of the relevant cognitive capacities. For a passage that is representative of this tendency in Kant's thought, consider again A184/B227, quoted earlier in this section.

practised, or put to use, when one sees for oneself how things are. In the same spirit, Kant concludes his presentation of the three maxims in the *Anthropology* – maxims which are designated in the third *Critique* as maxims of 'healthy human understanding' – by pointing again to experience as the ground on which this quality of understanding is developed.

> The most important revolution from within the human being is 'his exit [Ausgang] from his self-incurred minority [Unmündigkeit]'. Before this revolution, he let others think for him and merely imitated others or allowed them to guide him by leading-strings. Now he ventures to advance, although still shakily, with his own feet on the ground of experience. (Anth 7:229)[14]

The passage implies that the development of healthy understanding makes one fit – or, rather, as Kant implies, gives one the courage – to see for oneself how things are. Reading the passage in conjunction with the much earlier *Logik Blomberg*, we find a consistent set of claims: experience instructs common understanding; this instruction is not received from without, but rather by putting one's own capacities to use in seeing for oneself how things are; this yields a certain skill in thinking (as it is developed through practice and use) that is fundamentally required in order to be a healthy human being in the relevant sense; and this is why the outcome is conceived both as a matter of coming into cognitive maturity and as a coming into cognitive health. '[I]f someone does not have healthy understanding, he is a natural minor, a child. At least, then, we demand of everyone healthy understanding' (LB 24:21; see also KU 5:293 and 265).

But does the claim that healthy understanding is developed through experience entail that healthy understanding is a standard only of the *theoretical* use of cognitive capacities?[15] I don't think so. In the *Groundwork*, Kant clearly attributes to common human understanding both a practical and a theoretical engagement (see e.g. G 4:404). These distinct modes of its engagement will draw, respectively, on distinct principles: there are separate *substantive* requirements on each mode of thought. But this only reinforces what I have been claiming thus far, which at this point still has the status of a proposal: namely, that there should still be some *general* requirements on common human understanding, requirements that hold regardless of

---

[14] In one breath, Kant quotes here from his famous popular essay on enlightenment (Aufklärung 8:35) and alludes to his famous remarks about moral virtue as arising from a 'revolution' in a person's way of thinking (*Denkungsart*), from the *Religion* (6:47–8). Since the three maxims concern the manner of thinking (*Denkungsart*) that is required to make good use of one's cognitive capacities, the upshot seems to be that 'healthy' human understanding is the most basic human virtue: this, indeed, is what I will argue in Chapter 5.

[15] See note 6 in this chapter.

whether the thought at issue is theoretical (determining how things are in the domain of nature) or practical (determining what one ought to do). The argument of the *Groundwork* proceeds as an analysis from 'common moral rational cognition' – and, specifically, from the concept of a good will that 'already dwells in natural healthy understanding and needs not so much to be taught as only to be clarified' (G 4:397). The stated aim of the argument, then, is to make explicit the principle at work in common ethical thinking. And once that principle, the categorical imperative, is uncovered, Kant accordingly claims to 'have arrived, within the moral cognition of common human reason, at its principle, which it admittedly does not think so abstractly in a universal form but which it actually has always before its eyes and uses as the norm for its appraisals' (4:403).[16] There is a slight shift in terminology: Kant claimed initially that the concept of a good will is already present in common human *understanding*, but he speaks here of common human *reason* – presumably to indicate that the cognition at issue is practical rather than theoretical.[17]

This suggests that there is a general distinction to be drawn between common and cultivated understanding: the one is the power to judge *in concreto*, without explicit representation of the rules or principles governing these determinations; the other is a cognition of the rules or principles as rules, in universal form and in some kind of systematic order. This distinction will, of course, be articulated in distinct ways, depending on the principles at issue: these principles are the source of the relevant mode of knowledge and are, in that sense at least, *objective*. They are therefore *also* part of what it is for common understanding to be correct, and so 'healthy': one's thinking manifests a tacit appreciation of the appropriate substantive requirements on thinking correctly about objects in a certain domain.[18] But

---

[16] See also a similar remark after the first statement of the categorical imperative, at G 4:402.

[17] Thus, the cognition in question issues from the one substantive principle that can be traced to reason alone: the moral law. In the opening sections of the Transcendental Dialectic, Kant argues that pure reason alone cannot be the source of any theoretical synthetic a priori principles (A293–38/B349–96), pointing the way to his later presentation of the categorical imperative as a synthetic a priori practical principle (G 4:420; KpV 5:31).

[18] There are other differences between the way the common/scientific understanding distinction is drawn in theoretical and practical contexts – i.e. differences that go beyond the obvious fact that distinct objective principles are at work in each. One issue is whether the scientific presentation of the principles extends or enhances our knowledge in the relevant domain beyond what is possible for common or healthy understanding (i.e. without explicit, clear and systematic comprehension of the principles involved). If someone must *explicitly* grasp the principle of the permanence of substance in order to frame an experiment that can appropriately put nature to the question, so as to yield, in turn, knowledge of empirical natural law (see Bxiii), then scientific understanding conceivably renders us more discerning – more keenly appreciative – of what there is to be known than is possible through common understanding alone. Kant does not seem to allow this to be the case in

that still allows for the possibility that there are standards of correctness at work in healthy human understanding that are *subjective* in the sense that they concern the correct manner or spirit with which to engage one's cognitive capacities at all, at least when they are put to use in judging *in concreto*. These subjective standards, as I will argue in the remainder of the chapter, are the three maxims of healthy human understanding.

Before returning to the three maxims, let me take account of the epigraph of this chapter, which I draw from notes that Kant wrote as he prepared the *Prolegomena*. It can seem, from a cursory and historically unmoored reading of the *Prolegomena*, that Kant takes a disparaging attitude towards common and healthy understanding therein (see e.g. Prol 4: 259, 313–14, 369–70).[19] But Kant's remarks are targeted against the 'popular' philosophers of his day,[20] who appealed to common sense as a kind of 'oracle' (Prol 4:259)[21] or 'divining rod' (Prol 4:369) to settle matters in metaphysics, and who regarded the *Critique* as only so much 'long-winded pedantic pomp' (Prol 4:314).[22] Later, Kant encapsulates the same

---

the practical sphere: the 'practical faculty of judgment [praktische Beurtheilungsvermögen] . . . in common human understanding', he claims, 'can have as good a hope of hitting the mark as any philosopher can promise himself' (G 4:404). A related issue, implicit in this remark, concerns the role that wisdom plays on the practical side, which Kant presents as an excellence of practical reason that is in principle commonly attainable – i.e. it requires no abstract representation of the law, and so requires neither science nor philosophy to be cultivated. I will have something to say about wisdom in relation to healthy human understanding towards the end of this chapter.

[19] See also the scepticism about common understanding (as '*asylum ignorantiae*') noted at RMet-5637 [1780s] (18:275).

[20] For example, Christian Garve, co-author of the first major review of the *Critique* in 1782. Kant mentions elsewhere Garve's 'maxim' that 'every philosophic teaching be capable of being made *popular* (that is, of being sufficiently clear to the senses to be communicated to everyone) if the teacher is not to be suspected of being muddled in his own concepts' (MS 6:206). He denies that the maxim holds for his Critical philosophy (see also Kant's 7 August 1783 letter to Garve (10:339)), but since the Critical philosophy makes explicit the constitutive principles of the theoretical and practical engagements of human reason, he nevertheless allows that – at least on the practical side – 'its results can be made quite illuminating for the healthy reason (of an unwitting metaphysician)' (MS 6:206). Cf. Kant's 1799 open letter on Fichte's *Wissenschaftslehre*: 'I declare here again that the *Critique* is to be understood . . . from the standpoint of common understanding, yet just as it is sufficiently cultivated [cultivirt] for such abstract investigations' (12:371).

[21] Kant's essay 'What Does It Mean to Orient Oneself in Thinking?' disparages the appeal to common sense as an oracular source of metaphysical knowledge (substantive a priori claims). It addresses Moses Mendelssohn's 'maxim that it is necessary to orient oneself in the speculative use of reason by means of a certain guideline that he called *common sense* [*Gemeinsinn*] or *healthy reason* [*gesunde Vernunft*]' (Orientiren 8:133; alluded to at RL-2268 [1780s? or late 1770s?] 16:293; cf. LJ 9:57). The essay is complex, because it partly defends, partly criticises, Mendelssohn. In defence, Kant claims that Mendelssohn did not in fact appeal to common sense as an oracle for metaphysics, but rather rested his claims on a conception of healthy human reason; but he criticises Mendelssohn for supposing that a speculative theoretical demonstration of God's existence could be wrung from this appeal.

[22] See Kuehn (1987: 191–202) and Ameriks (2006) for accounts of this historical context.

frustrations when he notes that some 'praise' common or healthy understanding 'to the point of enthusiasm [Schwärmerei] and represent it as
a rich source of treasure lying hidden in the mind, ... its pronounce-
ment as an oracle ... more reliable than anything academic science offers
for sale' (Anth 7:139; cf. Orientiren 8:134). Kant is ambivalent about the
place of common or healthy understanding in metaphysics: this is because
his critical inquiry – which is supposed to take the first steps in putting
metaphysics on the sure path of a science – begins by illuminating what
is implicitly grasped in healthy human understanding itself, by providing the (putatively) comprehensive and systematic account of its principles. However, since Kant takes philosophical cognition to be 'rational
cognition from concepts' (A713/B741), its results are not *to be confirmed*
through some demonstration of their applicability to particulars.[23] Common understanding employs principles of which it has no explicit grasp,
and for which – a fortiori – it 'does not understand the justification' (Prol
4:259; cf. 4:369). Thus, the 'scientific' critical elucidation of these principles does not merely make them explicit: it should also provide this
justification.[24]

Kant's seemingly disparaging remarks about common and healthy
understanding in the *Prolegomena* are a reaction to the particular philosophical climate in which the *Critique* had been received. His point is
strictly methodological, and in no way amounts to any failure to appreciate the value of healthy understanding. He decries the methodologically
unmoored appeal to common sense in metaphysics as *Schwärmerei*; but he
remains – as noted in the epigraph to the present chapter –'an enthusias-
tic advocate of healthy human understanding'.[25] Indeed, he values healthy
understanding as the most basic human virtue: this is the idea that I
will develop and defend in the remainder of this chapter, and further in
Chapter 5.

[23] Its results should come, rather, from the analysis and systematic determination of concepts alone;
but this does not mean that its results should be unmoored from what can be appreciated through
healthy human understanding.

[24] Consider, moreover, the worry Kant raises in the Phenomena and Noumena chapter of the first *Critique*: 'If, therefore, through this critical investigation we learn nothing more than what we should
in any case have practised in the merely empirical use of the understanding, even without such
subtle inquiry, then it would seem the advantage that one will draw from it would hardly be worth
the expense and preparation' (A237/B296). His answer is that this critical investigation – the first
step of putting metaphysics on the path of a science – is not simply a matter of making these principles explicit: the systematic presentation of these principles should be *such as* to provide their
justification.

[25] *Schwärmerei* is consistently linked, in Kant's usage, with superstition and the presumption to have
insight into what lies outside of the bounds of possible experience. *Enthusiasmus*, by contrast, is just
sanguinity. In the epigraph, Kant expresses the latter.

2.4 The Three Maxims and the Requirement to Reflect-n

We have looked at some length into Kant's conception of healthy understanding and its three maxims; now I want to show in greater detail how these maxims offer a more nuanced version of the requirement to reflect-n, at least where the judging is *in concreto*.[26] Later, I will argue that this revised picture of the requirement to reflect-n can assuage the concern that was raised initially about it (in the Introduction), and which went unaddressed by our first-pass interpretation of it (in Chapter 1): namely, that a requirement to step back on the occasion of each judgment to consider the source of one's taking things to be a certain way simply issues the wrong demand.

At this point, the case for reading the three maxims as a further articulation of the requirement to reflect-n can be made rather quickly, at least in rough outline. We know now that common understanding is the power to judge *in concreto*, and that healthy understanding is this very capacity insofar as it meets some normative standard of correctness. The three maxims spell out that normative standard of correctness: they are, after all, the maxims of common understanding inasmuch as it is 'merely healthy (not yet cultivated)' (KU 5:293). These maxims do not concern what correctness requires in the objective sense; the objective principles requisite for engaging one's thought appropriately about objects in this or that domain (the principles of pure understanding, on the theoretical side; and the moral law, on the practical side) are not specifically in view here. That is why Kant underscores that he is not speaking here of the 'faculty of cognition, but rather of the *way of thinking* [*Denkungsart*] for making purposive use of it' (5:295). The maxims concern correctness in the frame of mind for putting one's cognitive capacities to purposive use, i.e. to know by means of them. In the remainder of this section, I will elaborate on this claim: I will argue that to form one's thinking according to the three maxims is to undertake, directly in the engagement of one's cognitive capacities, basic epistemic commitments required for making purposive use of those capacities.

[26] This is meant to allow that the requirement at issue in the claim that 'all judgments require reflection' may need to be differently articulated for judgment *in abstracto*. In Merritt (2015), I point out that there is a sense of 'reflection' that Kant appears to derive from German rationalist logic (particularly Meier), which is a comparison of concepts in order to set them into some systematic order; I suggest there that this is what Kant points to in the Amphiboly when he accuses Leibniz of reflecting merely logically where he ought to have reflected 'transcendentally'. This 'logical' notion of reflection surfaces in *Logik Jäsche*, when it is remarked that 'systematic cognition' is composed 'according to rules on which one has reflected [nach überlegten Regeln]' (LJ 9:139). Such reflection is surely necessary (if not sufficient) for correct judgment *in abstracto* – but it is not my topic here.

2.4.1   The Basic Epistemic Commitments

When Kant presents the three maxims in the *Critique of Judgment*, he attributes them to *sensus communis* – which often figures, in his own renderings, as the Latin gloss for common understanding (*gemeiner Verstand*).[27] He then says that by *sensus communis* he means

> the idea of a *communal* sense [die Idee eines *gemeinschaftlichen* Sinnes], i.e., a faculty of judging [Beurtheilungsvermögen] that in its reflection [Reflexion] takes account (a priori) of everyone else's way of representing in thought, in order *as it were* to hold its judgment up to human reason as a whole [gesammte Menschenvernunft] and thereby avoid the illusion which, from subjective private conditions that could easily be held to be objective, would have a detrimental influence on the judgment. (KU 5:293)

Kant refers here to a 'reflection' in the activity of judging, and he goes on to suggest that this 'operation of reflection' can be articulated in the formulas represented abstractly as the three maxims – underscoring, however, that common understanding does not conduct itself by representing the maxims explicitly (KU 5:294). Another thing to note here is that Kant's account of this 'reflection' in the passage seems to place special emphasis on the second maxim, *to think in the position of everyone else*: the reflection is presented as a matter of holding one's own judgment (a given mental state) up to the thoughts of everyone else *in order* to avoid a certain illusion. The illusion that is to be avoided is one that arises from taking 'subjective private conditions' to be 'objective': the former, he later elaborates, are those that 'contingently attach' to one's own judging, whereas the latter hold for anyone (KU 5:294). We can recall from Chapter 1 that Kant often presents prejudice in just these terms.[28] So, he is clearly alluding here to the idea that reflection-n is the antidote to prejudice. At the same time, the context of this allusion implies that it is through the adoption of the three maxims that one frees oneself from prejudice – and thus, presumably, reflects-n.

At the beginning of this chapter, I suggested that there are two thematic concerns at issue in the three maxims: originality and communicability, which are foregrounded in the first and second maxims, respectively. However, in the passage just quoted, Kant does seem to place special emphasis on the second maxim, and its theme of communicability. Why might this be? Although the three maxims have to be taken as a complete package in order for any one of them to contribute to the end of making purposive use

---

[27] The maxims *hold for* common understanding, and adequate adherence to them makes common understanding correct or 'healthy'.

[28] Noted in §1.4; see e.g. LJ (9:76); RL-2528 [1770s] (16:406).

of one's cognitive capacities,[29] it is the adoption of the second maxim that brings with it a basic epistemic commitment to the independence of the objects of knowledge from any particular point of view on them. The first maxim, *to think for oneself,* calls for one to care to be the source of one's own thoughts. On its own, the first maxim does not imply any recognition that there are distinct points of view on how things are: it just calls for one to think for oneself, which it is in principle possible to do without recognising alternative points of view. The second maxim requires one to think from the perspective of another,[30] and thus to recognise that multiple perspectives are possible on some matter of shared cognitive concern. The second maxim thereby brings in its tow a fundamental epistemic commitment: namely, the independence of any object of knowledge from the contingencies of any particular point of view on it.[31]

However, there is another basic epistemic commitment at work in the maxims, one that is linked to the theme of originality expressed in the first maxim, and again in the third. The first maxim calls for one to think for oneself: taken on its own, however, this implies nothing about the exercise and cultivation of *cognitive* capacities. In that regard, at least, the crucial move is made with the second maxim, as it introduces the commitment to the independence of objects. However, the third maxim, we can recall, is supposed to arise from a kind of fluency or merged 'skill' (*Fertigkeit*) with the first two (KU 5:295): so it returns to the theme of originality, but now with genuinely cognitive ends in view. The third maxim is *to think always consistently with oneself.* Of course, I must take an interest in the consistency of my own thoughts if I am to recognise them one and all as *my* thoughts. But it is not thoughts that I might have indifferently to their objective purport that is now at issue; rather, it is thought that lays claim to a point of view on how things are in a publicly available world.

When Kant speaks here of the 'reflection' of healthy understanding as a matter of holding one's judgment 'up to human reason as a whole' (KU 5:293), he again invokes the idea that reflection-n involves comparing a given mental state against some broader whole to which one is in some

---

[29] I have argued elsewhere that the thee maxims come as a complete package – as jointly required for making purposive use of one's cognitive capacities (Merritt 2009, 2011a, 2011b). A brief version of this argument was offered earlier in this chapter (§2.2); it relies on the idea that the first maxim addresses the prejudices of cognitive passivity, while the second addresses the prejudices of logical egoism. So we need both, and their synthesis in the third maxim, to make good use of our cognitive capacities.

[30] This is the non-ideal version of the second maxim, which expresses the minimal requirement at issue.

[31] Kant links the second maxim to the power of judgment. On Kant's conception of the objective and intersubjective validity of judgment as laying claim to 'what is the case in a public world shared with other thinkers', see also Kohl (2015, 310).

sense committed. The given mental state is some point of view on how things are; this is what is compared against 'human reason as a whole'. The implication is that the reflective person will accept the point of view in question if it is one that is in principle open to anyone to take, or reject it if it is not. Thus, it requires the ideal variant, *to think from the position of everyone else*. So, when the third maxim calls for one to care to be the coherent source of one's own thoughts, the coherence at issue can only be one that arises through fidelity to how things are independently of any particular point of view on them.

To sum up: as a package, the three maxims concern what it is to take the appropriate interest in one's own cognitive agency. This interest is not something that drives a separate activity of self-scrutiny: rather, it is simply *how* one stands to make good use of one's cognitive capacities, and thus is a proper part of the outward-directed activity of judgment. Thus, the three maxims concern *how* to know in general terms. Thematically, they point to two aspects of this broadly practical knowledge of knowing how to know: originality and communicability. To make good use of one's cognitive capacities, and so to know how to know, one has to care to be the source of one's own thoughts – for, even if one (say) accepts something on testimony, one must still care to integrate it into a coherent view of how things are. That is the first commitment. The second is that one must be committed to the independence of objects from any particular point of view on them. These two commitments can be summed up as taking the appropriate interest in one's own cognitive agency: and this, I submit, is how Kant ultimately comes to understand the normative requirement to reflect, or reflection-n.

Further, by presenting these maxims as the commitments of common human understanding, Kant suggests that they can be undertaken, perfectly adequately, directly in the cognitive engagement with particulars. The implication of their status as maxims of *common* healthy understanding, in other words, is that no stepping back from the occasion of judgment need be involved. Thus, if my thesis is correct – that these maxims articulate what it is to meet the normative requirement to reflect (for judgment *in concreto*) – then that requirement is met in adverbial fashion: it is met by considering how things are *in the right spirit*.

2.4.2   *The Normative Significance of the Two Variants of the Second Maxim*

In the concluding section, I will draw upon this result to respond to the lingering concern about Kant's claim that 'all judgments require reflection'.

Before that, however, I want to consider a puzzle about the normative significance of the three maxims that raises questions about their place in the systematic frame of Kant's thought. As we have just seen, in the *Critique of Judgment* the three maxims are principles of 'healthy human understanding', which is itself deemed 'the least that can be expected of one who makes claim to the name of a human being' (KU 5:293; quoted earlier). In the *Anthropology*, however, they are presented as maxims 'leading to wisdom' (7:200 and 228) – where wisdom is glossed as 'the idea of a practical use of reason that conforms perfectly with the law, [and] is no doubt too much to demand of human beings' (7:200). So, we have, on the one hand, a claim that the three maxims form the basis of a standard of cognitive 'health' that is 'the least' that can be demanded or expected of a human being; and on the other, a claim that they 'lead' to wisdom, which Kant indicates is a cognitive ideal that is 'too much' to be demanded of any given human being. To take full account of this, it will be necessary to consider the relation between moral and cognitive virtue by Kant's lights, which is my task in Chapter 5. Here, I will provide an initial account of these claims, by taking into consideration two further details about the presentation of the three maxims in the *Anthropology*.

The first detail is that the three maxims are presented twice in that work: Kant first presents them with the non-ideal variant for the second maxim, *to think in the position of another* (7:200), then presents them again with the ideal variant, *to think in the position of everyone else* (7:228). So, even though we find both variants throughout the textual record, it cannot be assumed that Kant changed his mind about the content of the second maxim from one text to another, since we find both in the *Anthropology*.[32] Closer attention to the two variants should help us understand the seemingly disparate normative upshot of the three maxims – as required for basic cognitive 'health', or as leading to 'wisdom'. To explain why, we will need to take note of another detail: as Kant gears up to present the maxims for the second time, he points out that the employment of the cognitive capacity – *in its theoretical and practical uses alike*, as he explicitly says – is directed by reason (Anth 7:227). Kant says that the 'demand that reason makes on the cognitive faculty' can be expressed in three questions, each lodged, as it were, by a distinct element of the higher cognitive faculty.[33] The grounds

---

[32] See Table 3. The earliest complete statement of the three maxims, as far as I can make out, occurs in RA-1486, which Adickes dates from the late 1770s; it has the non-ideal variant for the second maxim. The earliest complete statement of the three maxims with the *ideal* variant for the second maxim (that I am aware of) comes in KU (1790).

[33] Kant thus suggests that reason guides the entire use of the cognitive faculty *as* 'the faculty of ends' (for this gloss on reason, see KpV (5:59)).

for supposing that reason, in its general direction of the cognitive faculty, should be conceived as the faculty of ends is that the leading question concerns the determination of one's cognitive ends, and the remaining two questions concern the implications of this:

> *What do I want [to know]?* (asks understanding)[34]
> *What does it matter?*[35] (asks the power of judgment)
> *What comes of it?* (asks reason). (Anth 7:227)

Kant points out that it is comparatively easy to know what one's cognitive ends are, and so (in effect) to answer the first question. It is much harder, he suggests, to know what is relevant – what ought to *matter* to one – in light of those ends. This, he attributes to the power of judgment, which he illustrates with an example of a lawyer who has the 'talent for selecting what is exactly appropriate' – or salient – 'in a given case' (Anth 7:228). (As for the third question: as long as one is clear about what one wants to know, and what matters in relation to those ends, Kant claims that 'the verdict of reason follows by itself' (Anth 7:228).) So, a judgment, in Kant's view, cannot be an unmotivated statement that *p*: it is not merely to claim that *p*, but rather to claim this with a certain force. It is to maintain that *p* matters, is worth considering or paying attention to. Consider this in light of the fact that the second maxim calls for one to think one's way into the perspective of others 'in communication' with them, as Kant says twice in the *Anthropology* account (7:200 and 228). We do not simply communicate facts; we make claims on one another's attention. Judging at least potentially makes a claim on others about what matters, what is worth paying attention to.[36]

---

[34] Or, as Kant elaborates in the appended footnote, 'What do I want to assert as *true?*'
[35] I am following here Louden's translation; Makkreel (2014, 36) suggests 'What is at stake?' The German is '*Worauf kommts an?*', which might also be rendered 'What depends on it?' – i.e. 'What depends on its being true?', or 'How must the world be if whatever I want to assert is true is in fact true?' The account that I will offer of this question in the main text will show these translations not to be as far apart as they might initially seem. Makkreel (2014) discusses these three 'demands' of reason, linking them to the three maxims, epistemic character and wisdom along lines that are at times consonant with my arguments in this chapter.
[36] See *Blomberg* for interesting remarks about a natural human drive to communicate, noting that if someone were to find himself in conditions where communication were impossible (e.g. marooned on a desert island), his judgments would seem pointless and 'in vain' (LB 24:178). This remark belongs to a discussion that deals with themes reminiscent of the second maxim, and that regards a commitment to the second maxim as the antidote to logical egoism. The striking conclusion is thus: 'By instinct, the human being's understanding is *communicatio*. If it is to be communicative [mittheilend], it must really be sympathetic [theilnehmend], too' (LB 24:179). For discussion of this and similar remarks, in support of an account of the importance of testimony in Kantian epistemology, see Gelfert (2006), and along similar lines Mikelsen (2010). On the importance of communication to the interpretation of the three maxims, see also Deligiorgi (2002).

The second maxim, we have seen, is linked with the power of judgment. It is also presented in a non-ideal as well as an ideal variant. The non-ideal variant tells one to think from the perspective of another person.[37] This calls for one to consider what *matters* to that person, or ought to, in light of what she cares to understand. The non-ideal variant of the second maxim effectively recognises that different things are going to matter to different people, depending on their cognitive ends. Most of our cognitive ends are discretionary. It is a contingent fact about me that I have taken on this project; I need not have ever cared. But I did care, and this mandates, to some extent, what I need to pay attention to and come to grips with. So, although to judge that *p* is effectively to say that *p* matters, or is worth paying attention to, I may just be saying that *p* matters to me. I might recognise full well that it doesn't matter to you and is unlikely to matter to you: for example, I don't assume that my parents should care that much about Kant, at least not unless I can explain him properly – which, in this instance, may well involve showing why what he had to say on some topic should matter to any human being (a tall order, perhaps). Likewise, if *p* is my answer to some question that you put to me, the force of my claim may not be that *p* matters to me. (If I am simply conveying information, and do not take any special interest in your affairs, I might be relatively indifferent to the fact that *p*.) But my judgment that *p*, as a response to your question, acknowledges that *p* matters to you. The non-ideal variant of the second maxim suggests that judgment has this force, at least in the context of communication.

If the connection of the second maxim to the practice of judgment is to be understood in this way, then we can infer that the ideal variant of the second maxim calls for one to consider what ought to matter to anyone, regardless of discretionary cognitive ends. Since considerations of salience answer to ends, the ideal variant must effectively point to *obligatory* cognitive ends. But if the three maxims govern *common* understanding – the power to judge *in concreto* – then it must be the case that there are considerations arising from obligatory cognitive ends that mandate what, in the particulars, ought to figure as cognitively salient for anyone.[38]

---

[37] Although all of the maxims are formulated as positive commands, Kant says that the first maxim is 'negative' since it requires that one keep oneself *free from* the external constraints on thought that come into force when one cedes cognitive authority, without warrant, to others (7:228), whereas the second maxim is 'positive'. He does not adequately explain himself on this point. I surmise that he might mean that the second maxim, like an imperfect duty of virtue, does not set out exactly what one will need to do or refrain from doing. It simply calls for one to take an active interest in comprehending the mindedness, or point of view, of others. But it does not specify *which* others, or with regard to *which* objects of mutual cognitive concern.

[38] In Chapter 7, I will suggest that what ought to figure as cognitively salient for anyone are facts about the existence of actual persons.

Now, I think this tells us just enough to begin to come to grips with Kant's claim that the three maxims both are the standard of basic cognitive health (the least that can be expected of anyone) and lead to wisdom (more than can be expected of anyone). For, wisdom, by Kant's lights, is moral virtue (MS 6:405) – *human* wisdom is, at any rate.[39] In the *Groundwork*, Kant says that wisdom consists more 'in conduct [Thun und Lassen]' than in knowledge in the sense of '*Wissen*' (4:405). *Wissen* is the comprehensive mode of knowledge that Kant associates with reason: it involves the systematic grasp of some whole, rather than the piecemeal determination of isolated truths. Science, *Wissenschaft*, is the product of *Wissen*, when it is carried out according to the right method. Kant is not claiming that wisdom (*Weißheit*) has nothing to do with *Wissen*, but only that it cannot be reduced to it. So, Kant's point in the remark from the *Groundwork* is evidently that wisdom must be distinguished from some disinterested grasp of the complete order of things. It must instead be governed or shaped by some appreciation of what is most significant, what is most worth caring about, in this complete order of things. When Kant claims that the three maxims 'lead' to wisdom, he notes that wisdom can only be 'brought forth from oneself': 'not the least degree of [wisdom] can be poured into one by someone else' (Anth 7:200). Only you can make yourself wise. This is so for the same reason that healthy understanding cannot be acquired through instruction, but rather can only be formed through the practice of judging itself: you have to see for yourself what matters, in light of your cognitive ends. The ideal formulation of the second maxim suggests that one needs to appreciate what is salient in light of obligatory cognitive ends, and that this is the foundation on which wisdom, or moral virtue, can be cultivated. This is why, I think, wisdom is often presented as a matter of taking the appropriate perspective on things: the wise person is neither bothered nor unduly excited by trivialities. Consider the nature of wise words: while they may be consoling, they are not necessarily what a person wants to hear. They are consoling only if, and only to the extent that, the person who receives them is capable of stretching himself beyond his most readily available perspective on what matters. Colloquially, we say that a wise person has things in perspective. This is a perspective that is not only open to anyone to take, but indeed that anyone ought to take, on what matters.

[39] Kant notes that wisdom can be either a divine or a human attribute, and thus potentially obscures a distinction that should otherwise be drawn between holiness and virtue (KpV 5:11n). I return to this point in Chapter 7.

2.5   Conclusion

I have argued in this chapter that the requirement to reflect-n is articulated, at least where judgment *in concreto* is at stake, as the three maxims of common human understanding. This interpretation preserves the core claim of the initial interpretation: the three maxims concern the way of thinking – the general mindedness, or *Denkungsart* – required to make purposive use of one's cognitive capacities (KU 5:295). And so, the three maxims concern how to take the appropriate interest in one's own cognitive agency. This interest is internal to sound judgment: it is simply part of what it is to judge well. Reflection-n can therefore be conceived adverbially, in terms of the manner in which one puts one's cognitive capacities to use *in concreto*. It is not a separate, discrete activity: something further that one might 'do' on the occasion of judgment. Therefore, the assumption on which the demandingness objection rests is misplaced, and the objection can be dismissed by recognising that the interest that one ought to take in one's own cognitive agency is not an independent concern that needs to be invoked on the occasion of each judgment. Indeed, it is perfectly possible to be in flourishing cognitive health without expressly recognising that one takes this interest at all, much less that one takes this interest in the appropriate way. There is no independent concern that needs to be invoked anew on the occasion of each judgment.

One other result of this chapter needs to be underscored. The three maxims of healthy human understanding spell out, in general terms, what it is to take the appropriate interest in one's own cognitive agency. As we saw in Chapter 1, failure to do so leads to prejudice: thus, the three maxims plausibly spell out the normative requirement to reflect, at least where judgment *in concreto* is concerned. Two basic epistemic commitments are implicit in these maxims: one is a commitment to be the source of one's own thoughts (a requirement that remains binding even when one accepts claims on testimony), the other is a commitment to the independence of objects from any particular point of view on them. Now, it might seem that 'taking an interest in one's own cognitive agency' – reflecting-n, in other words – is an especially advanced cognitive development. In the next chapter, I will argue that this is not so: as soon as one is capable of genuine thought at all (and thus reflects-c), one must also take on the basic commitments proper to the three maxims, at least in some nascent way – a result that proves crucial to my project of rethinking the Kantian reflective ideal.

Table 3 *The three maxims*

	General designation	Formulations	Glosses on the individual maxims, or other notes
Critique of Judgment, §40 (1790)	'maxims of common human understanding' (5:294), associated with *sensus communis* (5:293–5) Concern 'the way of thinking [Denkungsart] needed to make a purposive use' of the 'faculty of cognition [Vermögen des Erkenntnisses]' (5:295)	1. Think for oneself; 2. Think in the position of everyone else; 3. Always think in agreement with oneself '1. *Selbstdenken;* 2. *An der Stelle jedes andern denken;* 3. *Jederzeit mit sich selbst einstimmig denken*' (5:294)	First = 'maxim of the *unprejudiced* way of thinking [Denkungsart]'; the maxim of a reason that is never *passive*' (5:294); the 'maxim of understanding' (5:295) Second = the maxim of 'a *broad-minded* [erweiterte] way of thinking' (5:294, 295); the maxim 'of the power of judgment' (5:295) Third = the maxim 'of the *consistent* [consequent] way of thinking' (5:294, 295); the maxim 'of reason' (5:295)
Anthropology from a Pragmatic Point of View (1798)	Maxims 'leading to wisdom' (see 7:200 and 228)	Kant's presentation of the three maxims in the *Anthropology* is distinctive for its handling of the second maxim: first, because it presents the second maxim as governing the *communication* of thought to others, and second, because it presents both **non-ideal** and **ideal** variants of the second maxim **Ideal variant of the second maxim:** *to think in the position of everyone else* (7:228) **Non-ideal variant of the second maxim:** *to think in the position of another* (7:200)	First = 'The first principle is negative (*nullius addictus iurare in verba Magistri*) [no one is forced to follow the words of the master], the principle of *freedom from constraint*' (7:228) Second = 'the second is positive, the principle of *liberals* who adapt to the principles of others' (7:228) Third = 'the principle of the *consistent* (consequent) (logical) way of thinking' (7:228)
Logik Jäsche (1800)	Called 'universal rules and conditions for avoiding error in general'; as in KU, associated with 'common human understanding' (9:57	The presentation of the three maxims matches Anth (7:200) – i.e. has the **non-ideal variant** for the second maxim '1) to think for oneself, 2) to think oneself in the position of someone else, and 3) always to think in agreement with oneself' (9:57)	First = maxim of 'the *enlightened* way of thinking [Denkungsart]' Second = maxim of 'the *broad-minded* [erweiterte] way of thinking' Third = maxim of 'consequent or coherent mode of thought' (9:57)

Reflexionen zur Logik	As general conditions for the avoidance of error' (RL-2273, as we find at LJ 9:57)	RL-2273 [1790s]: '(a) selbst denken. (b) sich in der Stelle eines Andern zu denken; (c) jederzeit mit sich selbst einstimmig zu denken' (16:294) RL-2564 [late 1760s]: 'Erstlich Selbstdenken. An der Stelle jedes andern zu dennken. also sein Urtheil an andern zu prüfen' (16:419)	The later RL-2273 has a full statement of the three maxims, with the non-ideal variant of the second maxim The earlier RL-2564 has the first and second maxim only, with the second maxim in the ideal variant
Reflexionen zur Anthropologie	RA-456 [c. 1790s] (15:188) RA-1486 [c. 1775–77] (15: 715–716) RA-1508 [c. 1780–84] (15:820) 'maxims of a mature reason [Maximen einer reifen Vernunft]' (15:822)	RA-456: a) Selbstdenken. b) In der Stelle jedes anderen. c) Jederzeit mit sich selbst einstimmig denken' (15:188) RA-1486: '1) Selbst denken; 2) an der Stelle anderer (für die Urtheilskraft); 3) mit sich selbst einstimmming (conseqvente Denkart)' (15:715; the maxims are repeated again at 15:716)	Ideal variant for the second maxim in RA-456; non- ideal variant in RA-1486 and RA-1508 RA-1508 glosses the first as the maxim of 'free (not slavish) thought', and the other two in the pattern of KU (5:294, 295)
Anth. Busolt (c. 1788–89])	'principles of thinking'	'1. Das Selbstdenken; 2. Das denken an die Stelle eines andern; 3. Das jederzeit mit sich selbst übereinstimmende Denken' (25:1480).	Non-ideal variant for the second maxim
Aufklärung (1784)	Implicit discussion of at least the first two maxims	The first maxim appears under the guise of the 'motto of enlightenment': 'Have courage to make use of your *own* understanding!' (8:35)	The essay dwells on the issues of communication and publicity that lie at the heart of the second maxim
Orientiren (1786)	Implicit discussion of the three maxims at 8:144–5 and 146–7n	'the maxim of always thinking for oneself is **enlightenment**' (8:146n).	Claims that any 'external power' that would take 'away people's freedom publicly to *communicate* their thoughts also takes from them the freedom to *think*' (8:144)
Correspondence	Allusion to the first two maxims in a letter of Kant to Mendelssohn dated 16 August 1783	'Few men are so fortunate as to be able to think for themselves and at the same time be able to put themselves into someone else's position and adjust their style exactly to his requirements. There is only one Mendelssohn' (10:345)	

Table 4 *Common and healthy understanding (distinguished from learned understanding)*

Common	Learned
Common human understanding is the capacity to judge *in concreto* (e.g. Prol 4:369) 'The common understanding is . . . the faculty to have insight into rules of cognition *in concreto*' (LJ 9:19; corresponds to RL-1579 [c1760s, possibly early 1770s] 16:19) • This involves an indistinct or unconscious grasp of rules: 'We arrange all of our judgments in accordance with these laws [of the understanding]. As a child in walking learns to observe the laws of movement, so too, in judging, does it seek to form itself according to those laws of the understanding. All this it does unknowingly, and it acquires the skill through practice' (LB 24:27) • People with common understanding (*sensus communis*) are 'knowledgable in the application of rules to cases (*in concreto*)'; they are distinguished from people of *science*, who are knowledgeable of 'the rules themselves before their application (*in abstracto*)' (Anth 7:139)	**'Cultivated' or 'refined' understanding** (KU 5:293; AColl 25:157; RL-1573 16:12, RL-1576 16:15) is the capacity to judge *in abstracto*: • Common understanding is distinguished from 'learned' understanding in the early *Logik Blomberg*(passim); learned cognition 'must be conscious of its rules and use them in accordance with reflection [nach überlegung gebrauchen]' (LB 24:27) • The later *Logik Dohna-Wundlacken* [c. 1792] suggests that the distinction might be more appropriately drawn between common and 'scientific' understanding (LD-W 24:717); this is how the distinction is drawn in Anth (7:139) • Common understanding is distinguished from 'speculative' understanding chiefly in the *Prolegomena* (4:369–70); see also RL-1629 [1780s] (16:47)
healthy human understanding = '*common understanding*, insofar as it judges correctly [richtig urtheilt]' (Prol 4:369; see also AParow 25:359) = 'the correct use' of the power of judgment (KU 5:169) = 'the faculty of judging correctly *in concreto*' (LB 24:22; see also LB 24:21). = 'the faculty of rules *in concreto*' (RA-423 [c. 1766–68 or possibly c. 1772], 15:171) 'Correct understanding is healthy understanding, provided that it contains an *appropriateness* of concepts for the purpose of its use' (Anth 7:198; cf. VKK 2:269). **Healthy understanding is required of everyone:** '[I]f someone does not have a healthy understanding, he is a natural minor, a child. At least, then, we demand of everyone healthy understanding' (LB 24:21); '*Common human understanding* . . . as merely healthy (not yet cultivated) understanding, is regarded as the least that can be expected of one who lays claim to the name of a human being' (KU 5:293; cf. 5:265)	**Cultivated understanding needs healthy (common) understanding:** 'Common and healthy understanding lies at the basis of all learnedness; [learnedness] becomes ridiculous if it is not grafted on to this stem' (LB 24:19); 'healthy understanding and healthy reason . . . provide a basis for all abstract higher cognitions . . . learnedness always presupposes healthy understanding, [as] art does nature' (LB 24:21)

CHAPTER 3

Attention, Perception, Experience

3.1 Introduction

My overarching aim in this book is to reconsider the Kantian reflective ideal. In Chapter 1, I showed that Kant draws a distinction between reflection as a constitutive requirement on thought (reflection-c) and reflection as a normative requirement of sound judgment (reflection-n). The normative requirement to reflect figures in Kant's various statements that *all judgments require reflection*: this is the account of reflection that appears in applied logic, and can be traced to quite early in Kant's career. The first-pass interpretation of the claim *all judgments require reflection* left us with a lingering question about what to make of the demandingness of the requirement – one that stems from the apparent suggestion that it is to be met with some deliberate effort on the occasion of each and every judgment. In Chapter 2, I drew attention to the conception of healthy human understanding that becomes a particular concern towards the end of Kant's career (mostly from 1790 onwards), and argued that Kant ultimately understands the requirement to reflect-n in terms of the normative standard of healthy understanding. Thus, the requirement to reflect-n properly lodges at the level of character, rather than piecemeal over individual acts of judgment: the requirement is to take the appropriate interest in one's cognitive agency, where this interest governs cognitive activity globally.

My arguments in this chapter will follow through on this line of thought, taking up an overarching aim that I set out in the book's Introduction: namely, to explain how the (in some sense) passive exercise of cognitive capacities in sensible experience should in principle be no less the expression of the self-determination proper to a rational mind than are overt efforts of deliberation and inquiry.[1] To do this, we need to understand the

---

[1] The passivity of experience is something that McDowell (1994) underscores. Sometimes, the point is disputed, on the grounds that experience is *cognition* (see e.g. Roessler 2011, 277). I mean here to pay due homage both to the Kantian view of experience as cognition and to the common-sense observation that experience is, at least in some sense, passive.

agency that is engaged in sensible experience. My object in this chapter is to show that experience, by Kant's lights, requires attention; that directed attention is the most basic engagement of the agency we need to have over own minds in order to be knowers at all; and that this agency is realised through taking on the basic epistemic commitments proper to healthy understanding.

To set the stage for this account, consider the remarkable opening words of Kant's *Anthropology*:

> The fact that the human being can have the 'I' in his representations raises him infinitely above all other living beings on earth. Because of this he is a *person*, and . . . through rank and dignity an entirely different being from *things*, such as irrational animals, with which one can do as one likes. (7:127)

Kant here contends that our capacity for first-person thought – which he immediately calls '*understanding*' (7:127) – is what most basically makes us persons, rather than things. He then says that the coming online of genuine thought is a developmental achievement, and points to a 'progress of *perceptions*' that has some 'crude beginning' in activities like tracking shiny objects and leads ultimately to '*cognition* of objects of the senses, that is, *experience*' (7:127–8). He wraps up the opening section of the *Anthropology* with the no less remarkable claim that childhood 'was not the time of experiences, but of merely scattered [zerstreute] perceptions not yet united under the concept of an object' (7:128).[2] He goes on to discuss attention and distraction in the ensuing sections of the *Anthropology*[3] – and the term for distraction, *Zerstreuung*, is cognate with the term he deploys for the 'scattered' perceptions of early childhood. Thus, Kant, taking experience to be empirical cognition, also takes it to require attention. What we stand to gain by thinking all of this through is a better understanding of what is basic to cognitive agency by Kant's lights.

I will begin by considering more closely what attention is, both in Kant's telling and in an important recent account of it; this will enable me to offer a brief reconstruction of the developmental story at issue – the progress of perceptions that leads to full-blown experience (§3.2). What I am chiefly concerned to understand, through this, is Kant's views about cognitive agency – an agency that should be fully engaged in experience, even if experience itself is in some sense a passive affair. The key to this account lies in

---

[2] It is because of this, Kant claims, that adults have no genuine memory of the period of childhood that he has in mind (Anth 7:128). I will examine this remark about the *zerstreute* perceptions of early childhood at some length in the course of this chapter.

[3] Anth §3, and §§5–7; he returns to the topic in Anth §47.

the idea that the most basic personal-level cognitive action is attention; by drawing jointly on the *Critique of Pure Reason* and the *Anthropology*, I will explain how and why experience requires attention by Kant's lights (§§3.3–3.4). This will enable me to return to the framing question about how sensible experience should in principle be no less the expression of the self-determination of a rational being than are overt efforts of inquiry and deliberation. The solution lies in distinguishing two distinct sides of the relevant notion of self-determination and seeing how both are at work even in sensible experience (§3.5).

3.2 Attention and Perception

When my daughter was not more than a few days old, she used to track with her eyes the movements of a white hoodie string that contrasted sharply against the black fabric of the hoodie itself, worn often by her father. She did this with rapt attention, held for a few seconds at a time. When she was several months older, I began to show her some picture books. In one, she would look attentively at the first pictures, which were all simple images with no more than two or three basic items (girl, cat, dog), again contrasting in clear ways against the background. When we got to the penulti-mate image – a suddenly complex tableau of many different dogs running around in a park, getting into various forms of mischief, and no longer contrasting clearly against the background – she would invariably start to cry. The fact that she would cry always at this point told me, of course, that something was bothering her. It suggested that she was aware, if not self-consciously of her engagement in the activity of looking itself, then at least of its suddenly going to pieces. I am going to assume that episodes along these lines are familiar to most people who have been involved in the bringing up of a child, and I will take them as pointing out a simple and obvious truth: that very young children, even newborn babies, are capable of doing things attentively (and very often do).

Juxtapose this starting point, now, against Kant's remarkable claim that (early) childhood 'was not yet the time of experiences, but merely of scat-tered [zerstreute] perceptions not yet united under the concept of an object' (Anth 7:128). There is quite a lot to take account of here, and it is an aim of this chapter to make some sense of the whole remark; but I am going to start by raising a question about what Kant might have meant by this talk of *zerstreute* perceptions given his own ensuing discussion of attention and distraction. My simple and obvious truth tells me that he cannot mean that children never perceive attentively – or, if he did mean this, then he was just flat wrong. However, the attention with which a neonate tracks a shiny moving object is engaged as a mechanical impulse of some kind, and, as we will see, it is not attentive in the sense that Kant has in mind when he suggests that experience requires attention.

To piece together Kant's developmental story about the 'progress of perceptions', we will first need to examine his discussion of attention and distraction in the *Anthropology*.[4] Following this, I will show how, and to what extent, Kant's remarks on attention can be merged with the basic elements of a compelling recent account of attention from Christopher Mole (2011). This will give us a better understanding of the difference between the attention involved in a neonate's tracking a contrasting string or a shiny object and the attention that Kant takes to be involved in full-blown experience – so that we can, in the end, offer a plausible account of what might drive the progress from *zerstreute* perceptions to full-blown experience by Kant's lights.

3.2.1   Attention and Distraction in the Anthropology

In *Anthropology* §3, Kant considers the 'voluntary consciousness' of one's representations, which he says is possible either by '*paying attention [das Aufmerken] (attentio)* or . . . *turning away [das Absehen]* from a representation of which I am conscious (*abstractio*)' (7:131). This 'turning away', he elaborates, is a 'real act of the cognitive faculty of holding off a representation of which I am conscious from combination with other representations in one consciousness' – and, on that grounds, should be distinguished from *distraction* (7:131). This presents abstraction as a matter of stopping a 'combination' of representations that might otherwise obtain. Thus, the dynamics of attention and abstraction – presented here as flip sides of the same coin, so that one attends *as* one disregards this or that – presuppose some kind of unified background of representations. But even though attention and abstraction are dynamically linked in this way, it remains possible to distinguish the two. To establish this, Kant observes that the deliverances of the senses sometimes obtrude upon our minds (7:131), as when we attend involuntarily to a sudden loud bang or an irritating insect's whine. The obtrusion need not be offensive: there is also the attention I might give, indifferently, to whatever happens to fall within my line of sight. Thus,

---

[4] The opening sections of the *Anthropology* move from claims about the first-person nature of genuine thought (in §1), to speculations therefrom about the sources of egoism (in §2), to questions about the agency that creatures capable of genuine thought have over their own minds through efforts of attention and abstraction (in §3).

attention, Kant concludes, does not manifest the same 'freedom of the faculty of thought and authority of mind' (7:131) as abstraction does. With this, he implies that there might be some sense in which abstraction is under one's deliberate control.[5]

Attention may or may not be voluntary: one may either direct one's attention, or one's attention may be seized by something. Distraction (*Zerstreuung*) likewise may or may not be voluntary. Distraction is the 'mere failure and omission' of attention (7:131); later, Kant says that it is 'the state of a diversion of attention [der Zustand einer Abkehrung der Aufmerksamkeit] (*abstractio*) from certain ruling representations through its dispersal on to other, dissimilar ones' (Anth §47, 7:206). Deliberate distraction is not the same thing as abstraction, although both involve making it such that one does not have present to mind what one might otherwise have present to mind: with deliberate distraction, it is a matter of some indifference where one's attention may then settle. A priest might want to banish from his mind the residual echoes of the sermon he gave earlier in the day (Anth 7:207), or I might wish for nothing more than to get an annoying television theme song out of my head; and so we might try fixing our attention on to other things.[6] But just as attention can be seized, it can also be disengaged, in ways not under one's control.[7] Involuntary attention and distraction presumably characterise the waking mental life of infants and very young children, at least for the most part.

Christopher Mole makes essentially the same point about attention in children: 'We do not think of children as great payers of attention, but this is not because they fail to attend. It is because their attention is easily caught and so is highly vulnerable to distraction. The state of attentiveness is one that children struggle to remain in, not one that they struggle to attain. The same thing goes for [non-human] animals' (2011, 70). Mole's motive

---

[5] It is appropriate to the 'pragmatic' mission of the *Anthropology* that Kant should then consider what the ability to abstract is good for: 'Many human beings are unhappy because they cannot abstract', he notes, such as the 'suitor [who] could make a good marriage if only he could overlook a wart on his beloved's face' (7:131–2). I think that what Kant means here is that this power of *attentio/abstractio* needs to be developed in order to attend properly to what matters, and to disregard what does not matter, in interpersonal relations: 'If the essentials are good, then it is not only fair, but also prudent, to *look away* from the misfortune of others, yes, even from our own good fortune. But this faculty of abstraction is a strength of mind that can only be acquired through practice' (7:132).

[6] Engaging again the 'pragmatic' mission of the *Anthropology*, Kant suggests that the ability to distract oneself deliberately belongs to an uncommon, yet highly valuable, art of 'mental diatetics', since it enables one to gather one's powers to ends of one's own choosing (7:207), whereas the echoing drone that the priest suffers in the aftermath of the sermon serves no purpose, and is ultimately debilitating.

[7] Kant calls intentional (*vorsetzlich*) distraction 'Dissipation [Dissipation]', and involuntary (*unwillkürliche*) distraction 'absence (*absentia*) from oneself [Abwesenheit von sich selbst]' – meaning, presumably, absentmindedness (7:206).

for making this observation, which he takes to be a matter of common sense,[8] is to suggest that it is a virtue of his model that it can so readily account for this fact, along with the corollary that for the most part the capacity to perform a task inattentively falls to the special sophistication of human adults (2011, 71). He offers no explicit diagnosis of why children are not great payers of attention, but the implicit one is roughly Kantian: their attention is *easily caught* (i.e. in ways outside their control), and because of this it is *easily surrendered*. In the next section, I want to bring out the elements and basic structure of Mole's account of attention, in order to see if it can help us to understand, ultimately, the Kantian idea that full-blown experience requires a certain agency over one's own mind that is plainly still lacking in neonates.

3.2.2 One Recent Account of Attention

Mole argues that attention should be conceived in adverbial terms – the manner in which something might be done – rather than as any sort of activity or process unto itself. With the rejection of the idea that attention is some sort of special process, it follows that there should not be any special faculty or capacity of attention that comes online at some point in a developmental story. What stands to be done attentively (or not) is a *task*, which Mole defines as 'an activity of the agent's the execution of which is under the guidance of the agent's understanding of that activity' (2011, 52). We will need to consider this conception of 'understanding' in a bit. First, let's consider how Mole conceives of a 'task', which he advertises as a 'regimentation of commonsense usage rather than an innovation' of the theory (52). Very roughly, a task is something that an agent is actively doing, and can be specified by adopting the agent's point of view, even though not every agent will be able to say what it is he is up to (52). Moreover, any given agent may be in a position to provide multiple equally sincere accounts of what task he is currently performing (52), and it is not obvious if we should be troubled by this flexibility in the identification of tasks. On Mole's view, any task has a 'background set' of cognitive resources that can be brought to bear in the service of that task, although any given performance of a task will likely engage only a portion of those resources at any given point. Since the agent's understanding of the activity guides any performance of the task, what belongs to the background set of resources as potentially

---

[8] See also Mole (2011, 54).

in the service of the task must be determined relative to the agent's current understanding of the task (61). A task is performed attentively – with 'cognitive unison' – when none of the resources in the background set is engaged in any way that is not serving the task itself. The attentive performance of a task has every resource either actively engaged or else poised and at the ready.

Since the cognitive unison theory defines attention as a particular way of performing *tasks*, we might think that it is not well suited to handle perceptual attention. But Mole explains why this does not follow: the theory counts *looking* at an object (a chair, say) as a task, because episodes of looking are normally guided by the agent's understanding of what looking is. '*Seeing* a chair,' by contrast, 'typically is not a task of the agent's, because episodes of mere chair seeing typically proceed without the agent deploying his understanding of seeing' (53). But what exactly is this curious notion of *understanding*? Mole's basic point is that an understanding makes a difference to how the performance of a task takes place: it plays a *guiding* role. At the same time, 'understanding' of this sort must be something that cats and infants are capable of, since *ex hypothesi* cats and infants can perform tasks attentively, and only a genuine task – only an activity that is guided by the agent's understanding of that task – stands to be performed attentively (or not).[9] What, then, is it to have an understanding of how to look, or how to explore things perceptually? Since tasks are to be specified from the agent's point of view, there is no fixed or absolute answer to this question. But since an 'understanding' in the relevant sense guides the performance of a task, it must most generally provide some capacity to 'deal with alternatives' (55). In order to account for how even infants and cats can perform tasks in a way that stands to be *attentive* and so requires *understanding*, in his sense, Mole opts to make the notion of understanding relative to various forms (and stages) of life:[10] all that it crucially takes is an ability 'to deal with *some* alternatives' (55). Somewhat unfortunately, Mole explains the general idea with an example of sophisticated mathematical understanding (55). But, as far as infants and cats go, his point must be that the infant who can track shiny objects might then be able to extend her tracking to objects less shiny,

---

[9] 'The cat can have stalking its prey as a task (and so can be counted by the cognitive unison theory as stalking attentively) because the way in which it stalks is under the guidance of the cat's understanding of stalking. The infant's perceptual exploration of the world can be among his tasks (and so can be performed attentively) because the infant conducts himself in a way that employs an understanding of how to explore things perceptually' (Mole 2011, 54).

[10] '[T]here is room for a notion of guidance by understanding according to which the requirements of understanding vary depending on the capacities of the creature in question' (Mole 2011, 54).

and the cat who stalks rats in the city might find the wherewithal to stalk bilbies in the bush.

If we allow that there are given interests proper to any form of life – an inflection of the natural 'drives' for movement and food and so on for each species – then there is plausibly, for the human species, a given interest in visual tracking, since this is a resource that normally needs to be cultivated in order for us to find our way about in the world. We could then say that an infant is *trying* to keep a certain shiny object in her sights, since we are prepared to regard the activity as guided by an intelligence. But there is no genuine thought in Kant's sense, no thought of tracking's being the thing to do just now: the infant just does it. There is, rather, something like a stimulus that leads to specific engagements of tracking, and a know-how or 'understanding' that develops as the infant handles alternatives (tracks items of different shapes, colours and sizes, or of different degrees of contrast against their backgrounds). That this development can take place suggests that this 'understanding' must most basically consist in some ability to recognise success and failure, even if there is as yet no conception of these or of the task itself.

Mole says that his model of attention is well poised to account for the readily observed fact that children and cats do so much of what they do attentively. His account of this is that the resources that they have available to bring to bear on their tasks is limited, so each task is served by a smaller background set, a higher proportion of which will need to be engaged in its performance. This leads to fewer latent resources in the background set that might be engaged in some manner that does not serve the task – and thus fewer opportunities to perform the task inattentively. The model is 'privative' because it accounts for a task's being performed attentively in negative terms: namely, in terms of there being no resources in the task's background set engaged in some manner that does not serve that task – 'an absence of irrelevant processing' (Mole 2011, 70). Mole argues for the model on the grounds that it saves the phenomena – the full range of phenomena, which includes the ready attention of cats and children. The privative cognitive unison model shows the inattentive performance of a task to be more sophisticated than the attentive performance, since it involves doing the task while also deploying resources in the background set in some way that does not serve that task – something, Mole points out, that children are scarcely capable of (71).

So, Kant's idea of early childhood as a time of *zerstreute* perceptions should not mean that a young child perceives inattentively. An infant can perceive with the attention that is appropriate to the as yet undeveloped state of her latently reflective mind. For this to be possible, she must perceive in a way that is guided by her 'understanding' (in Mole's capacious sense) of the task of perceiving. Take visual tracking to be one specification of the task of perceiving. Infant visual tracking is set into gear given the appropriate stimuli (a suitable thing to track), and supposing both that the necessary raw resources have come online (a suitably developed visual capacity) and that certain enabling conditions are in place (the infant is awake, not hungry, not tired). But, while her performance of the task may be guided by some sort of 'understanding' of the task itself, it is not an understanding that enables her to consider how to go on in light of any grasp of rule or standard. Her 'understanding' of the task is not only non-discursive, it is also non-evaluative: she has no sensitivity to reasons, and so no access to a thought about visual tracking as being worth doing.

3.2.3 The 'Progress of Perceptions'

Suppose now the child is a few months older and the father starts to play a game with her using a string. Bemused, he watches her track it assiduously; so he quickly flicks it over his shoulder. Where did it go? She is no longer tracking the string. Suppose then that they 'find' it together. Maybe the father makes it clear that he is bringing it back: the same string. The infant is conceivably in a position to recognise that the string *could* have been followed to the other side: for it was the same string that was there and has now been brought back. Such interactions are conceivably part of how a human being develops a readiness to find out about how things are in a publicly available world.

An infant's perceptions are *zerstreute* not because the infant perceives inattentively but – following through now on Kant's full claim – because they are 'not yet united under the concept of an object' (7:128). Attentive perceiving need not be united under the concept of an object. But what if it is? In that case, the perceiving is guided by a different sort of understanding of the task – one that is not just an ability to deal with alternatives (to track objects relevantly like the ones that one has already tracked) plus a sensitivity to the tracking's succeeding or failing at any given moment. She must now have something to which to refer her perceptions, something that unifies them as perceptions of an independent, publicly available world. Kant calls this the 'concept of an object'. If this perceiving is attentive, it is attentive in a new way. It is attentive because it is guided by a *conception* of the activity of perceiving: any given perception is such as can be referred to a rule or standard that it properly instances.

This standard, I propose, is grasped by putting one's cognitive capacities to use in concrete ways that can be elaborated from the string-tracking example. The infant's ability to put her own cognitive capacities to use is not independent of her recognising that there is a world to find out about, a world that obtains regardless of any efforts that she or anyone makes to find out about it. Perhaps the infant in my story begins to recognise this when her father returns the string to her line of sight: plausibly, she recognises that her father has kept track of the string all along. At some point, she might try to find the string before he shows it to her. If she can make this effort, she should have the beginnings of what could be called an understanding of the task by *Kant's* lights.

When we consider some such transition, we are of course not trying to explain how a mind that is not rational or reflective by nature becomes a mind that is rational or reflective by nature. We are assuming all along that we are working with a mind that is rational or reflective in its first potentiality. So, the difficulty lies more in considering what sort of occasioning stimulus could arouse the essentially reflective activity of such a mind, or genuine thought. We are talking, then, not only about certain sorts of visual stimuli that provide an occasioning stimulus by which *things go on in us* that lead to the development of certain resources, such as abilities for visual tracking. The development that we are interested in quite plausibly depends on play and communication, as well: for, the activity is acknowledged in such interaction, and it is from this that the infant plausibly acquires some rudimentary conception of it – enough so that she can set herself on the task, and continue the game.

Visual tracking is a resource, in us, for finding out about the world; but so are certain forms of thought. When an infant plays the sort of game that I have sketched, she is nascently capable of thought in Kant's terms; at least, we must say this if she is able to set herself on the task of looking for the string. To grant this is to suppose that she has some conception, however dim, of what it is to find out about things in a publicly available world. It does not seem implausible to me to suppose that the infant who plays the game that I have sketched takes a rudimentary interest in basic inquiry.

Now, my view is that full-blown experience as Kant conceives of it should depend on personal-level action, and in this section I have given some initial textual evidence for this view. But this is not an idea that plays any noticeable role in the *Critique of Pure Reason*. The *Critique* is largely given over to the pure, but domain-relative, project of Kantian transcendental logic: it is concerned with what is constitutively required for any thought about objects in the domain of nature at all. We should, then, not expect it to say much of anything about attention and its significance for the agency that we have over our cognitive lives, beginning with experience. Indeed, Kant notes there that 'attention [Aufmerksamkeit], its impediments and consequences' is a topic treated in *applied*, not *pure*, logic (A54/B79). And thus, if I am right to suggest that attention is among the most basic modes of personal-level cognitive action, then perhaps we should not be surprised that the *Critique of Pure Reason*, taken on its own, leaves us with a lot of unanswered questions about the Kantian view of the agency that we have, and need to have, over our own cognitive lives in order even to be capable of sensible experience.

In the next section, I will suggest that some of these problems can be resolved by continuing our reading of the early sections of the *Anthropology*, which move from a discussion of attention to an elaboration of the distinctively Kantian conception of experience. By reading that next stretch of the *Anthropology* in conjunction with a passing remark on attention from the *Critique*'s own Transcendental Deduction, I will attempt to bring out Kant's view of the agency involved in sensible experience.

3.3   Attention and Experience

In the previous section, we began to look into some of Kant's remarks on attention from the *Anthropology*. It turns out that those remarks are part of a longer discussion of the role of attention in empirical consciousness and full-blown sensible experience. One of my interpretive aims is to show this by demonstrating the direct relevance of Kant's initial remarks on attention (from *Anthropology* §3) to his discussion of the phenomenology of empirical consciousness in Anth §§5–7. My stake in this discussion turns on what it suggests about the agency that is necessary for, and necessarily expressed in, sensible experience. To make this case, I will be reading this stretch of the *Anthropology* in conjunction with certain claims from the *Critique*'s Transcendental Deduction: as we will see, there is considerable thematic overlap between the two texts in these areas, despite the fact that each pursues its own agenda.

3.3.1   *'Experiences are Made by Employing Observations'*

Let's begin with a remark about experience from a stretch of the handwritten manuscript for the *Anthropology* – the *Handschrift* (H) – that runs parallel to what is published as Anth §7.[11] In both texts, Kant says that experience is empirical cognition: he recalls, that is, the particular conception of experience that he argued for over the course of the Transcendental Analytic of the *Critique of Pure Reason*.[12] Here, however, Kant suggests that it *follows from* the fact that experience is empirical cognition that it is produced through some sort of personal-level activity.

> Cognition of an object in appearance (that is, as phenomenon) is experience... Therefore experience is the activity (of the power of representation[13]) whereby appearances are brought under the concept of an object of experience... and experiences are made by employing observations (intentional perceptions) and being reflective on their unification under a single concept [unter Einem Begriffe nachgedacht (reflectirt) wird]. (H 7:398)

I want to focus on the claim that 'experiences are made by employing observations' or 'intentional perceptions'. I will assume that to *observe* something is to perceive it attentively in a certain way. When an infant first attentively tracks a shiny object, she is not likely making an observation. Thus, what Kant seems to be saying here is that experiences are made by actively seeing how things are: and this, I think, requires attention in the sense that Kant presents in Anth §3 as engaged together with abstraction (*Absehen, abstractio*). To attend in this way is *at the same time* to disregard something else that I *could* attend to, and indeed could attend to in one and the same consciousness.[14] Further, observation is a personal-level activity: it is something that I do. An observation is not a representation that is generated in me by subagential processes that, as it were, go on behind my back.

We might then wonder where a passage such as this leaves the (putative) passivity of sensible experience. Consider now what Kant says about the passive character of sensible representations in Anth §7:

> Representations in regard to which the mind behaves passively, thus [representations] by means of which the subject is *affected* (this may be its affecting itself, or its being affected by an object), belong to the *sensible*... cognitive faculty. (7:140)

---

[11] On the textual status of the *Handschrift*, see Brandt (1999, 20–30).
[12] B147, B165–6 and B218; initially implicit at B1.
[13] Louden's CEWIK translation of the *Anthropology*, while generally excellent, makes some curious choices here and there – particularly in rendering *Vorstellung* as 'idea'. I could find no account of his rationale for this, and I have departed from his translation considerably in these sections.
[14] The *abstractio* at issue is a 'real act of the cognitive faculty of holding off a representation of which I am conscious from combination with other representations in one consciousness' (Anth 7:131).

Kant distinguishes here two ways in which one can have a sensible representation. The subject can be affected by itself (by its own mental activity), or the subject can be affected by objects. I am going to argue that having sensible representations in the first way (through self-affection) is a matter of perceiving attentively, and the second is not. Crucial to my case here is a passing remark about attention in the Transcendental Deduction: 'Every act of *attention* [*Aufmerksamkeit*],' Kant claims, 'can give us an example of' sensible representations that are had in virtue of self-affection (B156n). I take this to mean that any act of attention will affect one's phenomenology: attention makes an immediate difference to the sensory character of one's experience.[15] This is why attention is plausibly an example of self-affection, of the mind's affecting itself through the direction of its own thought. Such acts of attention occur at the personal level, and that is precisely why Kant supposes that self-affection should be in such plain evidence to anyone.[16]

Kant's remark about the passivity of sensible representations mentions not only self-affection, but also affection from objects (*full stop*, one feels compelled to add). We might at this point think that the latter are generated by subpersonal mechanisms of some kind: objects affect our senses, yielding sensible representations.[17] We don't have to *do* anything here. However, we need to be careful with this idea. To elaborate, let me begin with a recap: Kant appears to claim (in the *Handschrift*) that sensible experience requires a personal-level activity of some kind. I am proposing that this personal-level activity is what Kant points to as acts of perceiving attentively. We can recognise this while at the same time accommodating the passivity of sensible experience by taking a closer look at the remark about sensible representations: namely, that they can either be had in virtue of affection by objects full stop, or by self-affection – which is to say, by perceiving attentively. The latter is crucial to accounting for the agency over our own minds that Kant suggests is required in order to so much as enjoy sensible experience at all. Now, for reasons that I have already indicated, the argument of the *Critique of Pure Reason* does not take a ground-level

[15] Thanks to Markos Valaris for reminding me about this remark in the Transcendental Deduction, and for suggesting this straightforward interpretation of it.
[16] We are well placed now to appreciate why Kant is only remarking on attention *in passing* in the *Critique*. The *Critique*'s transcendental logic is a pure (but domain-relative) logic. As a pure logic, it abstracts from ground-level problems about how to make purposive use of our cognitive capacities: it is concerned with the *constitutive* requirements on thought about phenomenal objects. As a result, it doesn't have personal-level cognitive activity centrally in view. Applied logic does not abstract from ground-level problems about how to make purposive use of our cognitive capacities, and it *does* have personal-level cognitive activity in view. And attention, I am suggesting, is personal-level cognitive activity.
[17] Consider Kitcher (2012, 24–5) for a reading along such lines.

view of the agency we need to have over our own minds in order to so much as enjoy sensible experience at all. With that in mind, I want to take a closer look at how Kant's considered conception of experience emerges through the core arguments of the *Critique of Pure Reason*.

Kant's account of sensible experience as empirical cognition begins with one of the lessons of pure general logic. Pure general logic is concerned with the constitutive requirements on thought. The lesson concerns reflection-c, expressed in the famous motto:

> The *I think* must be *able* to accompany all of my representations, otherwise something would be represented in me that could not be thought at all, which is as much as to say that the representation would be impossible, or at least nothing for me. (KrV §16, B131–2)

This first-person voice is, minimally, an *intelligence*. But Kant's mission in the *Critique* is more specific: it is to understand how synthetic a priori judging is possible – i.e. to make claims that hold of necessity but yet pertain to matters of fact. Such cognition will include sensible representation as a necessary element – or a proper part – of it. Among the first moves that Kant makes in the Deduction is to point out (a) that sensible representations are among the representations that must be accompaniable by this intelligence's 'I think' (KrV §16, B132) and (b) that these representations are not unified under their own steam, but only in the 'I think', and so in virtue of some activity of this intelligence. Kant calls this activity combination or *synthesis*, 'an act of spontaneity of the power of representation . . . [of] understanding, in distinction from sensibility' (KrV §15, B130).[18] In this way, the lesson from pure general logic is transmuted into a doctrine of Kantian transcendental logic: the self-consciousness that is internal to thought as such must be inflected as a unity according to the principles that necessarily underwrite this synthesis, at least if this intelligence is to be admitted as a full-fledged knower embedded in an objective phenomenal world or the domain of nature. These principles are the principles of the pure understanding that Kant establishes in the aftermath of the Transcendental Deduction and argues are constitutive of experience.[19]

Now, when Kant first introduces the idea that the self-consciousness internal to thought (what I call reflection-c) must be inflected as a *synthetic* unity in transcendental logic, he indicates that the thinking subject can either be conscious of this synthesis or not (KrV §15, B129–30). A little

---

[18] Much of this paragraph up to this point recaps claims I argued for at greater length in Merritt (2011a).

[19] Although the 'mathematical' principles are constitutive and the 'dynamical' principles regulative of *appearances* (A178–80/B221–3), together they are constitutive of experience (A664/B692; cf. A236–7/B296).

later, he says that it follows from this that any given representation that this intelligence can enjoy '[a] contains a synthesis of representations, and [b] is only possible by means of the *consciousness* of this synthesis' (KrV §16, B133).[20] What [a] indicates is that any representation of an objective phenomenal world has a certain content in virtue of the necessary synthesis that makes the representation possible. But this synthesis, we have just learned, can *either* be conscious or not. I take it that an unconscious synthesis *could only be* one that goes on subagentially: it is not anything *done* at the personal level.[21] Yet, the further claim [b] indicates that any subagential synthesis that sensible experience might require itself depends on something that *is* done at the personal level. For the further claim [b] is that this intelligence's capacity to enjoy a sensible representation with a thinkable content depends somehow on the *consciousness* of a synthesis of representations.

What is it to be conscious of some such synthesis? I submit that it is to perceive attentively, in the manner mentioned in Anth §3: namely, where attending to one thing is at the same time disregarding something else that I *could* attend to, and indeed could attend to in one and the same consciousness. My agency infiltrates empirical consciousness, which gives me a whole over which my attention can run, more or less freely. And even if we accept the interpretation of Kitcher (2012) that I am given this whole in virtue of a subagential synthesis governed by the principles of pure understanding, nevertheless experience itself must require more than this subagential synthesis: I must also perceive something attentively. If I were incapable of *this* sort of attention (the sort that implicates *abstractio* and thus engages genuine thought), then by Kant's lights the only empirical consciousness that I could enjoy would be one that 'is in itself scattered [zerstreut] and without relation to the identity of the subject' (KrV §16, B133). This brings us back to the idea that experiences are made by employing observations, or intentional perceptions: the claim from the *Handschrift* is at least implicit in the context of Kantian transcendental logic.

3.3.2 *Attention and Clarity*

Let us now come down from the rarefied air of the Deduction, to consider how Kant works through some of the same ideas in the *Anthropology's* discussion of the phenomenology of empirical consciousness. Specifically of

---

[20] My emphasis. The [a] and [b] are also my additions, for ease of reference.
[21] See also Kant's remark about 'synthesis in general' as 'a blind though indispensable function of the soul, without which we would have no cognition at all, but of which we are seldom even conscious' (A78/B103).

interest is the distinction that Kant draws between clear and obscure representations. Clear representations, I will argue, are perceived attentively; but this attention also presupposes a unified background of unattended – obscure – representations,[22] at least if it is to be the attention that is proper to genuine thought, and hence involved in full-blown experience.

Kant begins by recalling the complaint that Locke raised against the very idea of having representations without being conscious of them.[23] Kant responds by claiming that we can be '*indirectly* conscious' of having certain representations without being 'directly conscious' of this; the representations that we are directly conscious of are '*clear*' and the representations that we are indirectly conscious of are '*obscure*'. The vast majority of our sensible representations, Kant maintains, are obscure (7:135, 136). Some of our representations are clear, and some of these are '*distinct*' as well – namely, if the clarity 'extends to the partial representations that make up a whole together with their connection' (§5, 7:135); cognition requires both (§6, 7:138). For present purposes, I am interested chiefly in the basic distinction between obscure and clear representation.[24]

What is it to be 'indirectly' conscious of a representation – that is, to have an obscure sensible representation? Since the distinction between obscure and clear sensible representation is drawn not long after the discussion of attention,[25] it is not implausible that attention figures in the distinction. Kant does not, I grant, say so explicitly – although he mentions in this context that a faculty of apprehension, glossed *attentio*, properly belongs to the cognitive faculty in general (7:138). So, I can only show that bringing Kant's recently introduced notion of attention to bear on the distinction between obscure and clear sensible representations provides a viable account of that distinction. A clear sensible representation, on my proposal, is one that is had in virtue of an act of attentive perception, and so through self-affection. An obscure representation is had in virtue of an affection by objects full stop: it is not attended. I will explain why it makes sense for Kant to say that we are only 'indirectly' conscious of obscure representations. I will also explain why Kant takes sensible experience to require both clear and

---

[22] For a similar point, see Waxman (1991, 227).

[23] This is one of the earliest claims that Locke makes in his *Essay Concerning Human Understanding*, and Leibniz naturally replies in his *New Essays on Human Understanding*. Indeed, much of Anth §§5–6 has a clear provenance in Leibniz's *New Essays*; for an account of this, see Heidemann (2012).

[24] I will effectively be considering clear ideas that are also distinct, but I will not have more to say here about Kant's conception of distinctness per se.

[25] Attention and abstraction are at issue in Anth §3; after an intervening section on self-observation (where he also makes comments questioning the viability of introspection, both in general and as a method in anthropology), Kant turns to clear and obscure sensible representation in Anth §§5–6.

obscure representation, so conceived. To proceed, let's look at the examples Kant offers in this context.

Kant likens clear representations to illuminated areas of a vast dark landscape, and then remarks that there seems to be something wondrous revealed about our own minds in our very capacity to enjoy clear representations. He likens this wonder to the divine performative speech act 'Let there be light!', presumably because the illumination of select areas of this dark landscape requires no noticeable effort – we need only *attend* (7:135). Taking a certain line of sight, something or other comes into view. What falls outside of this line of sight, from the margins of my peripheral vision inwards, remains obscure. Kant next offers the more complex example of a musician who

> plays a fantasy on the organ with ten fingers and both feet and also speaks with someone standing next to him. In a few moments a mass of representations is awakened in his soul, each of which for its selection requires still a special judgment as to its appropriateness, since a single stroke of the finger not in accordance with the harmony would be heard as a discordant sound. (7:136)

Kant complicates the example by having the musician carry on some kind of conversation as he plays: presumably, the point is that the musician's attention is divided. The example is also crafted to suggest an obscure mass of representations bubbling up in the musician in a manner not under his control. At the level of the musician's own phenomenology, the clear representations are simply those notes that it occurs to him to play next. And yet, these acts of attention – and this applies whether one is fixing on a note to play or fixing on a line of sight – are not simply happening to him. Certain notes are selected *from* the mass on grounds of their appropriateness, presumably in light of principles of harmony.

The examples of clear representations – and so, I am saying, attentive perception – are alike engagements of a point of view on how things are, or on what to do. This brings us to another complication of the musician example, which is that it concerns not a straightforward example of perceptual attention but attention as something like selection for action.[26] The thinking that it involves is practical rather than theoretical, and the notes that the musician represents clearly are the notes that he actually

---

[26] This is only a complication if we assume that perceptual attention must be, in some sense, *basic*. Maybe it is. At any rate, it seems to me that the musician example could be understood as an example of perceptual attention if 'perception' were conceived in a way that recognises the role that imagination (i.e. the singular representation of unperceived possibilities) might play in it. For an account of attention as 'selection for action', see Wu's chapter in Mole, Smithies and Wu (2011).

plays. What guides his activity can only be something highly general, and something which he needs not have expressly in view in order to guide his movements (since he is chatting away at the same time). But he is clearly long past needing to think explicitly about the movements of arms and legs required to generate the notes that occur to him to play; and we are led to imagine that he has internalised the principles of harmony so that he might so much as *select* each note. On Kant's telling, it emerges that 'the whole turns out so well that the freely improvising [phantasirende] musician would often wish to have kept in written notation some part of what he happily performed, which he perhaps otherwise with all diligence could not hope to bring off so well' (7:136). So, the point is not quite that he managed to improvise a coherent and compelling piece without thinking about it, but rather that he possesses acquired resources that enable him to generate interesting fragments that are loosely woven together – and to do this inattentively, in a scattered fashion, while talking to someone else, and so without conceiving clearly of the whole that he might bring into being.

My aim here has been to link Kant's remark about the passivity of sensible representations to the discussion of clear and obscure representations. Kant says that we have sensible representations either through self-affection or through affection from objects full stop. We may be tempted to think that the latter way of having sensible representations can be chalked up to subagential mechanisms in us. But we might resist this temptation on the basis of what I have been arguing – namely, that the distinction between two ways of having a sensible representation (either through self-affection or through affection from objects full stop) can be mapped on to the distinction between clear and obscure sensible representations. Kant says that we are *indirectly* conscious of an obscure representation: having it is not directly the result of any act of attention (which Kant says is self-affection). It takes attention to so much as divide empirical consciousness into a foreground and a background. Obscure representations figure in the background, in what I am not, now, attending to. (We are indirectly conscious of them, not wholly unconscious of them.[27]) So, our having them is not independent of some basic agency that we need to have over our own minds in order to be capable of thought at all. Thus, the idea that some sensible representations are had in virtue of affection from objects full stop does not entail that they are had in virtue of subagential mechanisms full stop.

---

[27] In addition to Kant's treatment of these issues in Anth §§5–6, see also KrV (B414–5n), KU (5:252). By contrast, some contemporary philosophers argue that attention is a necessary condition of consciousness: we cannot be conscious of anything without attending to it (for an example of such a view, see Jesse Prinz's chapter in Mole, Smithies and Wu 2011).

3.3.3 Recapitulation and Conclusions

Let me now recapitulate §§3.2–3.3 and draw some conclusions. There is a certain sort of attention that implicates abstraction – the two are flip sides of one coin. This sort of attention involves genuine thought in Kantian terms, and so (in my terms) requires reflection-c. Where basic empirical consciousness is concerned, such attention presupposes the principles of pure understanding. Without tacit grasp of these principles, Kant says, we would not be capable of experience, but only a 'rhapsody of perceptions' – nothing other than the *zerstreute* perceptions that he claims are the stuff of early infancy.[28] So, any act of perception that is attentive in the sense at issue makes tacit reference to an idea of the whole to which any given perception must belong. It is with this in mind that Kant says, in the Deduction, that 'the identity of apperception itself precedes *a priori* all of *my* determinate thinking' (B134). *My* determinate thinking will involve the ground-level engagement of my cognitive capacities, and it will always involve my attending to this or to that. So, Kant has said here that *my* determinate thinking presupposes the synthetic unity of apperception, the identity of apperception established through a certain tacit grasp of a battery of synthetic a priori principles.

But there is a complementary point that is not foregrounded in the *Critique*. It is that this synthetic unity cannot be wrought by subagential processes alone. Experience requires attention. Without attention, there can be no determinate point of view on how things are. And without that, it is not clear how we could countenance reflection-c and genuine thought.[29] When Kant claims that experience is empirical cognition, he underscores that experience involves genuine thought: and so, it requires reflection-c, that typically tacit handle on oneself as the source of a point of view on how things are. When we remain within the ambit of the mission of the *Critique of Pure Reason*, we abstract from the issues surrounding the ground-level engagement of our cognitive capacities, including 'attention, its

---

[28] Kant says this as he introduces the principles of pure understanding, echoing earlier remarks (such as KrV §16, B133, which I quoted in the main text): 'Now experience rests on the synthetic unity of appearances, i.e. on a synthesis according to concepts of the object of appearances in general, without which it would not even be cognition but rather a rhapsody of perceptions, which would not fit together in any context in accordance with rules of a thoroughly connected (possible) consciousness, thus not into the transcendental and necessary unity of apperception. Experience therefore has principles of its form which ground it a priori, namely general rules of unity in the synthesis of appearances' (A156–7/B195–6).

[29] For an interesting discussion of the problems around the idea of attention-free consciousness from a broadly Kantian point of view, see Roessler (2011, 287–9).

impediments and consequences' (A54/B79). Perhaps the most basic consequence of attention is that without it, we would not so much as have a point of view on how things are. This is again a way in which the question of personal-level *use* of our cognitive capacities has a certain priority over subagential processes – a priority that Kant, given the agenda of the *Critique*, is not always poised to bring to light.[30]

3.4   Spontaneity and Rational Self-Determination

I have argued that experience, in the full Kantian view, requires attention. This conclusion draws attention to the agency we have over our own minds even in putatively passive modes of cognitive engagement, such as sensible experience. Kant's interpreters have tended to suppose that his appeal to the spontaneity of the understanding in the first *Critique* is meant to account for this agency.[31] However, I have been suggesting that a Kantian account of this agency requires more than the 'pure' forms of inquiry (as we find in the first *Critique*) that abstract entirely from the personal-level problems of putting our cognitive capacities to use. Moreover, from the outset I promised a reconsideration of what it is to be reflective by Kant's lights that would allow for putatively passive modes of cognitive engagement – like sensible experience – to be no less the expression of the self-determination of a rational being than are overt efforts of inquiry and deliberation. My aim in this section is to follow through on that claim. To do that, we need to consider the concept of self-determination.

Let me begin by observing that 'self-determination' (*Selbstbestimmung*) is not really one of Kant's words: it scarcely appears in his published works, although it figures prominently in the German idealist tradition that followed him, and as a result is taken to have a Kantian provenance. In ordinary usage, 'self-determination' has general implications of autonomy or determining one's own principles and courses of action. As such, it is taken

---

[30] Merritt and Valaris (2017) further develops the account of attention presented in this chapter (especially in relation to the first *Critique*'s Analogies of Experience), and draws on it to address current debates about the role of understanding in perception and experience.

[31] This supposition is sometimes expressed in a tendency to take the 'spontaneity' of mind to be a certain freedom of choice; Tolley (2006) rightly disputes this reading of spontaneity, and points to Keller (1998, 7–8) and McDowell (1994) as examples of the confusion. I would point as well to the conception of a 'deeper' sense of 'spontaneity' that is engaged in choosing the principles constitutive of your will in Korsgaard (2009, 108). I was similarly confused about spontaneity in Merritt (2009). As I will suggest here, Kant's appeal to spontaneity is drawn from early modern rationalism, where it is clearly distinguished from freedom of choice – for a much more detailed account of this history, see Dyck (2016). See also Strawson (2003) on the 'involuntariness of spontaneity' – although I reject his broader account of mental agency.

to be an attribute that stands to apply only to *us*, not cats and infants, much less insects and plants; relatedly, it often takes on a political sense. But there is no direct conceptual connection between self-determination and choice, as I will explain. This is important to appreciate, as it enables us to see that the spontaneity of the understanding is just one of two aspects of the Kantian self-determination idea. The other side of the self-determination idea, as we will see, more closely resembles the suggestion from ordinary usage.

I want to begin, then, with a bit of conceptual analysis. I will start with the idea that the 'determination' of a thing is its being a certain way, whether this is a passing state or an abiding disposition of some kind. A thing is *self*-determined if it is itself the source of its way of being. When a thing is self-determined, both (a) the operative principles of its way of being come from the thing itself, rather than something external to it, and (b) nothing external obstructs the expression of these principles. From this, we can see that the concept of self-determination presupposes that a tenable distinction can be drawn between what is 'internal' and what is 'external' to the thing. This presupposition carries with it, I think, a claim about what sort of thing stands to be self-determined in the first place: namely, only what has a *nature* in roughly the Aristotelian sense.[32] An acorn becomes a tree only owing to principles of its own, and when it does this, it is 'self-determined' in the sense at issue. How can the principles come from the thing itself, when they are that in virtue of which it *comes to be* what it properly is? The principles can only belong to the thing as a member of a living species; they do not come from the individual.

The self-determination of things like oaks and bears will generally be quite unproblematic, as long as certain enabling conditions are in place – the right amount of warmth, water, nutrition, light or whatever. Enabling conditions are not sources of external determination, because they are simply what allows the thing to realise its own nature, or be what it properly is. The soil and moisture and so forth don't stand to make the acorn or shoot into anything other than an oak. But an oak does not become a *bed* owing to principles of its own: it becomes a bed owing to a carpenter, who treats the oak as matter for a bed that he conceives and builds. So, an oak or a bear fails to be self-determined either when it is in the course of perishing or when it is put to use and made to serve an alien purpose.[33]

[32] I am referring to Aristotle's conception of the nature of a thing as an internal principle of change and rest; for a classic study of the idea, see Waterlow (1982).

[33] This disjunction is inclusive: while an oak normally perishes before it can be made into a bed, a circus bear does not perish when it is trained to provide entertainment for humans.

Now, while Kant does not much use the term 'self-determination' (*Selbstbestimmung*), he does speak of the 'vocation' – *Bestimmung* – of living species, including the human being.[34] He is on record claiming that non-human animals 'fulfil their vocation [Bestimmung] automatically and unknowingly' (Päd 9:445), and if my conceptual analysis is sound, then this fulfilment is nothing other than their self-determination in the sense set out here. So, in Kant's view, an individual bear can be perfectly self-determined through a normal process of growth given the appropriate enabling conditions. Kant's point is not to deny that the normal process of growth for many non-human animals will only be possible in the pride, the pack or the hive; it is just that there is nothing further to be done for the non-human animal to live a life proper to its kind – and so for it to be fully self-determined – than for it to carry on according to its fixed original constitution, or instincts, of which it has no conception. Owing to this, the non-human animal faces no practical problem of what to make of itself. By contrast, the self-determination of the human being, the rational animal, is not possible without addressing this problem. This brings us to the familiar conception of self-determination as autonomy. Kant also expressly denies that an individual human being can fulfil the human *Bestimmung*: this can be done by the species, if at all (Päd 9:445; Anth 7:324). This is only partly due to the fact that the human *Bestimmung* consists in the perfection of our rational nature, which may be an ideal unattainable by us. It is also because we are jointly responsible for creating the enabling conditions – which include practices of communication, education, justice and so on – that make this fulfilment possible.

From the conceptual analysis, we learn that there is no inherent connection between self-determination and choice. An oak or a bear is self-determined in the unfettered realisation of its own form of life. Quite obviously, this does not require free choice. Now, I think that Kant invokes this conception of self-determination when he speaks of the 'spontaneity' of the understanding in the first *Critique*. First, it should be noted that he speaks of the understanding as having a nature in the sense that is relevant to the possibility of its self-determination. He does so at the outset of the *Critique*'s Analytic of Concepts,[35] where he proposes to undertake an '*analysis*' or '*dissection*' – *Zergliederung* – '*of the faculty of understanding* itself'

---

[34] I return to the eighteenth-century debate about the 'vocation of the human being' (*Bestimmung des Menschens*) and Kant's contribution to it in Chapter 5 (§5.3.1).

[35] This is the portion of the Transcendental Analytic (itself part of the Transcendental Logic) that deals with the nature of the understanding in the narrow sense (as the faculty of concepts for theoretical cognition).

to uncover the representations constitutive of its exercise (A65–6/B90–1). These representations are the categories: the pure concepts of the understanding. Kant thus gestures towards a developmental story, wherein these concepts are developed from 'seeds and predispositions in human understanding' on 'the occasion of experience' (A66/B91).[36] Experience is conceived here as the stimulus provided by objects affecting the senses, as it is in the famous opening lines of the *Critique*'s Introduction, where Kant nods to the empiricist idea that all of our knowledge begins in experience, with objects affecting the senses and thereupon 'arousing the cognitive capacity into activity' (B1).[37] This stimulus is an enabling condition of the development of the understanding: it is that stimulus by which the understanding comes to take its own proper form, not how it is thrown by an outside force. This constitutive form of the understanding can then be brought to light by the very 'same understanding', Kant says, gesturing towards the ensuing project of the Analytic of Concepts: the task is to 'exhibit' these concepts 'in their integrity [Lauterkeit], freed from the empirical conditions attaching to them' (A66/B99).

These remarks should be read in conjunction with Kant's earlier appeal to the 'spontaneity' of the understanding: 'the mind's power of producing representations from itself' (A51/B75). This 'spontaneity' is simply the understanding's unfettered engagement according to its own internal principles. This idea has its roots in early modern rationalism: Leibniz, for example, understands spontaneity as the self-determination of substances,[38] and spontaneous mental activity is that which arises unobstructed from the nature of the mind, i.e. from 'its own original constitution'.[39] A similar conception of spontaneity can be traced to Descartes as well.[40] Kant inherits this notion of spontaneity, but without conceiving of the mind as a substance: the spontaneity of the understanding

---

[36] This remark is related to Kant's implicit claim, at the end of the Deduction, that the categories are 'a priori *self-thought* [*selbstgedachte*] first principles of our cognition' (B167), and to his subsequent claim that the categories are not innate but 'originally acquired' (8:222–3). For an important reconstruction of the argument for the latter claim, see Longuenesse (1998).

[37] It is not, in other words, the 'full-blown' conception of experience as empirical cognition that Kant aims to establish in the core arguments of the Transcendental Analytic.

[38] See *Discourse on Metaphysics* §§32–3 in Leibniz (1989, 64); see also Leibniz (1981, 210).

[39] See 'A New System of the Nature and Communication of Substances, and of the Union of the Soul and Body' in Leibniz (1989, 143), and also 'Notes on Some Comments by Michel Angelo Fardella' (104).

[40] Consider especially the Fourth Meditation, where the meditator asserts that he has not been 'compelled by any external force' when he assents to what he clearly and distinctly perceives (AT VII:58; references follow the Adam and Tannery edition by volume and page, as given in Descartes 1985). The meditator analyses his self-determined state as follows: 'a great light in the intellect was followed by a great inclination in the will, and thus the spontaneity and freedom of my belief was all the

is its operation according to its own constitutive principles. The argument of the *Critique*'s Transcendental Analytic is given over to determining what these internal principles are: i.e. the principles of pure understanding that are derived from the categories. To say that these principles are constitutive of theoretical cognition is to say that we cannot fail to employ them and still be having a thought about phenomenal objects. Their governance over our thought about such objects is not something we are in any position to choose.

Now, the moral law stands in a parallel position, in the sense that the categorical imperative is constitutive of practical cognition. For Kant, practical cognition concerns the good to be realised in action, and all practical cognition is governed by the moral law. Here, I am bracketing questions about how precisely we should understand this claim: all I need is the recognition of the parallel elements in Kant's system. And the present point is that we are in no more position to choose the moral law than we are to choose the principles of pure understanding. If this is right, then it should follow that the 'spontaneity' of cognition is not something for the theoretical side alone (as is often assumed). For this spontaneity has been conceived in terms of the cognitive capacity's operation according to its own constitutive principles.

Now let's consider the other side of the self-determination idea, which comes to light when we consider the personal-level problem of how to put one's cognitive capacities to use. This side of the self-determination idea does involve the will: it involves a commitment to the principles, and to their correct application in judgment. And, while no one chooses the principles that are constitutive of theoretical and practical cognition, there might be a sense in which a person is responsible for the particulars of her cognitive constitution. Of course, we have to be careful with this idea: to a large extent, these are cognitive resources inherited with a particular language, society and intellectual tradition – we don't exactly choose these, either. But we are rationally required to submit these cognitive inheritances to criticism. Without a doubt, this is central to Kant's conception of our

greater in proportion to my lack of indifference' (AT VII:58–9). Although the meditator links self-determination with freedom, he distinguishes them. Further, the freedom in question is expressly *not* a freedom to choose one thing over another: it is the freedom of rational necessitation, of being compelled by the clear and distinct perception of innate ideas, i.e. by the unobstructed recognition of the nature of the mind in 'its own original constitution', to borrow Leibniz's phrase. Thus, here again the appeal to spontaneity tracks a conception of self-determination that is, as such, independent of the will; see also Third Meditation (AT VII:36) and *Principles of Philosophy* (AT VIII:21). For a more extended argument against the common reception of Descartes as a 'voluntarist' about judgment, see Stevenson (2011, 97–101).

self-determination: surely, it is at work in the very idea of a 'critical' philosophy, and in his popular writings on enlightenment (*Aufklärung*).

So framed, the two aspects of the self-determination idea seem quite far apart from one another. Kant, moreover, never makes resoundingly clear how they come together in a single conception of our self-determination.[41] But the two aspects are, in effect, simply another way of framing the distinction between constitutive and normative requirements to reflect. Thus, we might be able to think about the two sides of the self-determination idea by returning to the main line of thought in this chapter: namely, about how reflection-c and reflection-n are conjointly in play in sensible experience. To establish the connection between the two aspects of the self-determination idea, we will need to consider the context of the remarks in the Transcendental Deduction and the *Anthropology* that led to my conclusion that experience, by Kant's lights, requires attention.[42]

The context of those remarks is a broader discussion of self-consciousness and the sense in which I can cognise myself as a thinker, an intelligence. The Kantian motto concerning the reflective nature of the rational mind is expressed in the first person: 'The *I think* must be *able* to accompany all of my representations'. This *I think* is the self-consciousness that is internal to thought: pure apperception, or reflection-c. Later in the Deduction, Kant considers its bearing on the possibility of cognising oneself as an intelligence, and remarks: 'I have . . . no *cognition* of myself *as I am*, but rather merely as I *appear* to myself' (B158). The initial, and merely negative, point is that pure apperception is a logical consciousness of oneself as the subject of thinking, and not as an object of synthetic a priori knowledge. Kant says this clearly in the *Anthropology* as well (7:134n), and it is of course the guiding principle of his critique of the dogmatic conclusions of rationalist philosophy of mind in the Paralogisms chapter of the first *Critique*'s Transcendental Dialectic. The second, and positive, claim concerns the possibility of cognising oneself as an intelligence – although neither as a noumenal object, nor as a phenomenal object (since an intelligence, as Kant understands it, is no such thing).[43] The positive point

---

[41] McDowell (2009, 90–107) identifies two aspects of the (broadly) rationalist conception of self-determination, roughly along the lines just indicated here, and asks more or less this question. While he doesn't answer it directly, he suggests that the Kantian account risks collapsing into a kind of uncritical dogmatism. I am not going to take up McDowell exegesis in this book, so I won't attempt to articulate and address his concern about the risk of 'one-sidedness'. That said, I take myself to be connecting dots in Kant's thought that should show how this sort of worry need not arise.

[42] Those passages were: Anth (7:134n–142), with H (7:397–9); and KrV §§24–5 (B152–9).

[43] See e.g. A556/B584.

follows through on the idea that pure apperception (or reflection-c) is a consciousness of oneself as the subject of thought. The positive point is that I can cognise myself, as an intelligence, only in the concrete engagement of my own thought – which is to say, as I appear to myself. When Kant says this, he is repeating something he said earlier: the very remark to which he appended the claim that every act of attention provides an example of the mind's being affected by its own thought. Here is that original claim:

> [i]f we admit . . . that we cognise objects only insofar as we are externally affected, we must also concede of inner sense that by means of it we intuit ourselves only insofar as we are inwardly affected *by ourselves* – i.e. as far as inner sense is concerned, we cognise our own subject only as appearance, but not in accordance with what it is in itself. (B156)

There are exceedingly difficult interpretive questions about these remarks, and more generally about Kant's distinction between pure apperception and inner sense, which I cannot pretend to address here.[44] I will confine myself to a point that is relatively simple, and that bears directly on the fact that the remark about attention is appended to this claim. When Kant says that I cognise myself, as an intelligence, only as I appear to myself, he must mean that this self-cognition is possible only in the actual engagement of my own thought – which includes every act of attention in sensible experience.

Let me revisit the basic elements of that account of experience. Recall Kant's distinction between sensible representations that are had in virtue of affection from objects full stop and sensible representations that are had in virtue of the mind's affecting itself, as it does in any act of attention. I argued that this tracks Kant's distinction between obscure and clear sensible representations. Obscure sensible representations are had in virtue of affection from objects full stop, and may even be the result of unconscious syntheses; but in order to so much as have a *point of view* on how things are, I need to perceive something clearly, or attentively.

Thus, the full account of experience needs to recognise the agency involved in experience, which is most basically engaged in acts of attention. Kant says that every act of attention provides an example of the mind's affection of itself through its own activity; and it is in this self-affection

---

[44] The idea of 'inner sense' has its roots in Locke, who supposes that there is a special kind of impression left by mental activity that can register in consciousness through inner sense. Kant gives every indication of rejecting this conception of inner sense, and particularly the idea that inner sense has its own 'manifold' (i.e. special impressions left by mental activity, à la Locke: see B67). For illuminating discussion of this point, see Valaris (2008).

that I cognise myself as an intelligence, as we have just seen. I have suggested that these acts of attention are the most basic engagement of our cognitive agency. The normative requirement to reflect, which is spelled out through the three maxims of healthy understanding, calls for taking an appropriate interest in one's own cognitive agency. This allows for radically non-introspectionist conclusions to be drawn about the Kantian reflective ideal.[45] The reflective person is not bent on stepping back from every episode of taking things to be a certain way in order to determine whether it has its source in a 'spontaneous' act of the understanding or in the mechanisms of prejudice. Rather, a central question that the reflective person bears in mind, and continually returns to, is: *What am I paying attention to, and why?* This is an essential part of what it is to take an interest in one's own cognitive agency – and one, it seems to me, that is often overlooked in Kantian discussions of cognitive agency.

The normative requirement to reflect is articulated through the three maxims of healthy understanding, and these maxims make plain that reflecting in this way is not a private affair: the second maxim secures this, and without it there would be no way to distinguish the reflective person from the logical egoist. Human understanding, Kant is on record as saying, is 'by instinct' communicative (*mittheilend*, LB 24:179). The reflective question at issue – *What am I paying attention to, and why?* – is therefore not isolated from one's participation in a shared practice of judgment, which should itself engender standing questions about the adequacy of the cognitive resources operative within that practice. Once we recognise this, we find ourselves in territory that is more readily recognisable as the ideal of cognitive autonomy conceived as a kind of public enlightenment. And it is by connecting these dots that we can begin to see how the Kantian reflective ideal can in principle be fully realised in putatively passive exercises of cognitive capacities, such as sensible experience.

3.5 The Relation between Reflection-c and Reflection-n

In Chapter 1, I made a point of *distinguishing* constitutive and normative notions of reflection: we need this distinction, I argued, in order to countenance the range of ways in which Kant talks about reflection. For some sense of 'reflection' seems to be going on by default inasmuch as one thinks at all; but in another sense of the term, one could fail to 'reflect'

---

[45] Relatedly, the received interpretation of Kantian inner sense effectively takes it to be empirical introspection, i.e. a consciousness of mental goings on that is modelled on sense perception. For a powerful challenge to the received view, see again Valaris (2008).

as one ought, and yet still be thinking and judging. So, a distinction was drawn, and traced to the textual record, between constitutive and normative requirements to reflect. However, this leaves us with a question about their relation to one another. The remaining task of this chapter is to answer that question.

I have been considering Kant's remarks on attention and its role in empirical consciousness. I have distinguished the attention that is involved when an infant tracks a contrasting or shiny object (or when a cat stalks its prey) from the attention that is involved in full-blown perceptual *experience* as Kant understands this. When Kant gestures towards a developmental story that leads from a time of shiny-object tracking to genuine experience, he is pointing to a transition wherein one becomes capable of genuine thought, and reflects-c. The experiencer must have a tacit handle on herself as the source of a point of view on how things are, which the *mere* shiny-object tracker still lacks. Such reflection must already meet the basic constitutive requirements on thought about a certain kind of object: in Kant's terms, this apperceptive self-consciousness is inflected as a synthetic unity according to the principles of pure understanding. In the story I told, an infant comes to reflect-c once she recognises that there is a world to find out about; and recognising that there is such a world brings certain *substantive* commitments along with it (the principles of pure understanding). In the terms of Table 2, reflection-c is domain-relative from the beginning, as long as we are speaking in developmental terms. (That is, it is not as if an individual first has a tacit grip on herself as the source of her own thoughts full stop, and then at some later stage recognises that these thoughts concern independent objects in a publicly available world.) At the same time, recognising that there is a world to find out about does not take place in isolation: the basic skill of inquiry at issue presupposes some kind of communication with others who have a point of view on how things are. This brings us into the territory of the fundamental epistemic commitments of the three maxims of healthy understanding: (through the second maxim) a commitment to the independence of objects from any particular point of view on them, and (through the first maxim) a commitment to engage one's own capacities to find out how things are.[46] And as we saw in Chapter 2, Kant speaks of a 'skill' with the three maxims, taking healthy

---

[46] As already noted, the second commitment mentioned here is not in itself disparaging of the proper epistemic role of testimony: I might accept a claim on the basis of testimony, but to do this I need to integrate it into a coherent point of view on how things are – which is every bit a matter of putting my own capacities to purposive use. See Chapter 2, §2.4.2, 36.

understanding itself to be a skill and a certain 'merit' (*Verdienst*).[47] So conceived, healthy understanding is far too much to attribute to an infant who is just finding her way about in the world. However, our story suggests that the coming online of genuine thought (reflection-c) can only be coeval with some nascent meeting of the normative requirement to reflect that is articulated through the three maxims: the child who recognises that someone else kept track of the string all along must also appreciate that the string is an object in a publicly available world. My conclusion, then, is that while reflection-c and reflection-n are conceptually distinct, in reality the coming online of genuine thought (and thus reflection-c) puts one on a continuum that leads (although not inevitably) towards healthy understanding.

My other aim in this chapter concerned the question of how (what we might refer to in shorthand as) *passive* exercises of our cognitive capacities should in principle be no less the expression of our rational self-determination than overt efforts of deliberation and inquiry. The Kantian self-determination idea seems to involve two very different things: on the one hand, the understanding's operation according to its own timelessly constitutive principles, and on the other, the ongoing, and always historically determinate, project of submitting the principles of a shared cognitive inheritance to critical scrutiny. One way to reconstruct the Kantian self-determination idea might be to explain how these might be flip sides of the same coin. That is not the approach that I have taken here, in large part because my inquiry in this book has not been about the nature of *concepts*, and thus has not put on offer the resources needed to reconstruct the Kantian self-determination idea in quite these terms. I also think that such an approach stands to leave mysterious how sensible experience should in principle be no less the expression of our self-determination than overt efforts of inquiry and deliberation; and in my view, we need an account of this possibility to send away the Kantian caricature of the reflective ideal. My account begins with the agency we need to have over our own minds even in sensible experience; this agency, I suggest, is most basically engaged in acts of attention. In practice, a person's acknowledgement of the normative requirement to reflect includes a standing sensitivity to the question of what one is paying attention to, and why. Reflection-n is an aspect of object-directed thought, not an introspective speculation. Such a conception of reflection-n would seem to play a natural role in any account of what it is to submit a shared cognitive inheritance to critical scrutiny. If this is right, then the account that I have offered here should complement, and pave the way for, a reconstruction of the Kantian self-determination idea as it is more familiarly cast in terms of the ideal of cognitive autonomy conceived as public enlightenment.

PART II

Virtue

This permanent awareness of what was *so*, regardless of her whims of the moment, regardless of what it would be pleasant to believe, or not pleasant, this solid bedrock was what she was, what she was about. What could there be in its place if you were differently constituted?

What use (the question came) had she ever made of this supposedly valuable possession? What use did she ever intend to make of it?

Clare, in Elizabeth Harrower's *The Watch Tower*
(Harrower 2012 [1966], 220)

CHAPTER 4

Conceptions of Reason and Epistemic Normativity

4.1 Introduction

In Chapter 2, I argued that Kant ultimately takes the normative requirement to reflect to lodge at the level of character, rather than piecemeal
over individual acts of judgment. This transition in Kant's thinking about
the normative requirement to reflect happens in his later writings (1790
onwards), and centres around the three maxims of healthy human understanding. In the next chapter, I will argue that Kant's notion of healthy
human understanding is a conception of *general* cognitive virtue – *general*, because the cognitive normativity at issue holds whether theoretical
or practical cognition is at issue. Now, we might wonder how this general standard of cognitive normativity gets inflected when the cognition at
issue is either specifically theoretical (and concerns phenomena) or practical (and concerns good action). In Chapter 5, I will explain that Kant does
not countenance a special notion of *theoretical* cognitive virtue at all. However, there is a distinct notion of virtue that comes to light when the general
standard of cognitive normativity is inflected for the specially *practical* use
of our cognitive capacities: and this, as I will explain in Chapters 5 –7, is
nothing other than moral virtue. This is the *specification thesis*: that moral
virtue is general cognitive virtue inflected for the specially practical use of
cognitive capacities.

The specification thesis presupposes a certain view about Kant's conception of reason: namely, *reason is a single cognitive capacity admitting of
distinct theoretical and practical employments*. My chief aim in this relatively
brief chapter is to argue that the textual evidence overwhelmingly supports
ascribing this conception of reason to Kant: this is my task in §4.2.

But despite the textual evidence, not all scholars ascribe this conception
of reason to Kant: indeed, it is something of a minority view. Thus, it
is widely supposed that only the theoretical exercise of reason is genuinely
cognitive: from that point of view, the 'practical cognition' that Kant speaks

about throughout his ethical works has no grounding in anything basic about cognition as such that would be shared with theoretical cognition as well. This prevailing view informs an influential body of work on epistemic normativity in Kant, rooted in the groundbreaking work of O'Neill (1989). Although there are important confluences between my project here and that body of work, it also differs in significant ways that can be traced to competing interpretations of the Kantian conception of reason. In §4.3, I compare the two projects, identify the confluences, but raise concerns about some of the assumptions about the Kantian conception of reason that drive the competing account of epistemic normativity. Finally, I face a lingering objection that might be raised about my specification thesis: doesn't it run afoul of Kant's claims about the primacy of practical reason? As I explain in §4.4, there is a narrow sense in which Kant invokes this idea in the second *Critique* which is orthogonal to my concerns in this book, while there is a broader sense in which he invokes this idea here and there across many works that is fully accommodated within my argument.

4.2   Reason as a Cognitive Capacity

That Kant draws a distinction between theoretical and practical employments of reason is entirely uncontroversial. It is quite plain that this is the division on which the critical system is set out, and by which Kant stands to address the problem of metaphysics raised in the prefaces of the first *Critique*. This problem, in briefest overview, is that metaphysics has not made any progress since its inception, and requires a change in its method if it is ever to attain the status of a science (*Wissenschaft*). Kant goes on to argue, in the Transcendental Dialectic, that some questions of traditional speculative metaphysics cannot be answered, while others – those concerning '*God, freedom*, and *immortality*' (Bxxx; B7; B395n; A789/B826) cannot be ignored, but remain to be addressed in the context of an examination of the practical employment of reason (KpV 5:132–4). This leads to the systematic division of critical philosophy into its 'theoretical' and 'practical' branches, each presenting the principles constitutive of thought about objects in the respective domains of nature and freedom. This then gives rise to a substantive question about how the two bodies of rational cognition, theoretical and practical, are to be united in a single system – arguably the problem that Kant sets himself in the third *Critique*.

That there is, for Kant, a division between the theoretical and practical employments of reason is, therefore, entirely uncontested, since the entire system of critical philosophy is structured around it. However, it is often supposed that only the theoretical employment of reason is, by Kant's lights, genuinely cognitive. But there is considerable textual evidence that Kant took both the theoretical and the practical employments of reason to be genuinely cognitive: modes of *knowing*. At the outset of the *Groundwork*, Kant divides rational cognition into that which is '*material* and concerned with some object' and that which is '*formal* and occupied only with the form of the understanding and of reason itself and with the universal rules of thinking in general, without distinction of objects'; he then divides material, or substantive, rational cognition into two kinds: theoretical and practical (G 4:387). In the second-edition Preface to the first *Critique*, Kant makes clear that he takes rational cognition (*Erkenntnis*) to be either theoretical or practical, where these modes of rational cognition are distinguished most fundamentally by the manner in which each relates to its object:[1] theoretical rational cognition merely determines an object that is given through sensible intuition, whereas practical rational cognition does not merely determine its object 'but also *makes it actual*' (Bix-x). The sole objects of practical reason are the good and the evil: the good as what is to be realised, and the evil as what is to be avoided, in action according to a rational principle (KpV 5:57–60). Practical cognition is efficacious: its object is the good realised in action.

Further, Kant speaks often of practical cognition (*Erkenntnis*), both in prominent locations in the published works and in the Nachlass. There are many references to 'practical cognition' and 'common moral rational cognition' – the practical cognition of ordinary moral life – throughout the *Groundwork* (4:389, 390, 392, 393, 403, 409, 411, 420, 447). There are likewise many references to practical cognition in the second *Critique*: practical cognition is 'cognition that has to do only with the determining grounds of the will' (5:20); it is a cognition of obligation (5:38); it is 'a cognition insofar as it can itself become the ground of the existence of objects and insofar as reason, by this cognition, has causality in a rational being' (5:46).[2] The record of Kant's logic lectures also includes regular mention of practical cognition, often in distinction from theoretical cognition (LJ 9:69, 86; LB 24:250; LD-W 24:699; WL 24:900). Thus, on the face of it, there should be no reason to think that, for Kant, the practical exercise of reason is, owing to its efficacity, somehow not genuinely cognitive.

Another set of passages on the unity of reason provides further textual evidence for the idea that reason is at bottom a cognitive capacity by Kant's lights. These passages are arguably somewhat more ambiguous, because,

---

[1] As Engstrom (2009) helpfully puts it.   [2] See also KpV (5:29, 30, 57, 65, 66, 73, 103).

while they always mention two distinct employments of reason (theoretical and practical), they do not always make explicit that they are two employments of a single *cognitive* capacity. In the *Groundwork*, Kant mentions that it should be possible 'to present the unity of practical with speculative [theoretical] reason in a single principle, since there can in the end be only one and the same reason, which must be distinguished merely in its application' (G 4:391). He does not provide an account of this unity in the *Groundwork*, and in the second *Critique* we find him still hoping for 'insight into the unity of the pure rational faculty (theoretical as well as practical) and to derive everything from one principle – the undeniable need of human reason, which finds complete satisfaction only in a complete systematic unity of its cognitions' (KpV 5:91). However, Kant also makes fully clear, right before this last remark, that he takes reason to be at bottom a cognitive capacity: 'Now, practical reason has as its basis the *same cognitive faculty* as does speculative reason insofar as both are *pure reason*' (KpV 5:89; first italics my emphasis). And, when he revisits the issue, he points out that 'it is still only one and the same reason which, whether from a theoretical or a practical perspective, judges according to a priori principles' (KpV 5:121) – thus, as long as we take it that the activity of *judging according to a priori principles* can only be cognitive, an activity that puts us in a position to *know* some object, then again it should follow that reason, by Kant's lights, must at bottom be a cognitive capacity. Kant repeatedly infers from the idea that reason is a single cognitive capacity – a premise he seems not to question – to the idea that there can only be one system of rational cognition in the end (see also MS 6:207; A835/B863).

I do not think, in light of this textual evidence, that it should be controversial to suppose that reason is at bottom a cognitive capacity, admitting of distinct theoretical and practical employments.[3] Yet, many (perhaps even most) Kantians and Kant scholars tend towards the opposing view that reason is *not* at bottom a cognitive capacity, but rather a cognitive capacity only in its theoretical exercise. This reading of Kant might be traced to a different set of passages, which we will consider next. Kant begins the preface to the third *Critique* by referring to '*pure reason*' as '[t]he faculty

---

[3] We might still ask what it *means* to say that reason is a cognitive capacity in its practical, or will-determining, exercise. Schematically, we can say that an object of knowledge must be something that obtains independently of any particular effort to come to cognitive terms with it; 'the good', by Kant's lights, is the object of practical reason. This sketch raises many questions about the object of practical reason and how it could plausibly 'obtain' independently of any particular exercise of practical reason. Such questions are tied to the debate between constructivism and realism in Kantian ethics, and to the distinct conceptions of practical reason mustered by opposing parties to this debate, which I address in Merritt (2017a). Since I will be arguing that moral virtue is a certain kind of cognitive virtue, I will have more to say about practical reason as a cognitive capacity from that angle in Chapters 6 and 7.

of cognition from a priori principles', and says that the 'investigation of its possibility and boundaries in general' is the 'critique of pure reason' in a broad sense that is evidently meant to align with Kant's own critical project in general (KU 5:167). He then says that his work entitled *Critique of Pure Reason* was concerned with pure reason only in its theoretical use, so that this work has to do 'merely with our faculty to cognise things [Dinge] a priori, and thus concerns itself only with the *cognitive faculty* [*Erkenntnißvermögen*] to the exclusion of the feeling of pleasure and displeasure, and the faculty of desire' (KU 5:167). On a quick reading, Kant seems to say that only the first *Critique* is concerned with the cognitive capacity, which may give the impression that only the theoretical exercise of reason is genuinely cognitive. However, he began by identifying reason as a cognitive capacity, so when he says that the first *Critique* is concerned only with the 'cognitive faculty', he evidently means this in a narrower sense.

Furthermore, he says in this passage that the first *Critique* is concerned with our capacity to cognise *things* a priori, which plausibly means things in the strict sense, i.e. spatio-temporal objects in the domain of nature. If this is so, then the force of the remark is to distinguish the work of the first two *Critiques*. The first is concerned with our capacity to cognise *things* a priori; the second is concerned with our capacity to cognise the good efficaciously, in the determination of the will. After all, his aim in this immediate context is to point out that feeling and desire are irrelevant to the critical account of the a priori principles of theoretical cognition; but since practical cognition is the efficacious determination of the will by rational principles, the faculty of desire is presumably not irrelevant to its account. Thus, his express point is to say that a distinction between cognition and volition tracks the division between the theoretical and practical exercises of reason: the former distinction, in this case, takes cognition to be specifically theoretical, the domain of understanding in the narrow sense (KU 5:168). Kant retraces these same points in the opening section of the Introduction a few pages later: philosophy can be divided into the theoretical and the practical, but in each case 'the concepts that refer to the principles of this rational cognition' – which, again, may be either theoretical or practical – 'must also be specifically distinct' (KU 5:171). And similarly, at the outset of the second *Critique*, Kant distinguishes the faculty of cognition from the faculty of desire, respectively at issue in the theoretical and the practical branches of critical philosophy (KpV 5:12 and 15) – perhaps giving the impression that only the theoretical employment of reason is genuinely cognitive.[4] But he

---

[4] There is one other passage in the same vein, at KpV (5:120) – from the section on the 'primacy of practical reason' – which I save for §4.4.

thereupon refers to a 'cognition' that 'lies at the basis' of the practical use of reason (KpV 5:16), which should cast this impression into doubt. Thus, while it is true that in some passages Kant links the theoretical exercise of reason with *cognition* and the practical with *volition*, this is consistently done under the umbrella of the idea that reason is at bottom a cognitive capacity, equally so in its respective theoretical and practical employments.[5]

4.3 Epistemic Normativity and Background Conceptions of Reason

The groundbreaking work of O'Neill (1989) first drew serious scholarly attention to Kant's three maxims of healthy understanding,[6] and with that, to the very idea of a notion of epistemic agency in Kant's philosophy. O'Neill reasoned from the incontestable – but at that point still neglected – premise that thinking is something we do, and from this proposed that the principle that properly governs choice about action – the categorical imperative – must, by extension, govern choice about how to think (1989, 27).[7] She takes it that Kant's remarks about the primacy of practical reason from the second *Critique* suggest that the categorical imperative must be the supreme or highest principle of reason tout court (3), and proposes – although without a clearly set out textual argument – that the three maxims of healthy understanding are none other than the categorical imperative as it is applied to epistemic practices of thought, judgment and communication (25).[8]

For O'Neill, the categorical imperative and the three maxims are alike in that they alike 'offer only negative instruction' (25). Her account of this is rooted in her view of the universalisation test, or CI-procedure, as it is

---

[5] If the textual evidence is so overwhelming that Kant takes reason to be at bottom a cognitive capacity – equally so in its theoretical and practical employments – then why *is* this a minority view? The answer may lie in the influence of constructivist interpretations of Kantian ethics – wherein it is often (but not always) assumed that taking practical reason to be a *cognitive* capacity is at odds with the ethics of autonomy. This is too large a topic to take on here, but for considerations challenging this assumption, see Wood (2008 – passim, but especially remarks on moral truth at 51, 64 and 114), Elizondo (2013, 14–17) and Merritt (2017a). Cf. Engstrom (2009, 14), who powerfully underscores that the practical exercise of reason is genuinely *cognitive*, but takes *truth* to be at issue only for theoretical cognition.
[6] O'Neill focuses on their framing as principles of *sensis communis* in KU (O'Neill 1989, 25).
[7] See Gardner (2006, 267) for scepticism that O'Neill's conclusion that the categorical imperative guides theoretical reasoning 'in any important or interesting sense' should follow from the fact that thinking and judging (even theoretically) is something that we *do*.
[8] Kitcher (2011, 238–48) endorses O'Neill's position on the categorical imperative as the supreme principle of reason and the basis of specially epistemic normativity, but without making much of the three maxims per se.

carried out under the Formula of Universal Law (i.e. to act only under that maxim that one can will as a universal law). That procedure offers negative instruction in the sense that it only serves to rule out those maxims that could not serve as universal laws: it does not offer positive instruction about which maxims one should adopt. Likewise, on her view, the three maxims only 'constrain understandings, indeed practices of communication, that can be shared in any *possible* community' (25). But one puzzling feature of this proposal is that the three maxims are indeed formulated in positive terms: *to think* for oneself, *to think* in the position of another (or of everyone else), *to think* always consistently with oneself. They concern the way of thinking (*Denkungsart*) that is required if one is to make purposive use of one's cognitive capacities: it is not clear what exactly is 'negative' about this.

Alix Cohen (2014b) offers a clearer account of this point, and more generally of the possible role of a universalisability test for epistemic normativity. First, she points to a clear textual basis for thinking that a universalisability test might be applicable to what we might think of as the conduct of a cognitive agent, drawing our attention to this remark from Kant's 'Orientation' essay:

> To make use of one's own reason means no more than to ask oneself, whenever one is supposed to assume something, whether one could find it feasible to make the ground or the rule on which one assumes it into a universal principle for the use of reason. (Orientiren 8:146n; quoted by Cohen 2014b, 322)

The point of this, Cohen argues, is to rule out prejudice as one's source for taking things to be a certain way. So, the person who makes use of her own reason properly considers whether the source of her taking things to be a certain way could be a universal principle for the use of reason. What are some examples of the sorts of maxims that would be tested? Cohen considers *I will ignore evidence in cases when it falsifies a belief I desire to be true*, and argues that the attempt at universalisation leads to a contradiction in the will, since we are epistemically dependent beings who rely on *one another's* sound beliefs – and if this maxim were universalised, I could never know whether another's beliefs were based on objective grounds, or on what the other merely wishes to be the case (2014b, 323–4).[9]

Thus, Cohen gives us an account of the idea that the three maxims offer only negative instruction. And, quite plausibly, the account she provides

---

[9] Cf. Elizondo (2013, 12), who argues that the basic epistemic commitment of 'cognitive judgment in general involves a commitment to universal agreement on the basis of truth' – by my lights, the addition about what is effectively *respect for truth* is crucial.

of the universalisation test for more specific maxims of cognitive conduct provides a partial account of the sources of epistemic normativity by Kant's lights.[10] But one might still contend that the three maxims do not obviously offer 'merely negative' instruction. For the three maxims call for certain basic epistemic commitments – to the independence of objects, and to making use of one's own cognitive capacities (which, again, does not rule out the judicious acceptance of testimony and the like) – in arriving at a view of how things are. This is what I argued in Chapter 2. That said, there is much that I endorse in the general spirit of Cohen's account of Kant on epistemic normativity. I endorse her inference that there must be, for Kant, a deep analogy between our status as moral agents and as cognisers (Cohen 2014b, 328). Here, I would adduce the further evidence of Kant's *Anthropology* §1, which begins with the idea that possessing the capacity for first-personal thought – *understanding* in the broad sense of the term, as he explicitly says there – most fundamentally accounts for our status as persons, rather than things (7:127; quoted in Chapter 3, §3.1). Second, I endorse Cohen's further inference that, on the basis of this deep analogy, 'autonomy is not just the remit of practical reason' (2014b, 328).[11]

A third point of concurrence is rather more ambiguous. Cohen and I agree that Kant's various remarks about the unity of reason are relevant to reconstructing his principles of epistemic normativity. However, on my view, these passages are relevant because they contain some of the clearest statements of Kant's view that reason is a cognitive capacity admitting of distinct theoretical and practical *cognitive* employments. Now, Cohen draws attention to *Groundwork* (4:391), where Kant says that the distinct theoretical and practical employments of reason are nonetheless employments of a single faculty, and thus that the nature of reason can be grasped through some unifying principle. But, by my lights, it is striking that Cohen concludes her quotation of that remark with the offhand gloss that this principle is the categorical imperative (2014b, 329). For Kant does not there (or anywhere, as far as I know) say what that unifying principle is: indeed, he consistently presents it as an unresolved puzzle.

My view is that Kant takes reason to be a cognitive capacity admitting of distinct theoretical and practical employments. I take seriously the idea that there should be some common core to these two employments, something very basic that could be said about reason simply from the recognition that it is at bottom a cognitive capacity. This is not intended to be a solution

---

[10] That said, I find Cohen's concluding suggestions – where she aligns the three formulas of the categorical imperative with the three maxims, respectively (2014b, 330) – to be less promising.

[11] See Chapter 3, §3.4.

to the problem of the unity of reason. For *that* problem, as Kant presents it, has to do with the systematic unification of two bodies of substantive rational cognition – about the domains of nature and freedom – under a single principle.[12] My point is simply that given that Kant takes reason to be at bottom a cognitive capacity, we might expect there to be some basic standard of its good use; that Kant articulates this standard through the three maxims; and, finally (as I will argue in the next chapter), that the three maxims point to a general standard of cognitive virtue.

Why is it assumed that the unifying principle of reason must be the categorical imperative? On this, O'Neill mentions Kant's discussion of the 'primacy of practical reason' in the second *Critique*, which I will consider next. However, neither O'Neill nor Cohen elaborates on the grounds for taking the categorical imperative to be the highest principle of reason, and thereby treating the three maxims as its *extension* in some putatively distinct epistemic realm. If the textual considerations I adduced in §4.2 are on target, we should question whether there is any distinct epistemic realm at all. Rather, there are only distinctly theoretical and practical employments of reason, both of which count as 'cognitive' on some basic terms that might be sketched out through the three maxims. Further, rejecting the idea that reason, by Kant's lights, is a cognitive capacity comes at a cost on other fronts as well: this denial has promoted the curious alliance in contemporary metaethics between expressivists like Allan Gibbard and Kantian constructivists like Christine Korsgaard. Taking ethics to be practical on their terms 'implies that the business of ethical judgment cannot be to cognize at all', as Elizondo (2013, 2) aptly puts it – a conclusion that is plainly at odds with what can only be deemed a litany of textual evidence showing that Kant takes the practical employment of reason to be genuinely cognitive.

4.4   Kant on the Primacy of Practical Reason

In the next chapter, I will be arguing for the specification thesis. This thesis, as I noted earlier, presupposes that reason, by Kant's lights, is at bottom a cognitive capacity admitting of distinct theoretical and practical employments. I have adduced the textual evidence for attributing this conception of reason to Kant. Now, I want to take care of a lingering worry. Does my specification thesis run afoul of Kant's remarks about the primacy of

---

[12] Klemme (2014, 122) makes a similar point in criticising the view, rooted in O'Neill (1989), that the categorical imperative is the unifying principle of reason.

practical reason? As I will explain, there is both a narrow and a broad sense in which Kant invokes the 'primacy of practical reason':[13] the narrow sense is orthogonal to my concerns in this book, and the broad sense is perfectly well accommodated by the interpretive arguments I make.

Let me begin with the narrow conception of the primacy of practical reason. As we have already noted, Kant argues in the Transcendental Dialectic of the first *Critique* that certain questions of traditional speculative metaphysics do not admit of any answer, and proposes that certain other questions – those having to do with the existence of God, freedom and immortality – can also only be addressed in practical philosophy. In the second *Critique*, Kant returns to this problem, arguing for the 'primacy of pure practical reason in its connection with speculative reason' (KpV 5:119). Here, Kant begins by claiming that 'every faculty of the mind' has a certain '*interest*', taking the interest of the speculative use of reason to be 'the *cognition* of the object up to its highest a priori principles' and the interest of the practical use of reason to be 'the determination of the *will* with respect to the final and complete end' (KpV 5:120). Notice, first, that Kant speaks of the *speculative* versus practical employments of reason, rather than the *theoretical* versus practical employments (see also G 4:391 and KpV 5:89). Claims about the real existence of given entities are theoretical; claims about the real existence of entities that cannot be met with in the senses – *God exists, the will is free, the soul is immortal* – are speculative-theoretical. The chapter on the primacy of practical reason specifically concerns the relation between practical and *speculative* reason: it sets the stage for a larger argument that the interests of speculative reason must give way to accommodate the interests of practical reason, which Kant contends necessarily depends upon the assertion of the preceding propositions (about God, freedom and immortality) as practical *postulates*.

The narrow sense of the primacy of practical reason concerns the introduction of the practical postulates not only into practical philosophy, but ultimately into a unified system of rational cognition. Nothing that I have to say in this book bears particularly on these postulates. Nor am I particularly concerned with the problems of speculative metaphysics in this book. The primacy of practical reason, in this narrow sense, is orthogonal to the concerns of this book.

The broader sense in which Kant invokes the primacy of practical reason has to do with its place in a teleological conception of reason. In Chapter 5, we will see that Kant distinguishes the 'original' or 'natural' vocation or

Bestimmung of the human being (the rational animal), which consists in the development of healthy understanding, from the 'second and higher' *Bestimmung*, which consists in the cultivation of the will. This distinction accords perfectly with the primacy of the practical in the broader sense, for it suggests, again, that while the cultivation of our cognitive capacities is fundamental to this 'original' *Bestimmung* – we cannot realise our rationality without it – the end for which this is all done is ultimately the cultivation of the will, or practical reason. Or, as Kant says (somewhat in passing, at this point) in the third *Critique*: 'in the end all the effort of our faculties must be directed to the practical and united in it as their goal' (KU 5:206). The specification thesis at issue in the next chapter – that all virtue, by Kant's lights, is cognitive virtue, and moral virtue is a certain specification of the basic cognitive virtue that goes by the name of 'healthy human understanding' – should not be confused with any claim about what is the most important exercise of reason, or what is its highest calling, again by Kant's lights. The highest calling of reason, as I have made plain, consists in the cultivation of specifically practical cognitive capacities; thus, the specification thesis fully accommodates Kant's broader conception of the primacy of practical reason. Let's now turn to the task of establishing the specification thesis.

CHAPTER 5

Cognitive and Moral Virtue

a correct and healthy understanding is always bound up with righteousness [– or], at least, the other way around.

from Kant's handwritten notes on logic[1]

5.1 Posing the Question

What was Kant's view of the relation between good epistemic and moral
character – or, as I will say, between cognitive and moral virtue? The epigraph to this chapter invites us to ask this question – at least if 'healthy
understanding' should turn out to refer to a conception of cognitive virtue,
and 'righteousness' to be a way of speaking, at least loosely, of moral
virtue. One aim of this chapter is to establish that 'healthy understanding' is indeed a conception of basic cognitive virtue by Kant's lights; and a
range sources reveals Kant's readiness to speak of good moral character as
'righteousness'.[2]

The epigraph does not itself *answer* the question, of course. This is not
only because it is a handwritten note, rather than a text that Kant prepared for publication, but also because the remark itself is noteworthy for
its hesitation and uncertainty. The remark, in its first phrase, suggests that
wherever there is healthy understanding (cognitive virtue), there must also
be righteousness (moral virtue). This could mean a dependence relation

---

[1] 'ein richtiger und gesunder Verstand ist jederzeit mit Rechtschaffenheit verbunden, wenigstens
umgekehrt' (RL-2564 [c. 1764–68? or 1769?] 16:418). The remark is mistranslated in the CEWIK
translation (*Notes and Fragments*, 46), where the subject (*gesunder Verstand*) is rendered 'healthy
reason'.

[2] In a familiar passage from the *Critique of Practical Reason*, Kant speaks of the respect that is wrung
from him when he recognises in 'a humble common man' a degree of 'righteousness of character
[Rechtschaffenheit des Characters]' that he is not aware of in himself (KpV 5:77). For identification of
righteousness with good character, see RA-1497 [1775–77] (15:768). For the suggestion that virtue is,
or partly consists in, righteousness, see Kant's preparatory sketches for *Religion* [c. 1793–94] (23:120)
and RMor-6792 [early 1770s]: 'Tugend besteht in rechtschaffenheit und Wohlwollen, in so fern beyde
thätig sind' (19:162).

running in both directions: the two can only emerge together. Or, it could mean a dependence relation running only from cognitive virtue to moral virtue: where there is cognitive virtue, there must also be moral virtue. At any rate, Kant then hesitates and suggests that he commits himself to a dependence relation running only in the other direction: righteousness is 'bound up with' healthy understanding – or: where there is moral virtue, there must also be cognitive virtue. This would allow for there to be cognitive virtue without moral virtue.

My aim in this chapter is to reconstruct Kant's considered answer to the question the epigraph raises for us. I will do so chiefly by drawing upon his account of character in the *Anthropology* and his introductory remarks on virtue in the Doctrine of Virtue (or *Tugendlehre*) of the *Metaphysics of Morals*. My goal is to ascribe the *specification thesis* to Kant: moral virtue is specification of general cognitive virtue, and general cognitive virtue goes by the name of 'healthy understanding'. To follow through on this goal, I will of course need to explain why it makes good sense to think of *moral* virtue in such terms, and adduce the textual basis for attributing it to Kant: this is the work of Chapters 6 and 7, which focus on moral virtue as such. Here, I am trying to establish why it makes sense to take healthy understanding to be a notion of cognitive *virtue* at all. I begin by considering the relative absence of Kantian ideas from contemporary virtue epistemology, and in this context I draw some preliminary boundaries around what can plausibly count as a Kantian notion of epistemic virtue (§5.2). I then argue that healthy understanding must count as good cognitive *character* (§5.3). To take the further step of showing why good cognitive character should count as cognitive *virtue* on Kantian grounds, I turn to Kant's remarks about natural and moral perfections from the *Metaphysics of Morals*, Doctrine of Virtue (§5.4). This is where I return to the question of the epigraph, and argue that Kant does indeed commit himself to the dependence of moral virtue on general cognitive virtue (but not the other way around). Now, moral virtue is moral perfection. Healthy understanding is a *natural* perfection. But, I argue, healthy understanding has a unique status among the possible natural perfections of a human being. And this shows us why it is plausible to conceive of it, on Kantian grounds, as a kind of *virtue*. From here, I reconstruct the Kantian conception of cognitive virtue.

I speak here of reconstruction, rather than straight exegesis, since Kant spoke explicitly only of *moral* virtue, which he regularly presented as the *strength* of one's disposition to act from one's recognition of moral requirement (MS 6:380, 394, 409). Such talk can give the impression that Kant takes virtue to be composed of separable cognitive and motivational states:

recognition of moral requirement is one thing, and the readiness to be appropriately motivated by it is another. To the extent that we are more likely to think of motivational force (rather than cognition) as admitting of degree, it may then seem as if the 'strength' of virtue characterises the putatively separable motivational component – so that the adequacy of one's appreciation of moral requirement has, in itself, *no bearing* on one's readiness to be appropriately motivated by it. But this picture of Kantian moral virtue fails to take adequate account, as I will argue, of its cognitive basis. According to my thesis, moral virtue should be rooted in the correctness of the capacity to judge *in concreto*, which (as we know from Chapter 2) is nothing other than 'healthy understanding'. Hence, moral virtue should consist chiefly in the adequacy of one's capacity to appreciate moral requirement *in concreto*, rather than a capacity to apply rules, represented *in abstracto*, to a given situation. As a result (to be elaborated in Chapters 6 and 7), Kantian virtue can ultimately be understood as a readiness to see facts about one's situation as themselves requiring certain responses of attention and action. This still allows that cognitive and motivational aspects of moral virtue may be notionally distinguished, but it does not readily allow for their functioning separately at the level of individual psychology.

5.2   Kant and Contemporary Virtue Epistemology

Questions about the distinction, and relation, between moral and intellectual virtue have concerned philosophers working on virtue in recent years, typically from the side of epistemology. The Kantian thesis that I aim to defend in this and subsequent chapters is largely off the radar of contemporary discussion. Perhaps this is because contemporary discussion is overwhelmingly rooted in (various interpretations of) Aristotle, and to some extent Hume, and so it speaks freely of 'the virtues' – and without, by and large, displaying any particular interest in the question of their unity.[3] Kant, by contrast, doesn't really speak of 'the virtues' at all, but of *virtue*;[4] and if my thesis is correct, he takes virtue to have a cognitive basis. Thus, on my reading, the historical roots of the Kantian conception of virtue are broadly Socratic – but I am not going to make a detailed and historically grounded

---

[3] Cooper (1998, 234–5) remarks on the extreme unfashionableness of this idea in contemporary work on virtue, surmising that it may be due to the discussion on moral dilemmas (e.g.) in the wake of Williams (1973).

[4] He does, however, recognise various 'duties of virtue', which we might recognise as dimensions of one single unitary virtue; cf. MS (6:447).

case for that claim in this book.[5] Nor can I attempt anything approaching an exhaustive account of Kant's absence from contemporary virtue epistemology, which is diverse and voluminous (and ever-expanding). But Kant's being off the radar of contemporary discussion of virtue should be noted and accounted for,[6] at least to an extent that might contribute to our drawing some preliminary boundaries around a plausibly Kantian conception of cognitive virtue.

Some contemporary virtue epistemologists take an epistemic virtue to be any resource of mind that reliably attains good epistemic ends – chiefly, true beliefs. Thus, for such reliabilists, the faculty of visual perception can count as an intellectual virtue as long as it is reliable in these terms.[7] It is the dispositions themselves that are reliable (or not), and they qualify as virtues (or not) on the basis of their reliability alone, independently of any characteristic motivations or interests on the part of their possessor, such as respect for, or love of, truth. Moreover, from this point of view, a virtue can be a gift: it is not necessary to *do* anything to acquire the virtues, apart from submitting to a normal process of growth; and because of this, one need not be held *responsible* for the virtues that one has.

The reliabilist's conception of epistemic virtue might remind Kant scholars of his comment about '*talents* of mind [*Talente* des Geistes]' from the opening lines of the *Groundwork*. The talents of mind are named as 'understanding, wit, power of judgment', and come up for mention together with certain 'qualities of *temperament*' (Kant names specifically 'courage, resolution, perseverance in one's plans') as 'gifts of nature [Naturgaben]' (4:393).

---

[5] Kant's relation to the Socratic thesis that virtue is knowledge, and its development by the Stoics – and how, specifically, Kant's interest in these ancient sources might have shaped his views on ethics and moral psychology – is a topic for a separate study. For an illuminating historical discussion of the virtue-is-knowledge thesis and complementary claims about the unity of virtue from the Socratic dialogues of Plato through the Stoics, see Cooper (1998).

[6] James Montmarquet is an interesting exception to this rule, claiming that 'we *do* owe respect both to moral and epistemic norms', and drawing the relevant notion of respect from Kantian moral theory (Montmarquet 1993, 48–50) – a move which is not at all alien to my effort to reconstruct the Kantian conception of cognitive virtue in this chapter. However, Montmarquet goes on to suggest that the difference between epistemic and cognitive virtues should be conceived as a difference in their respective *subject matters* – they answer to norms that are *different in content*; nevertheless, the basic nature of the responsibility at work in each (the beholdenness to norms) remains the same (1993, 49–50; see also 109–10). I would accept that there is a difference in content if it were specified that epistemic norms are essentially norms governing belief about the phenomenal world; but the basic conception of cognitive virtue that I take to be at work for Kant is healthy understanding, the norms governing which are *general* (i.e. abstract from the content of thought) – and therefore do not, in and of themselves, call for this specification.

[7] See e.g. Ernest Sosa's 'Reliabilism and Intellectual Virtue' and 'Knowledge and Intellectual Virtue' both collected in Sosa (1991, 131–47 and 225–44, respectively). Sosa's views have evolved since then, to accommodate aspects of a 'responsibilist' take on epistemic virtue in Sosa (2015).

128 Virtue

They count as *gifts* not only because having them is normally a benefit of some kind, but also – and chiefly – because a person does not *do* anything to acquire them. And that is precisely why Kant would never take the talents of mind to be epistemic *virtues*. His express point is that they are not good in themselves: they can be 'extremely evil and harmful if the will which is to make use of these gifts of nature, and whose distinctive constitution is therefore called *character*, is not good' (4:393). So, he implies, their status as resources aimed at any genuine good depends upon the will or the character of the person who possesses them, and stands to put them to use.

As we will see in the next section, Kant conceives of individual character as a matter of what a person makes of herself: she is responsible for it. By Kant's lights, a person cannot be praised for having the talents of mind mentioned in the *Groundwork*, nor blamed for lacking them, since having them, or not, is not dependent on anything that she does or doesn't do. We might then expect Kant's conception of cognitive virtue to align more closely to that of those who conceive of epistemic virtue in 'responsibilist' terms, as an appropriately motivated disposition for knowing that is acquired through what one does.[8] The appropriate motivation is typically conceived as a certain desire or respect for truth.[9] Because of this, the responsibilist may be inclined to see epistemic and moral virtues as more closely aligned with one another than will the reliabilist. Indeed, some responsibilists openly resist drawing a firm distinction between moral and epistemic virtues,[10] while others maintain the distinction but argue that they are nevertheless *not* different in kind. Linda Zagzebski, for example, marks the distinction by classing the epistemic virtues as a subset of the moral virtues (1996, 137–58).[11] Every epistemic virtue should then be a special sort of moral virtue. Does this arrangement moralise the epistemic

---

[8] Whether or not this disposition must be reliable as well: Zagzebski (1996) incorporates reliability into her responsibilist conception of epistemic virtue, Montmarquet (1993) does not.

[9] For example, Zagzebski (1996, 158).

[10] See e.g. Roberts and Wood (2007, 60). According to Driver (2003), failure to draw the distinction conflates what common sense readily recognises as distinct. Consider the muddle that Montmarquet wades into when he invokes 'a normative level which is, at once and equally, ethical end epistemic' (1993, 109), while at the same time insisting that any given virtue always 'carr[ies] a tag as more ethical than epistemic, or the reverse', so that, in the end, 'the distinction between . . . morality and epistemology . . . is ultimate and irreducible' (110).

[11] Heather Battaly (rightly, it seems to me) questions whether Zagzebski should be committed to this arrangement: 'the Aristotelian moral virtues appear to be a special subset of the responsibilist intellectual virtues, rather than the other way around' – since they satisfy all criteria for intellectual virtue, along with additional criteria that make them distinctively moral (2014, 185–6). A comment by Baehr (2011, 207, n. 2) is indicative of how completely off the contemporary radar this idea is.

virtues inappropriately? It shouldn't, Zagzebski responds, as long as we conceive of ethics in broad terms, as 'a system for fulfilling human nature' (255–8). Although my thesis maintains that moral virtue is a specification of general cognitive virtue (and thus effectively has the classificatory relationship the other way around), still for Kant the cultivation of cognitive virtue falls under the scope of a morally obligatory end. This may raise similar concerns about 'moralism', which I will suggest can be addressed by appreciating how a similarly broad conception of ethics figures for Kant as well.[12]

I have been suggesting that the question of how to distinguish moral from epistemic virtues is more pressing for those who take moral and cognitive virtues alike to be dispositions of character that are acquired through what one does, and so for which one can be held responsible. One way to begin to distinguish moral from epistemic virtues is to establish their independence from one another. But it is just this independence that Kant seems inclined to reject in the epigraph. And yet, from a certain perspective, their independence from one another can seem like the most obvious thing in the world. Lacking basic levels of intellectual power should hardly make a person morally bad: moral virtue must be independent of cognitive virtue. Thinking this, Julia Driver reminds us that Forrest Gump 'wasn't the sharpest tack, but he was sweet and kind' (2003, 373). The relevance of such an example depends upon how it is elaborated in relation to a particular conception of moral and epistemic goods, of knowledge and of virtue. The Kantian thesis that I aim to defend claims that moral virtue is cognitively grounded. By the lights of this thesis, the kindness of Gump may well issue from his having grasped something very well indeed; and his knowledge, although perhaps in some sense limited, may nevertheless

---

[12] Together with this, Zagzebski conceives of epistemology as a branch of ethics (1996, xv). This move is alien to Kantian thought. Whatever his importance may be to the history of epistemology, Kant does not in fact conceive of epistemology as a discrete area of inquiry. In the *Groundwork* Preface, he endorses what he presents as the ancient Greek division of philosophy into the 'sciences' of 'physics, ethics, and logic', taking logic to be a merely 'formal' inquiry inasmuch as it does not have to do 'with determinate objects and the laws to which they are subject' (G 4:387). Kant does a lot of what would be recognised today as epistemology under the scope of logic, and many of the particular concerns of virtue epistemology fall for Kant under the heading of applied general logic. But epistemology is also pursued in the 'material' branches of philosophy (physics and ethics), where he accounts for the nature of knowledge inasmuch as it concerns objects in the domain of nature or the domain of freedom, and is respectively either theoretical or practical. So, it would not occur to him to locate epistemology as a branch of ethics. See also Annas (2001, 33) on this point as regards Zagzebski's drawing from ancient tradition.

be perfectly keen knowledge of the most valuable kind.[13] If so, a figure like Gump provides no counterexample to this thesis.

Observations made in a similar spirit might be marshalled to call into question the dependence of cognitive on moral virtue. Surely, there is no reason to suppose that a brilliant physicist has, by dint of her cognitive powers, any particular moral goodness: she may be unconscionably neglectful of her children, spouse or students; she may be vain, or a small-minded yet adept purveyor of academic politics, or insatiably hungry for praise – and so on. The brilliant physicist has well-honed skills of inquiry in a particular domain: exceptional talents or resources, developed at her own discretion. These are cognitive excellences, and nothing prevents Kant from recognising them as such. But virtue, by Kant's lights, is not a disposition that is acquired through the adoption of discretionary ends. The exceptional skills of inquiry of a great physicist *are* acquired through the adoption of discretionary ends. So an observation like this is irrelevant to the question of the relation between moral and cognitive virtue, at least from a Kantian point of view. If Kant allows for the independence of cognitive from moral virtue, it must be on some other grounds. This also tells us that if healthy understanding should count as cognitive virtue, it will not *simply* be because it is an acquired state of character for which its possessor can be held responsible; it must *also* be because healthy understanding can only be cultivated through the adoption of rationally required – as opposed to discretionary – ends.

The boundaries that I provisionally draw around a plausibly Kantian conception of cognitive virtue are these. First, it must be a disposition of character acquired through what one does: it cannot be a given endowment of mind, whether basic or exceptional. Second, it must be acquired through one's commitment to rationally required ends.

5.3   Healthy Understanding as Good Epistemic Character

My aim in this section is to make a case that the notion of 'healthy understanding' introduced in Chapter 2 is, for Kant, good epistemic character. I will begin by looking into Kant's conception of character, focusing first

---

[13] See Kant on 'the *simpleton* [der *Einfältig*]': 'he . . . cannot grasp *much* through his understanding; but he is not therefore stupid, unless he grasps it incorrectly. "Honest but stupid" . . . is a false and highly reprehensible saying. It is false because honesty (observing one's duty from principles) is practical reason. It is highly reprehensible because it presupposes that anyone would deceive if only he felt skilful [geschickt] enough to do so, and that he who does not deceive merely displays his own incapacity' (Anth 7:204–5).

on the account in the *Anthropology*: here, I will draw attention to Kant's claim that character, strictly speaking, is a matter of one's 'way of thinking' or *Denkungsart*.[14] The argument that healthy understanding is good epistemic character will rest on (a) drawing attention to the idea (noted, but not dwelled upon, earlier) that healthy understanding is a certain 'way of thinking' or *Denkungsart*, and (b) showing that this way of thinking – or, as I shall sometimes say, *mindedness* – is categorically required. There will remain a pressing problem about the implications of this view: for, surely good moral character must be a categorically required mindedness, by Kant's lights, if anything is. So, what is their relation to one another? I address that question in §5.4.

5.3.1 Character

In the opening lines of the *Groundwork*, Kant glosses character (*Charakter*) as the 'characteristic constitution [eigentümliche Beschaffenheit]' of a person's will (4:393) – it comes up precisely where Kant says that the various 'gifts of nature' (talents of mind and qualities of temperament) can only be conditionally good, depending on the goodness of the will that puts them to use. If a person's character is the distinctive constitution of her will, then it is not to be understood (at least not primarily) in terms of given resources or dispositions of mind – i.e. anything that might fall under the scope of gifts of nature or *Naturgaben*. Character is a matter of what a person makes of herself, although this may be largely a matter of how she plays the hand that she is dealt.

In the *Anthropology*, Kant distinguishes between individual character and the character of the species.[15] His position on the character of the species is his somewhat belated contribution to the debates around the 'vocation of the human being' (*Bestimmung des Menschen*) that arose in the mid-eighteenth century.[16] '*Bestimmung*' in its most basic usage means

---

[14] For an important earlier study on Kant's conception of character, with illuminating historical remarks on the notion of a *Denkungsart*, see Munzel (1999).

[15] Kant also indulges at length in reflections on 'national character', 'the character of the sexes' and the character 'of the races' in this and his other anthropological writings. I cannot enter into these remarks here. For helpful discussion of Kant's conception of national character, and its relation to philosophy of history, see Louden (2011, 150–63). For a well-argued account of the development of Kant's views on race, together with discussion of the interpretive debates on the issue, see Kleingeld (2007); see Mikkelsen (2013, 3–18) for another angle.

[16] Philosophical discussion of the *Bestimmung* of the human being originated in a public debate between Thomas Abbt and Moses Mendelssohn (which was itself a response to the considerable popular influence of Johann Joachim Spalding's 1748 *Betrachtungen über die Bestimmung des Menschen*). For accounts of this, see Kuehn (2009), Brandt (2003) and Wood (2003).

'determination'; and in this context, it is the determination that makes a thing what it is. But the term takes on a teleological sense where the *Bestimmung* of the human species is at issue, where it is typically rendered 'vocation' in English translation. Kant follows ancient tradition and adopts the formula *rational animal*, but he lays special emphasis on the idea that the realisation or cultivation of this rationality – our nature – is an achievement of some kind. This rational essence is not itself a given endowment, but rather a perfective *to be realised* through what we do and what we make of ourselves.

> [I]n order to assign the human being his class in the system of animate nature, and so to characterise him, nothing remains for us than to say that he has a character that he himself creates, insofar as he is capable of perfecting himself according to ends that he himself adopts. By means of this the human being, as an animal endowed with *rational capability* [*Vernunftfähigkeit*] (*animal rationabile*), can make out of himself a *rational animal* (*animal rationale*). (Anth 7:321–2)

In the anthropological writings, Kant is mostly concerned with the *Bestimmung* of the entire species, which he claims consists in human 'perfection'.[17] But he also discusses individual character in the *Anthropology*. Moreover, as we will see, self-perfection plays a central role in his account of virtue in the *Metaphysics of Morals*: the individual is called to perfect herself, to make herself fit for her own essential rationality. I am chiefly concerned with individual character, rather than with the character of the species as such.

Kant presents individual character as 'what belongs to a human being's faculty of desire (what is practical)' – and so, presumably, what can be said of a person's character inasmuch as it is expressed in attitudes of pursuit and avoidance (Anth 7:285). Individual character is a matter of

> what is characteristic in (a) his *natural* aptitude or disposition [*Naturell* oder Naturanlage], (b) his *temperament* or sensibility [*Temperament* oder Sinnesart], and (c) his *character* purely and simply, or way of thinking [*Character* schlechthin oder Denkungsart]. (Anth 7:285).

Kant draws a line in this list, separating (a) and (b) from (c). The line is supposed to distinguish character as it depends 'on what nature makes of

---

[17] See also MAM (8:115), Päd (9:445); MC (27:470–1).

the human being' from character as it depends on 'what the human being *makes of himself* (Anth 7:292).[18] To make this clear, allow me to present the preceding quotation regarding individual character in tabular form:

		What is characteristic in an individual's
GIVEN	Character as it depends on 'what nature makes of the human being' (7:292): individually characteristic inflections of *Naturgaben*.	(a) '*natural* aptitude or disposition [*Naturell* oder Naturanlage]' (b) '*temperament* or sensibility [*Temperament* oder Sinnesart]'
	'THE LINE'	
MADE	Character as it depends on 'what the human being *makes of himself* (7:292).	(c) '*character* purely and simply, or way of thinking [*Character* schlechthin oder Denkungsart]' A sense of temperament distinct from (b) – namely, temperament that depends on habit – should fall here.

It is worth considering the viability of *the line*, which Kant draws again and again.[19] Many parents will claim that that their children were *characteristically* certain ways, more or less from birth. Perhaps some of this may be chalked up to parental fantasy. Nevertheless, if we are prepared to admit the notion of character at all, then it seems fair to say that there must be some given materials on which the development of character has to work, and some given dispensation of these materials might very well count as characteristic. Perhaps, then, the line can be allowed – it can be recognised that nature makes something of each one of us – but we need to consider very carefully what this can be. Kant goes on to spell out the above-the-line aspects of character as a range of normal human possibilities, which can be assumed to receive a certain congenital inflection in any given individual. And this, I think, provides us with the best guide to interpreting the passage about individual character.

---

[18] Kant initially says that the first two aspects of individual character 'indicate what can be made of the human being' – implicitly, *by others*, in a social environment – whereas the last indicates 'what he is prepared to make of himself' (Anth 7:285). Kant may be thinking, in the first instance, of how the given aspects of a person's character can be useful for pedagogical purposes – how one's character is such as can be shaped by others – but it is clear that the point extends beyond the prerogatives of education, and holds whether the shaping is wise and benevolent, or not.

[19] It is implicit in the opening lines of the *Groundwork* (4:393) and at Anth (7:285); it is explicit at Anth (7:292). See also RA-1125 [c. 1773–78] (15:502); RA-1497 [c. 1775–77] (15:768).

Consider first the idea of a 'natural aptitude or disposition'.[20] Kant elsewhere mentions the 'natural dispositions [Naturanlage]' that are characteristic *of our species*: they are, first, the 'natural drives for food, sex, rest,
movement' that are characteristic of animals generally, and second, 'the
drive for honour and to enlarge our knowledge' that is characteristic of
rational animals in particular (MS 6:215).[21] The natural dispositions are
the given interests of our species. An interest, Kant tells us, is '[t]he satisfaction that we combine with the representation of the existence of an
object' (KU 5:204). So, there will be certain objects the existence of which
we (as rational animals) are prone to take satisfaction in, owing to a given
dispensation of mind. The given interests of any particular individual will
be these drives inflected in some particular way: anyone will take an interest in moving his body, but only some will have an ingrained affinity for
sprinting. Kant works along similar lines in his account of temperament
as an aspect of individual character. Anyone, in his view, will have a temperament based on one of four basic temperaments (which he lists as the
sanguine, the melancholy, the choleric, the phlegmatic), and any more specific inflection of temperament, such as cheerfulness or stubbornness, will
just be one of these basic modes of temperament considered concretely
with regard to its normal causes (Anth 7:291).[22]

But the line does not hold up all that well under pressure. Above all, there
seem to be at least two senses of 'temperament' – the one just sketched,
which we might (with some generosity to Kant) admit above the line,
and another that would have to fall below it. For in this stretch of the
Anthropology, Kant makes a point of distinguishing temperament (*Sinnesart*) from any disposition that is founded on habit (7:286. As long as we

---

[20] Kant's explicit discussion of the first aspect of individual character ('*Naturel*' or natural disposition)
in the *Anthropology* is unclear and underdeveloped (7:285–6): he begins by talking about what looks
to be a person's temperament (e.g. he talks about things like irascibility), and then claims that natural
aptitude has to do with 'the *feeling* of pleasure or displeasure', whereas temperament has to do with
'the *faculty of desire*' – and so not with mere feeling, but with how a person characteristically acts
from sensible incentives (Anth 7:286). This is confusing, not least because Kant presents the *entire*
discussion of individual character in terms of what is characteristic of a person's 'faculty of desire'
(7:285). For this reason, I draw on other sources to interpret what he means by 'natural aptitude' in
this context.

[21] Kant divides his list just as I indicate here, but the glosses are my own. I mentioned this passage
in Chapter 1 (§1.5.3). On the drive to know, see also Orientiren (8:139n). Without appropriate
cultivation, the natural desire to know is actually itself a cause of error: on this, see LJ (9:74), LB
(24:187), WL (24:817).

[22] Kant does not elaborate on the details of how the relatively 'thin' modes of temperament on his
fourfold metric become relatively 'thick', and concretely familiar, modes of temperament like these.
Moreover, the discussion of temperament in the *Anthropology* is cloaked in a guise of architectonic
tidiness that makes it hard to take seriously: he insists that there are 'only *four* simple temperaments',
and models the division on that of the four syllogistic figures in logic (Anth 7:286)!

admit very basic Kantian points about the reflective nature of the rational mind – enough to recognise that we commit ourselves to principles directly in action itself, even when our action is thoughtlessly habitual – then we should be able to see that a disposition formed on habit will belong to what one makes of oneself (however unreflectively), and should therefore fall below the line. Even if there is some 'given' character of temperament, this can only be something that gets shaped in its environment, where it elicits certain responses from others, and responds itself in turn, eventually forming itself (at least in one aspect) as, say, a distinctive sense of humour. And *that*, surely, is a disposition (of *temperament*, I would say) that is formed on habit – intelligent habit – and it brings with it certain commitments to values (to what is worth doing, on what occasion, for what end), no matter how thoughtless a person may in fact be about these commitments. So while we may be able to acknowledge that there are given materials on which the development of individual character has to work – the *Naturgaben*, one and all – it doesn't seem that there is all that much we can say about them, beyond the type of generalised anthropological speculation that Kant puts on offer.

Now let's consider what falls below the line a little more closely. In his handwritten notes, Kant claims that making maxims for oneself is tantamount to *Denkungsart*; otherwise, a person's characteristics are a matter of temperament, or *Sinnesart*.[23] The remark sheds light on the claim from the *Anthropology* that character in the strict sense is a matter of one's way of thinking, or *Denkungsart*: character is a matter of a person's commitment to principles.[24] That is why Kant claims that character in the strict sense – as *Denkungsart* – is not something that one has by nature; rather, a person 'must always have *acquired* it' (Anth 7:294). We should challenge this, since most of what we would ordinarily recognise as a person's temperament must be acquired as well: this is what I just argued. Moreover, Kant also allows that 'temperament' or *Sinnesart* is a way of speaking of a person's character: when we speak of a person's having '*this* or *that* character' – as opposed to moral character, which can 'only be one, or nothing at all' (Anth 7:285) – we mean his temperament (*Sinnesart*) (Anth 7:292; also 7:285). Thus, Kant appears to invoke two notions of temperament (*Sinnesart*): one is temperament as a given dispensation of nature, the other is temperament that is largely shaped by habit and is an expression of one's

[23] 'Sich maximen machen: Denkungsart. Sonst Sinnesart' (RA-1518 [1780s] 15:870).
[24] See also RA-1230 [c. 1776–78] (15:541) and RA-1125 [c. 1773–78] (15:502), where he says that character *consists* in *Denkungsart*.

contingent practical commitments. This should be a perfectly viable conclusion to draw, given the Kantian position on the essentially reflective
nature of the rational mind.

   Although I do not advocate taking all of Kant's anthropological speculations especially seriously, I do think that there is something of interest to
learn by following through on his remarks about individual character. The
items above the line (natural aptitude and temperament) are presented as
a scope of possibilities that can be assumed to receive some particular congenital inflection in any given individual. The character of individuals will
therefore be some specific determination within what is generally, or normally, possible in the species. But character in the strict sense, for Kant,
should be a matter of a particular rational animal forming itself according
to its own essential standard. And thus, what we say of the individual on
this score should be true of the species as a whole. In the next two sub-
sections, I will draw on these ideas to consider the possibility of epistemic
character.

5.3.2   Cognitive Character

Let me begin by making a simple historical observation that should immediately head off any objection to the effect that cognitive or epistemic character wasn't anything Kant ever thought about. As I noted in Chapter 1,
Kant lectured on logic for several decades, using as his textbook G.F. Meier's
Auszug aus der Vernunftlehre. The final section of Meier's text is devoted
to an account of 'the character [Character] of a learned person' (1752, 146–
55),[25] which seems to have served as a kind of blueprint for Kant's discussion
of individual character in the *Anthropology*. Meier, like Kant, distinguishes
between given and made aspects of general learned character, and does so
using terminology that Kant seems to have taken up in his own account.
Meier marks the division between given and made aspects by dividing his
picture in the following way. First, there are the natural aptitudes and temperament requisite for learnedness: the umbrella term he uses is 'the learned
Naturel (*natura erudita*)' (147–48, §§529–35) – the same term (*Naturel*[26])
that figures in Kant's item (a). He includes in this 'learned Naturel' a set
of raw cognitive resources that he calls 'the mother wit'; he also says that

[25] Meier considers both the *general* character of a learned person (i.e. regardless of the particular
domain of learnedness) and the *special* character (i.e. what is required for learned character in a
given domain). My remarks here focus on the former. Translations of Meier are my own, although
I consulted the recent translation of Bunch in Meier (2016).
[26] Spelled *Naturell* in the Academy edition of the *Anthropology*.

the mother wit must be accompanied by a temperament that 'agrees' with it, so that a person is not only inclined to attain learned cognition, but also disposed to exercise his cognitive powers properly to that end (147, §531). Thus, the mother wit and this temperament together make up the natural aptitude of the learned, or the 'learned *Naturel*'. Second, there are certain skills (*Fertigkeiten*) to be acquired through practice that are requisite for learned character (148–9, §536), which he distinguishes from its natural aptitude. So, again, we have a division between given and made aspects of character, only here the character at issue is general learned character – *general* in the sense that it is not specified as learnedness in any particular domain. The 'made' aspects of character fall under a notion of acquired skill – an idea that I will take up further in the next chapter.

Now let's take a closer look at the given cognitive resources that belong to the 'mother wit'. Meier says that the mother wit consists of:

(a) **reason** (*ratio*), the faculty to understand distinctly the connection of things... which must be predisposed by nature to become healthy, far-reaching, strong, thorough and beautiful.

(b) **understanding** (*intellectus*), the faculty of distinct cognition... which must be predisposed by nature to become far-reaching, profound, pure and beautiful. Consequently, a great attentiveness, reflection, consideration and abstraction belong to the mother wit.

(c) a **beautiful spirit** (*ingenium pulchrum*), the proportion of cognitive powers by means of which a person is predisposed towards beautiful thinking. (Meier 1752, 147, §530)

I am not going to worry here about how Meier might arrive at this account of the mother wit; what interests me is just that these are given cognitive resources – cognitive faculties, one might say – which are such as properly to develop in certain ways (to become healthy and so on). This should ring a bell for readers of the first *Critique*, who may recall that Kant there likens the power of judgment 'to the so-called mother wit, whose lack no school can make good' (A133/B172). There are scant references to the 'mother wit' in Kant's corpus, and it seems not to be a term he was inclined to use when speaking in his own voice (hence the 'so-called').[27] Thus, he is clearly alluding to Meier, who notes that this 'Naturel' is a matter of congenital good luck (1752, 147–8, §532). If you lack it, there is nothing that you can do to

---

[27] I have been able to find only one other reference to the mother wit in the published corpus (Anth 7:139). From the handwritten notes, I have been able to find only RA-480 [c. 1776–89, possibly earlier or later] (15:203) and RA-1498 [c. 1775–77] (15:776).

come to acquire it. Kant says the same thing of the power of judgment, adding that it is a 'talent which wants not to be taught, but only practised' (A133/B172; see also Anth 7:199). This, too, is reminiscent of Meier on the mother wit: for it is a given cognitive resource that is *such as* properly to develop in certain ways, presumably through the possessor's own efforts of putting it to use. But the talent should be distinguished, as a *Naturgabe*, from the properly developed capacity.[28] Talents of mind are given cognitive aptitudes that do not themselves make for good or bad character. Character, rather, will be a function of how these endowments – and others – are put to use. Kant indicates as much in his handwritten notes on anthropology: 'Character is the general governing principle in a human being of the employment of his talents and distinctive qualities. Therefore it is the constitution of his will and is good or evil' (RA-1113 [c. 1769–78] 15:496).

Nevertheless, while Kant nods to Meier, and likewise draws a distinction within cognitive character between natural aptitude and what can only be acquired through one's own efforts, he has a very different point to make. In this context, Kant distinguishes the power of judgment from the understanding, conceived as the faculty of rules.[29] There is a sense in which the understanding can be developed through the agency of others, Kant allows, namely inasmuch as it can be 'taught' or 'equipped' with the concepts and cognitive endowments of a particular language, society and intellectual tradition.[30] The power of judgment is the aptitude to appreciate that a given case falls under a particular rule, and this is what Kant claims cannot be taught. A person has to appreciate the relevance of a rule to the cognitive determination of particulars for herself. As Kant points out in the *Anthropology*, this is not a matter of running around with a rule in one's hand (as it were) looking for instances that fall under it; rather, it is a matter of having a range of conceptual resources at one's disposal and being able to appreciate which of these is *appropriate* in any given case (Anth §41, 7:197). As Kant makes these points, he implicitly distinguishes the given talents of understanding and power of judgment (i.e. as *Naturgaben*) from

---

[28] In other words, talents as *Naturgaben* should be distinguished from the cultivation of these talents in a manner requisite for character. For example, at G (4:393), Kant mentions understanding and the power of judgment both as 'talents of mind' – i.e. as given cognitive resources – but he also makes much of the idea that they ought to be cultivated as healthy understanding (soundness of judgment *in concreto*). Consider also RA-404 [c. early or middle 1770s?], where Kant remarks that 'understanding is either talent or merit [Talent oder Verdienst]' (15:163).

[29] Rather than in the broad sense, as the intellect (as distinguished e.g. at A131/B169).

[30] The understanding, as the faculty of rules, is 'capable of being instructed and equipped through rules' (A133/B172).

the same facilities as they are developed through use. That much aligns with Meier. More pointedly, though, Kant's allusion to Meier's notion of the mother wit lightly mocks the idea of a learnedness that floats untethered to the basic virtue of healthy human understanding. For Kant makes a point here of deriding the character of the learned one who can discourse thoroughly on a particular subject matter but yet is helpless when it comes to appreciating the concrete relevance of any of the rules that he teaches (A134/B173). There is nothing absurd about the contrapositive: someone who can make good use of her own cognitive capacities by judging *in concreto* about things but yet takes up no learned endeavour. Learnedness is, as it were, optional: someone might choose to put her mind to use in learned projects, but she is not required – by dint of her status as a rational being – to do so. Kant thereby implies that, by contrast, healthy understanding is not optional, to be cultivated (or not) at one's own discretion; rather, it might be a categorically required mindedness, and would count thereby as good cognitive character.

5.3.3 Good Cognitive Character

Why should we take healthy understanding to be a conception of *character*? Recall Kant's claim, introduced in §5.3.1, that character in the strict sense is a matter of a person's 'way of thinking' or *Denkungsart*. (I will mostly leave *Denkungsart* untranslated in what follows.) And recall from Chapter 2 that Kant presents healthy understanding as a function of a person's *Denkungsart*: the three maxims are collectively identified as the '*way of thinking* [*Denkungsart*] for making purposive use' of one's cognitive capacity (KU 5:295). Each maxim is in turn glossed as the determinant of a certain way of thinking: 'The first maxim [*to think for oneself*] is the maxim of the *unprejudiced* way of thinking, the second [*to think in the position of everyone else*] of the *broad-minded* way of thinking, the third [*to think always in agreement with oneself*] of the *consistent* way of thinking' (KU 5:295). So, if, by Kant's lights, (a) character is a matter of a person's *Denkungsart* and (b) healthy understanding is a certain *Denkungsart*, then (c) healthy understanding might be a notion of cognitive character. What would it mean for healthy understanding to count as *good* cognitive character by Kant's lights? In the *Critique of Practical Reason*, Kant explains the concept of the good as 'a necessary object of the faculty of desire . . . in accordance with a principle of reason' (5:58). Good cognitive character would then be something that no one is at liberty to be indifferent about realising in herself. Good cognitive character would have to be a categorically required mindedness.

My aim in this subsection is to show how Kant conceives of healthy understanding in these terms.

My argument goes by way of Kant's claim that character, strictly speaking, is a matter of a person's 'way of thinking' or *Denkungsart*. We have to
be careful with this, for Kant mentions a great many *Denkungsarten* across
his writings, and even if we set to one side what he variously presents as the
moral *Denkungsart*,[31] we will still find a great diversity of *Denkungsarten* of
pointedly epistemic significance. One set of examples is rooted in Kant's
claim that his critical philosophy proposes to underwrite an 'altered method
in the way of thinking' for metaphysics (Bxviii; see also Bxi–xii, Axi n),
to overcome the variously 'dogmatic' and 'sceptical' *Denkungsarten* that he
blames for (what he regards as) the sorry state of metaphysics.[32] Another set
of examples comes from Kant's discussion of wit and discrimination (*Witz*
and *Scharfsinnigkeit*) as the 'very different way[s] of thinking' required in
some particular proportion of any investigator of nature (A654–5/B682–3).
It is worth taking a closer look at Kant's account of wit and discrimination, for two reasons. First, doing so will bring into view concrete, and relatively straightforward, examples of epistemic *Denkungsarten* (whereas any
further study of Kant's remarks on dogmatism, scepticism and criticism as
Denkungsarten would get us tangled up in his view of the problem of metaphysics – a distraction, for present purposes). Second, Kant's presentation
of wit and discrimination as epistemic *Denkungsarten* in the first *Critique*
stands at odds with his presentation of them as inborn 'talents' of mind in
the *Anthropology*:[33] the interpretive issue is that as *talents*, they would figure above Kant's line, whereas as *Denkungsarten*, they would fall below that

---

[31] For example, *sittliche Denkungsart* (KpV 5:127 and MS 6:387); *moralische Denkungsart* (KU 5:210);
a *Denkungsart* 'devoted to the morally good' (KU 5:298) or that 'well-founded *Denkungsart*' that is
established through the cultivation of moral feeling (KU 5:299); a *Denkungsart* 'trained to the good
or especially receptive to such training' (KU 5:301); *Denkungsart nach moralischen Gesetzen* (KpV
5:160); and, of course, the 'revolution' in the *Denkungsart* that grounds the cultivation of true virtue
(R 6:47–8). Kant also mentions fraudulent moral *Denkungsarten*, such as: the 'unreliable, superficial,
fanciful way of thinking' where one takes oneself to have transcended moral duty (*windige, über-
fliegende, phantastische Denkungsart*, KpV 5:85); or the 'inner opinion regarding [one's] magnanimity
and noble, meritorious way of thinking' (*edler verdienstlicher Denkungsart*, KpV 5:157). Somewhat
more neutrally, see Kant on the Stoics, whom he claims 'put the incentive and the proper determining ground of the will in an elevation of the *Denkungsart* above the lower incentives of the senses'
(KpV 5:127n; cf. KU 5:274) – the problem he sees, I think, is that the *incentive* of morality should
not be to elevate one's own *Denkungsart* in this way, i.e. that self-care should not be what drives the
moral enterprise.

[32] These are discussed in turn in the Discipline of Pure Reason section of the *Critique*'s Doctrine of
Method, with scepticism presented as a *Denkungsart* at A757/B785. See also RA-2663 [c. 1773–76?,
possibly early 1770s?] (15:458); RA-2666 [c. 1780s?, possibly late 1770s?] (15:459); RL-2670 [c. early
1790s] (16:460); RM-5645 [c. 1785–88, possibly c. 1780–84] (18:293).

[33] As talents, recall also G (4:393) – at least for wit.

line – and only then would they count as possible aspects of character in the strict sense. Addressing this interpretive puzzle will help us to distinguish healthy understanding from any other cognitive *Denkungsart*.

Let me begin with a characterisation of wit and discrimination that is itself neutral on their status as either given talents of mind or acquired *Denkungsarten*. A person with wit takes a particular interest in the systematic completeness of knowledge, and is accordingly attentive to the identity of seemingly disparate phenomena under one and the same rule. A person with discrimination takes a particular interest in the diversity of phenomena, and is accordingly attentive to distinguishing what initially seem to be the same in kind. Their attention is drawn in characteristically different ways, and they find *satisfaction* in different sorts of movements of thought. The person of wit is geared up to find cognitively significant similarities in what initially appeared distinct and unconnected, and is 'as it were hostile to heterogeneity [der Ungleichartigkeit gleichsam feind]' (A655/B683); the person of discrimination will look hard at what seem to be the same, at the ready to spot cognitively significant differences, and is presumably likewise 'hostile' to identity.

This much is consistent with Kant's presentation of wit and discrimination in the *Anthropology*, where he discusses them as talents of mind (Anth §44, 7:201). First, he presents them as 'exceptional talents' of particular faculties of mind. Wit is an 'exceptional talent' of the faculty of wit itself. It is the capacity to light upon general rules by which to unify thought; its exceptional talent consists in making it possible to notice 'even the smallest similarity' among apparently diverse objects. Discrimination (*Scharfsinnigkeit*) is an 'exceptional talent' of the power of judgment. Here, Kant presents it as 'a matter of noting the differences in a manifold that is identical in part', so that its exceptional talent consists, not surprisingly, in making it possible to notice 'even the smallest dissimilarity' among apparently identical objects (Anth §44, 7:201). Later, in a separate discussion of the 'talents in the cognitive faculty', Kant explains the notion of a talent as an 'excellence of the cognitive faculty which depends not on instruction but on the subject's natural disposition [natürliche Anlage]' (Anth §54, 7:220). He underscores that these talents are congenital excellences of mind: a person who has them did not do anything to acquire them, but possesses them through the fortunes of birth.[34]

---

[34] The talents of the cognitive faculty that Kant lists in Anth §54 are: wit, sagacity (or 'gift of inquiry') and genius (or 'talent for inventing'). The account of wit is consistent with the earlier mention of wit as a talent (from Anth §44). But sagacity and genius are newly mentioned as talents – and we

Now let's consider the account of wit and discrimination in the first *Critique*, where they are presented as *Denkungsarten*. Wit and discrimination are presupposed there as ways of thinking required for the *theoretical* exercise of cognitive capacities, and thus where the unity and diversity of *phenomena* are at issue. Plausibly, the sound investigation of nature requires some measure of each, if it is not to become entirely unmoored. Someone at the extreme end of 'wit' would take no interest in particularity, and would in some sense fail to *perceive* the phenomena; and someone at the extreme end of 'discrimination' would take no interest in generality, and would in some sense fail to *think* about the phenomena. In the *Critique*, Kant presents the unification and specification of thought as interests *of reason*. Rational knowledge is comprehensive and systematic, and wit and discrimination answer to the interests of reason as it is trained on comprehensive and systematic knowledge of the domain of nature. Kant also suggests that any given individual will be predisposed to think in a way that answers more to the one interest than to the other. Presumably, it is in light of this that wit and discrimination figure as *talents* – that is, as this or that congenital inflection of the cognitive resources proper to our kind, at least along one dimension of their power.

As *Denkungsarten*, however, wit and discrimination must be expressions of commitments undertaken in the conduct of one's thought. Of the two characters in question, Kant says:

> Each believes his judgment comes from insight into the object and yet he grounds it solely on the greater or lesser devotion [Anhänglichkeit] to one of the two principles, neither of which rests on any objective grounds, but only on the interest of reason, and hence could better be called 'maxims' than 'principles'. (A667/B695)

Kant is pointing to a certain cognitive self-deception here. He presents a person of wit who *takes* his judgment to come from some insight into how things are independently of any particular point of view on them, when in fact it comes from a devotion to the satisfaction of his inborn talents of mind. When this is the case, the *Denkungsart* in question does not accord

---

might, in light of Anth §44, wonder what happened to discrimination. Sagacity is briefly presented as a kind of lucky knack for inquiry – a tendency always to turn over the right stone, as it were (Anth 7:223–4). But I think Kant misrepresents his case when he says this; saying so, at any rate, only mystifies sagacity. It might be better explained as a readiness to light upon precisely what, in one's circumstances, stands out as calling for a harder look, given a particular cognitive end of discovery. Concretely, this might be understood as an acute sensitivity to what appears to be out of place, as it fails to accord with a given theoretical framework or set of expectations about how things are. And if that is right, then it should be akin to discrimination as discussed in Anth §44, as a certain aptitude to appreciate what *stands out* as not adequately captured by given rules.

with the basic epistemic commitments of healthy human understanding, which I argued in Chapter 2 include a commitment to the independence of objects from any particular engagement of our capacities in relation to them.

But the *Denkungsarten* of wit and discrimination – even when taken to relatively extreme degrees – are not *necessarily* at odds with the basic epistemic commitments of healthy understanding. That is: Kant's point is not to advocate a kind of middle way, or perfect balance between the two. That a person develops one or the other way of thinking may have some basis in the engagement and gratification of given proclivities of mind. But the commitment she thereby undertakes – to pursue the unification, or the specification, of thought – may be pragmatically well-founded. Her particular commitment may be precisely what leaves her most suitably positioned to make the best, or most purposive, use of the available resources of mind. As long as she hews to the second maxim, and seeks out alternative perspectives on the matters at hand – whether to further specify or to defragment her own view on how things are – there need be no epistemic liability. When such conditions are met, wit and discrimination should count as discretionary and epistemically permissible aspects of cognitive character. They are discretionary because they are cultivated in light of a certain cognitive end – *scientific* knowledge of material nature – and it is up to the individual whether or not to care about this. They are permissible because making the appropriate commitment (given one's available resources) should be a proper part of how one makes 'purposive use' of one's cognitive capacities, at least for the sort of knowledge in question.

How, then, do we distinguish the *Denkungsarten* of wit and discrimination from healthy understanding – the *Denkungsart* required to make purposive use of one's cognitive capacities? What I have just said suggests an answer. First, what makes wit and discrimination discretionary and permissible when they are pragmatically well-founded is that they answer to a cognitive end that one is equally at liberty to adopt or not to adopt. Healthy understanding, by contrast, is the way of thinking that answers to some highly general end of knowing. Is a person equally at liberty to adopt this end or not to adopt it? I don't think so. Allow Kant the idea that there are given cognitive resources, an epistemic *Naturell*: these resources will come online in any normally functioning human being, at least to some extent. The resources will be put to use. And there is something that a person is after, inasmuch as she puts them to use. There is, in that sense, a telic drive internal to them: the desire to know is a proper part of what it is to come into the use of one's cognitive capacities. This is so basic, so fundamental, that we scarcely ever think about it. But while it may be the case that we all desire by nature to know, we don't, simply in virtue of that, have an adequate pragmatic grasp of *how to know*. To acquire this, we need to cultivate, appropriately, the relevant resources. And this, conceivably, is to make something of oneself, or to develop cognitive character.

Healthy understanding is not (as wit and discrimination can be) a discretionary aspect of cognitive character. Kant, as I have noted,[35] presents healthy understanding as the 'the least that can be expected of one who makes claim to the name of a human being' (KU 5:293) – where 'expect' clearly takes the sense of 'demand' or 'require' (see also LB 24:21). This is not a one-off remark. He says it twice more in the *Critique of Judgment*: once in the Preface, where he claims that the correct use of the power of judgment is 'so necessary and generally required that nothing other than this very faculty is meant by the name 'healthy understanding'' (KU 5:169), and once later, when he mentions healthy understanding and moral feeling[36] as two aspects of human nature that can be 'required' and 'demanded' of everyone (KU 5:265).[37] Thus, healthy understanding, by Kant's lights, is a categorically required mindedness – and, therefore, good cognitive character.

5.4   Natural and Moral Perfection in the Doctrine of Virtue

I have just argued *that* Kant takes healthy understanding to be a categorically required mindedness, which would make it good cognitive character. Now I want to explain *why* he conceives of healthy understanding in this way, by accounting for its relation to moral virtue. To do this, we need to turn to Kant's account of virtue in the *Metaphysics of Morals* – and I will

---

[35] See Chapter 2, §2.3.
[36] That is, the 'disposition [Anlage] to the feeling for (practical) ideas, i.e. to that which is moral' (KU 5:265).
[37] Kant also says that 'the minimum that one can demand from a reasonable human being' is to have *character*, and that 'the only proof within a human being's consciousness that he has character is that he has made truthfulness [Wahrhaftigkeit] his supreme maxim' (Anth 7:295). The interpretation of this remark is problematic, given Kant's views about our uncertainty over what our maxims are (see Introduction, §0.2, note 8). How can a person have 'proof', exactly, that she has made truthfulness her supreme maxim? The remark has received rather little attention from commentators; the chapter on truthfulness in Wood (2008), for example, passes it over. James Mahon, who has written quite a lot on the Kantian moral prohibition against lying, mentions it in that context. As a result, though, he reads it as claiming that the least that we can demand of one another is not to make false declarations about the content of our own mental states; see Mahon (2009, 219). But this greatly distorts what truthfulness is: a person who does not generally care to know how things are, and wants only to report accurately on her own mental states, should hardly count as its paradigm.

need to begin with some stage-setting remarks about that text, particularly around its claim that the cultivation of virtue falls under the scope of a morally obligatory end of self-perfection (§5.4.1). Within this self-perfection, Kant distinguishes natural and moral perfections. As we will see, healthy understanding is a natural perfection, yet it is a natural perfection like no other. Taking account of this will enable me to return to the epigraph, and to draw conclusions about Kant's commitments about the relation between cognitive and moral virtue (§5.4.2). On the basis of this, I will reconstruct the Kantian conception of cognitive virtue (§5.4.3).

5.4.1 Self-Perfection as an End that is a Duty

The *Metaphysics of Morals* is a work in moral philosophy in a broad sense. It is divided into two parts: a doctrine of right (*Rechtslehre*) and a doctrine of virtue (*Tugendlehre*). In drawing this division, Kant proceeds from a general conception of duty as 'the *necessitation* (constraint) of free choice through the law' (MS 6:379). The division between duties of right and duties of virtue tracks a distinction in the nature and source of the constraint that is at work in each. Duties of right rest on 'an *external constraint*', since they can be coercively enforced: juridical law provides individuals in a state with incentives for particular actions and omissions. Duties of virtue, by contrast, rest on 'self-constraint', because they call for the free adoption of certain morally obligatory ends (MS 6:379, 394). Thus, while 'I can indeed be constrained by others to perform *actions* that are directed as a means to an end' – e.g. to perform the actions that make actual social relations of right – 'I can never be constrained by others *to have an end*: only I can *make something my end*' (MS 6:381; also MS 6:239). Others might be able to make me do certain things, but they cannot make me care about anything in particular, or see to it that my actions are the expression of my active interest in certain ends. Kant's doctrine of virtue – *Tugendlehre* – outlines the disposition, or character, that follows from the free adoption of certain morally obligatory ends. It is accordingly concerned with moral requirement governing not action, but rather the dispositions of actions.[38]

Let us grant Kant the basic parameters of his *Tugendlehre*: that the moral law determines certain morally obligatory ends, and that the duties of virtue follow from the free adoption of these ends, so that virtue is to be

---

[38] For Kant, this is ethics distinguished from the broader notion of morality: *Tugendlehre* is *Ethica* (MS 6:379).

conceived as self-constraint. What is it to adopt an end? In the *Groundwork*, Kant distinguishes willing an end from idle wish: willing calls for a mustering of all of the resources at one's disposal to realise the end (G 4:394).[39] The morally obligatory ends at issue are one's own perfection and the happiness of others (MS 6:385), which are unified in the idea of making the 'human being as such' one's end (MS 6:395).[40] Strictly speaking, Kant says, duties of virtue are 'wide' or 'imperfect', because they do not command particular actions or omissions, only the adoption of the relevant ends.[41] For present purposes, we can restrict our focus to the duties of virtue to oneself that follow from the end of self-perfection. This is because we need to bring Kant's distinctive ethical perfectionism to light in order to reconstruct his view of the relation between cognitive and moral virtue.[42]

Kant explains that he invokes 'perfection' in a general teleological sense, as 'the harmony of a thing's properties with an *end*' (MS 6:386).[43] One and the same knife could be perfect for skinning figs, wedging open a particular door and dislodging splinters. One thing can have several perfections, Kant notes: in principle, as many as it has ends for which it is fit (MS 6:386). The basic conception of perfection in play is fitness for ends.[44] Here, though, we are talking about self-perfection as a morally obligatory end: this must be a requirement to make oneself fit for certain ends. But which ends? Kant answers that question by considering the source of the obligation: granting the premise that self-perfection is a morally obligatory end, the source of the obligation can only be one's own rational nature, as a human being. Recall now Kant's view that the rational nature of a human being is *such*

[39] See also Kant on the self-deception involved in taking 'a wish for the deed' because one 'has a really good end in mind' (MS 6:430).

[40] Although Kant does not here provide any dedicated account of how, precisely, these ends are prescribed by the moral law, he does offer a brief explanation of why *one's own* happiness and the perfection *of others* cannot be morally obligatory ends. For the first, there can be no duty to have as one's end something that anyone 'already wants unavoidably'; and for the second, since the perfection of a human being consists in his capacity 'to set his end in accordance with his own concept of duty', this perfection is something that only he can bring about in himself (MS 6:386).

[41] So, despite speaking of perfect duties to oneself and to others in an account of the duties of virtue, he maintains that 'imperfect duties alone are . . . *duties of virtue*' (MS 6:390).

[42] I will make a few basic points about this; for an extended discussion of Kant's distinctive brand of ethical perfectionism in historical context, see Guyer (2011).

[43] Kant dubs this teleological conception of perfection 'qualitative' or 'formal', and distinguishes it from a 'quantitative' or 'material' notion of perfection that he glosses as 'the concept of the *totality* of the manifold which, taken together, constitutes a thing'; the latter is the notion of perfection at work in 'transcendental philosophy' (MS 6:386). Kant mentions this other notion of perfection only to set it aside, but for an account of its roots in Wolff, see Guyer (2011), and for illumination of the relevant notion of 'transcendental philosophy', see de Boer (2011).

[44] Kant claims that there is an etymological link between such fitness (*Tauglichkeit*) and virtue (*Tugend*) (MS 6:390); I have no idea whether he is right about this, but I consider its implications in Chapter 7.

as to be developed or perfected: the human being is by nature 'an animal endowed with a rational capability (*animal rationabile*)' and is called to realise or perfect this rational capability, to 'make out of himself a rational animal (*animal rationale*)' (Anth 7:321). So, he is saying that a human being is required to take an active interest in making himself fit for the humanity that is proper to him, since his nature is given to him as a kind of task, and not merely as a given endowment. From this, Kant infers that 'this perfection must be put in what can result from his *deeds*, not in mere *gifts* for which he must be indebted to nature' (MS 6:386).

The end for which the human must make himself fit is the realisation of his rational nature. From this, Kant draws initial conclusions about the specific content of the duty:

> This duty can be nothing other than the *cultivation* of one's *faculties* (or natural dispositions), the highest of which is the *understanding* as the faculty of concepts, and thus also of those concepts having to do with duty, but at the same time also [the cultivation] of one's *will* (of the moral way of thinking) so as to be sufficient for all duty in general.
>
> Sie kann also nichts anders sein als *Cultur* seines *Vermögens* (oder der Naturanlage), in welchem der *Verstand* als Vermögen der Begriffe, mithin auch deren, die auf Pflicht gehen, das oberste ist, zugleich aber auch seines *Willens* (sittlicher Denkungsart) aller Pflicht überhaupt ein Gnüge zu thun. (MS 6:386–7)[45]

One interpretive puzzle in this passage is what exactly Kant means by 'natural dispositions', and whether it is appositive to 'faculties'. In §5.3.1, I pointed to a passage from the *Metaphysics of Morals* that explains the 'natural dispositions' as drives characteristic of the human being: they were the 'natural drives for food, sex, rest, movement' that are characteristic of animals generally and 'the drive for honour and to enlarge our knowledge' that is characteristic of *rational* animals in particular (MS 6:215). If that is what Kant has in mind here, then the upshot of the passage will be that self-perfection consists of the cultivation of these drives. However, Kant focuses particularly on the understanding as a *faculty* that requires cultivation under this duty, and while this might readily be thought of as cultivating the drive 'to enlarge our knowledge' – i.e. the basic desire to know – it must surely also be a matter of developing the faculty itself, which Kant glosses here as the 'faculty of concepts'.

Indeed, Kant claims that the understanding, conceived as the *faculty of concepts*, is the 'highest' of the faculties to be cultivated. I think that

---

[45] Since we will be reading the passage closely, I have put the complete original German alongside my own translation.

we should avoid being satisfied with the idea that the 'highest' faculty must be vaguely more important, or dignified, than the others – whatever exactly this might be taken to mean. Perhaps we can draw a quick lesson from Kant's division between sensibility and intellect (understanding in the broad sense[46]) as the lower and higher cognitive faculties, respectively. One of the aims of the central arguments of the first *Critique* is to establish that sensibility figures as a *cognitive* capacity – a source of knowledge about objects – through its relation to the intellect. Thus, the higher cognitive faculty makes the lower cognitive faculty *what it is*, qua cognitive capacity. Taking this as a guide, Kant's point here is conceivably this: the understanding is the 'highest' among all given resources for realising one's nature as a rational animal, because it is that in virtue of which any of the other ('lower') resources can function as such resources at all. The realisation of rational nature can perfectly well take shape through the cultivation of capacities for certain forms of movement (e.g. in sport), but this is an expression of rationality because it goes through some grasp of what one has reason to do in the first place, which requires an understanding in the broad sense that Kant sets out here.

What I want to puzzle over, though, is the striking claim that comes next: to cultivate the understanding is at once – *zugleich* is Kant's word – to cultivate the will. What could this mean? We might consider it in light of the epigraph at the outset of this chapter. As we can recall, Kant first asserts there that healthy understanding (cognitive virtue) 'is always bound up with' moral virtue. This may mean that they are always bound up with *one another*, signalling a dependence relation running in both directions: the presence of the one entails the presence of the other. And if that is so, then it will presumably also follow that cultivating the one is 'at once' to cultivate the other – as Kant's *zugleich* seems to suggest. However, we should also remember that healthy understanding is a *general* standard of cognitive normativity: general, because it holds for theoretical and practical exercises of our cognitive capacities alike. And this, in the end, tells against a strong biconditional interpretation, a dependence relation running in both directions. For while healthy understanding requires a commitment to – and, indeed, as I will argue, *respect for* – truth, it does not obviously require a commitment to particular substantive ends. Moral virtue, by contrast, does: it requires a commitment to the value of humanity. This still allows

---

[46] That is, in the sense that comprises understanding as the faculty of concepts, the power of judgment and reason; see A130–1/B169.

for Kant to be committed to a dependence relation running in one direction: moral virtue depends upon general cognitive virtue. Healthy understanding, then, will provide a necessary background for the cultivation of the will. Indeed, this is precisely what Kant commits himself to in the epigraph, after his hesitation: where there is moral virtue, there must also be general cognitive virtue – but not the other way around.

Now, Kant distinguishes natural and moral perfections quite sharply from one another, and he clearly takes healthy understanding to be a natural perfection.[47] However, as we are about to see, healthy understanding is a natural perfection like no other. This will help us to understand why healthy understanding should count as cognitive *virtue*.

5.4.2 *Perfection as Fitness for Ends, Discretionary and Non-Discretionary*

Natural perfection, Kant explains, is the 'cultivation of any *capacities* at all [aller *Vermögen* überhaupt] for the advancement of ends set forth by reason' (MS 6:391). Why is this an end that is a duty – a duty of virtue? The answer that Kant gives turns on a conception of humanity as characterised by the capacity to set and pursue ends freely: this distinguishes us from non-rational animals (MS 6:392). Self-perfection as such is therefore a matter of making oneself fit to set and pursue ends freely. Natural perfection, in particular, is fitness for discretionary ends: Kant deems it perfection for a 'pragmatic purpose [Absicht]', since it is cultivating the resources of 'spirit, mind and body' required to take the means to one's ends (MS 6:444). If natural perfection is the cultivation of resources for discretionary ends, it follows that the resources in question do not involve – as proper parts of them – the readiness to act from any particular incentive. If I have decided to try to teach myself some Latin because I might want to make a closer study of the Stoics, what moves me to do this is my growing interest in the Stoics. The resource that I aim to cultivate is some skill to read Latin independently; the motivation that drives me to do this is (at least arguably) not a proper part of the resource itself.

Moral perfection, by contrast, is fitness 'for a moral purpose' – or for non-discretionary ends (MS 6:446). There are things that a person is morally obliged to care about, to be attentive and appropriately responsive to, where there is no leave to be indifferent. Moral perfection is making

---

[47] See the division as it is drawn at MS 6:387 (immediately following the passage just quoted) and a little later, still in the introduction, at MS 6:391–3, as well as his elaboration on the end of self-perfection in the main text (§§19–21 MS 6:444–7): in these places, Kant gives clear signals that the perfection of cognitive capacities should fall under the scope of natural perfection.

oneself fit for those ends. Further, moral perfection is not a fitness to perform morally correct actions from any incentive; rather, it is a fitness to perform such actions from a particular incentive – namely, one's recognition of moral requirement. Moral perfection must centrally consist in the cultivation of that incentive, which is just how Kant presents it in this context (MS 6:387). This is why Kant says that the end of moral perfection is 'narrow and perfect *with regard to* its object', since to acquire this perfection is to adopt a particular end, namely to value humanity appropriately in oneself and in others; but '*with regard to* the subject it is only a wide and imperfect duty to himself', since it does not mandate precisely when, how often and how rigorously one should deliberately consider the incentives on which one acts (6:446).

The distinction that Kant draws between natural and moral perfections tracks a distinction that he draws, typically somewhat more implicitly, between the natural and moral *Bestimmung* of a human being. Although his remarks on the issue are scattered, he claims that the 'natural' *Bestimmung* of a human being consists in the 'development of all talents' (RA-1454 [1778–89] 15:635–6). He likewise mentions the 'original' vocation that consists in progress towards enlightenment and accordingly calls for the appropriate cultivation of cognitive capacities (Aufklärung 8:39). In a similar vein, Kant remarks that enlightenment should be 'easy *in thesi*': easy, that is, when one abstracts from certain epistemic liabilities of the human condition, and imagines a person 'who wants only to be commensurate with his essential end and desires not to know what lies beyond his understanding' (KU 5:294n). The specific point is that we are not normally like that, so enlightenment is difficult '*in hypothesi*' (i.e. under the human condition). What I want to draw attention to, though, is Kant's claim that the 'essential' end of the human being should consist in something like the development of a frame of mind where one is poised to make good use of one's cognitive capacities.[48] These scattered references to the 'original' or 'natural' *Bestimmung* of the human being can be matched against references to our 'second and higher' *Bestimmung*, which consists in the cultivation of the will (see KpV 5:87 and G 4:396).[49]

---

[48] The context of the note at KU 5:294 is, moreover, a discussion of the three maxims.
[49] On the 'first' and 'second and higher' *Bestimmung* issue, cf. the letter from C.A. Wilmans to Kant, which Kant had published as the appendix to Part I of his *Conflict of the Faculties* (7:69–75). Wilmans writes: 'Thus it is morality, not understanding, which first makes us human beings' (7:72). Note that Kant explicitly withholds his full endorsement of Wilmans's letter (7:69n), although we cannot be certain on which points (but compare here Anth. §1, discussed in Chapter 3, §3.1). What is important for present purposes is that the cultivation of the will is the second and *higher* human

Still we face the question of where to locate the cultivation of one's cognitive capacities in the distinction between natural and moral perfections. I have marked that distinction by taking natural perfection to be fitness for discretionary ends and moral perfection to be fitness for non-discretionary ends. But here we should distinguish the cultivation of cognitive capacities in light of some discretionary end – e.g. the cultivation of particular research skills suitable for a chosen métier, say among one of the learned professions (see MS 6:445) – from the development of healthy understanding, which, as we saw, Kant repeatedly claims can be demanded of anyone, and thus must be required independently of discretionary ends. Someone who has acquired certain skills that are the resources appropriate to a chosen way of life need not engage these skills from any particular motive, since she may have chosen this or that way of life ('a trade, commerce, or a learned profession', 6:445) for any number of reasons. Such observations accord fully with the account of natural perfection I have provided here. Next, I will argue that healthy understanding differs precisely in this: that it calls for the engagement of one's cognitive capacities from a particular interest, which should be conceived as respect for truth. Healthy understanding is still a natural perfection, since much of the time, at least, it is a resource to be deployed for discretionary ends. However, since healthy understanding includes a motivational component as a proper part of the 'fitness' or perfection in question, it is structurally similar to moral perfection. I will account for this first by elaborating a bit on Kant's conception of moral perfection, or virtue, and then by sketching how we might conceive of healthy understanding along analogous lines. This will allow me to explain why Kant should be committed to taking moral virtue to be a specification of general cognitive virtue, or healthy understanding.

5.4.3 Kantian Cognitive Virtue

Although Kant elaborates on the idea of virtue by identifying a range of 'duties of virtue' in the *Metaphysics of Morals*, he maintains a general conception of virtue as the strength of the disposition to do one's duty from the recognition of duty.[50] Prima facie, there are two elements at work in virtue

---

Bestimmung; thus, if my earlier suggestion (in §5.4.1) for interpreting Kant's 'higher' and 'lower' talk is correct, it should follow that it is only inasmuch as we answer the 'higher' calling for moral self-perfection that any natural perfection can truly contribute to the realisation of our rational nature.

[50] There are various ways that Kant says this. Virtue is continually presented as the strength of the moral disposition (see e.g. MS 6:380, 390, 394–5, 409). Conceived in general or 'formal' terms –

so conceived: the capacity to recognise what morality requires of one and the readiness to be moved by this recognition. Although on my interpretation of the Kantian conception of virtue these do not really come apart, I will consider them separately for now. Consider first the capacity to recognise moral requirement. According to Kant, the categorical imperative is constitutive of reason in its practical employment.[51] It follows from this that anyone will have some grasp of moral requirement – however dim – just as soon as she comes into the practical use of her reason, which is just as soon as she is able to think about what she has reason to do. On Kant's view, then, the capacity to appreciate moral requirement is a proper part of what it is to be able to make use of practical reason at all: it is given along with coming into the use of one's reason. Structurally, we have something that aligns with Kant's claims about character under consideration in this chapter: for, I have just identified a particular sense in which the capacity to appreciate moral requirement is a given endowment; and yet, this is presumably a capacity that must be developed or cultivated in certain ways in order to acquire virtue.

Now consider the putatively distinct motivational component of virtue: the readiness to be moved by one's recognition of moral requirement. In the *Metaphysics of Morals*, Kant invokes the idea of 'the mind's receptivity to concepts of duty as such' (6:399), which means, in effect, our readiness to be impressed by the recognition of moral requirement. Kant's discussion of this receptivity has roots in his earlier discussion of respect for the moral law;[52] here, he offers a fourfold elaboration of this receptivity as moral

---

that is, where we abstract from moral ends – virtue is the strength of one's disposition to act from one's recognition of moral requirement, or as Kant says, from the motive of duty (6:387, 391, 395). When that abstraction is lifted and the ends that are duties are brought into view, the unitary formal conception of virtue refracts into various 'duties of virtue' that Kant seems prepared to conceive as a list of the virtues (6:447).

[51] This is an example of a claim from the core arguments of Kant's critical philosophy that, as I noted in the Introduction to this book, I shall take for granted. But the basis of the claim is something like this. Kant marks the distinction between theoretical and practical reason by noting that the theoretical employment of reason merely determines its object (which is given to it from elsewhere), whereas the practical employment of reason does not only determine its object but also makes it actual (Bix-x). The object of practical reason – what is *known* through the exercise of practical reason – is the good realised in action (see also KpV 5:44, 46; A301–2/B358 and A327–8/B384–5). Therefore, *if* reason can be practical, it must be able to determine the will; and to do this, it must itself be the source of ends. Only a synthetic a priori practical principle – that is, a practical principle that has direct substantive implications about necessary and universal value a priori – could be the source of ends. Such a principle, Kant argues, can only be the moral law (KpV 5:30), which for imperfectly rational beings (like us) is a categorical imperative.

[52] Respect for the moral law is mentioned only briefly in the *Groundwork* (at 4:401n), but is the chief topic of Chapter III of the *Critique of Practical Reason*, 'On the Incentives of Pure Practical Reason' (KpV 5:71–89). I will return to the topic of moral feeling, respect, etc. in Chapter 7.

feeling, conscience, love of human beings and respect (MS 6:399–403). For now, though, I focus just on a general conception of the receptivity in question. What I want to draw attention to is Kant's claim that the various dimensions of this receptivity are 'natural dispositions of the mind [natürliche Gemüthsanlagen] to be affected by concepts of duty' (MS 6:399). We have again the idea of a given endowment that there can be no obligation to acquire – a point that Kant reiterates several times throughout this discussion (beginning at 6:399). Someone who lacked the capacity to be impressed by his own recognition of moral requirement could not be brought to acquire this capacity, nor held responsible for lacking it. Rather, there can only be an obligation 'to *cultivate* and to strengthen' this natural disposition (MS 6:399–400). However, while Kant claims that 'every human being' has this receptivity as a natural endowment, he also considers the possibility that someone might lack it (MS 6:399). Here, we need to be careful about what we make of this receptivity as a natural endowment: it is a receptivity to *concepts of duty*, so it can only come online together with the practical exercise of reason. It is therefore 'given' in the same rather specialised sense that the capacity to recognise moral requirement is given. Thus, what Kant means when he says that every human being has this receptivity is that it belongs to the nature of the rational animal (the imperfectly rational being who does not unfailingly act from recognition of moral requirement). And what Kant allows when he imagines that someone might lack this receptivity is the possibility that some particular human being could be congenitally defective in an extreme and fundamental way – so as to be physically alive but 'morally dead' (MS 6:400).[53]

This way of explicating Kant's conception of moral virtue distinguishes the cognitive and motivational aspects of it, the one being the ability to recognise what morality requires of one, the other the readiness to be moved or impressed by this recognition. I've indicated already that this distinction won't hold up when the cognitive basis of moral virtue is interpreted along the lines that I am proposing in this book.[54] Let me take a first step towards establishing that view by elaborating a bit more on the implications of Kant's conception of virtue as it has been set out thus far. I have identified a sense in which the capacity to appreciate moral requirement and the receptivity to concepts of duty are given endowments: they are alike proper to rational animality, and so are given with one's coming into

---

[53] On the possibility of such a 'death', see the insightful discussion of conscience in Kennett (2015) – and particularly her remarks on lack of conscience as psychopathy.

[54] I am introducing this claim in this chapter, and I develop it further in Chapter 7.

the practical use of one's reason.[55] This means that the lack of virtue can be conceived neither as a complete failure to recognise moral requirement nor as a complete failure to be impressed by one's recognition of moral requirement. This helps to explain why Kant draws on the model of strength for moral virtue: strength admits of a degree that can be measured by the 'magnitude of the obstacles it could overcome' (MS 6:397). The recognition of moral requirement and the basic readiness to be impressed by it must be present in the morally quick (if not the morally dead). Lack of virtue and vice must then be conceived in terms of an insufficiency of resources to overcome obstacles that befall any practical thinking that a human being is capable of. What are these obstacles? Kant claims here, in a parenthetical aside, that 'in us, these are inclinations' (MS 6:397). But this must be recognised as the misleading shorthand that it is. For, as I argued in Chapter 1, there can be nothing culpable about inclination as such on Kant's view; inclination and the other sources of prejudice (custom and imitation) are given features of human psychology that we stand no chance of doing away with. What is to be 'overcome' can only be our readiness to be driven to unreflective views about how things are and what is worth doing that are forged under the steam of inclination and other sources of prejudice.

For this reason, I want to suggest that the model of strength governs Kant's entire picture of virtue, and not the putatively separable motivational component alone. Clues about how to follow through on this suggestion can be found at the end of the long introduction to the *Tugendlehre*, where Kant nods to a broadly Stoic conception of virtue as self-mastery (MS 6:407ff.). This is where Kant discusses affect and passion in the *Metaphysics of Morals*; here, I will focus just on what he says about affect, which he analyses as a certain '*weakness* in the use of one's understanding' that is paired with a certain 'strength of the movement of the mind [Gemüthsbewegung]' (MS 6:408; my emphasis). The picture is one where a certain cognitive weakness leaves one vulnerable to being overcome by forces that, as it were, blow in from without – that is, quite independently of the 'use of one's understanding'. The very idea that lack of virtue would partly consist in a 'weakness in the use of one's understanding' indicates that the model

---

[55] Although both are given endowments of rational animality, presumably in Kant's view these given endowments *can* come apart, since the capacity to recognise moral requirement should be a given endowment of a perfectly rational being, while the *receptivity* to concepts of duty will not be. This might be inferred from Kant's invocation of the perfectly rational being, or holy will (see KpV 5:72). It might lead us to wonder whether the given capacity to appreciate moral requirement in a holy will stands in need of cultivation: does a holy will *learn*? Considering this question stands to teach us something about Kant's conception of human virtue, so I will return to it in Chapter 7.

of strength should apply to the whole package – the putatively separable cognitive and motivational aspects alike.

What might it mean for the use of one's understanding to be *weak* in this context? Since Kant does not give us much guidance about how to interpret this remark, we can proceed from the rather safe supposition that the understanding is the faculty of concepts, and that in this context we are concerned with concepts of duty. Thus, the use of one's understanding should refer to one's recognition of moral requirement. Now, this does not by itself entail that the recognition of moral requirement should be *in concreto*: rooted, that is, in adequate attention to the morally salient aspects of one's situation. A use of one's understanding – a deployment of concepts of duty – can of course be carried out *in abstracto* as well, whenever one has a general thought about moral requirement (e.g. 'I should be honest', as a general rule). But Kant is quite clear that common understanding is lacking in nothing when it comes to morals, at least in principle: cognition of moral laws *in abstracto* is not required.[56] So, I will assume that the talk of the 'use of one's understanding' should indicate – perhaps chiefly – the capacity to recognise moral requirement *in concreto*. What then would it be for this capacity to be *weak*? It would mean that it has insufficient resources to overcome external interference on its own operations. So, although a person who is prone to affect must have some appreciation of moral requirement, his understanding may be 'weak' in the sense that he does not thereby fix attention sufficiently firmly on what in his situation is morally salient, and possibly provides him with indefeasible reasons to do certain things. The person whose understanding is 'weak' in this way is left *exposed* to the particular sort of overwhelming feeling that Kant takes affect to be.[57]

I now want to consider if there is anything about this brief sketch of the 'strength' of moral virtue that carries over to, or has some analogue in, Kant's idea of healthy human understanding. In Chapter 2, I argued that the three maxims articulate basic epistemic commitments required in order to make purposive use of one's cognitive capacities – that is, to know by means of them. I pointed to two commitments in particular: a commitment to one's own cognitive agency, and a commitment to the independence of objects. Consider now two people who respect one another's intelligence and knowledge over a given domain disagreeing about a matter

[56] As I noted in Chapter 2, §2.3. See also A425/B453 on the resources of moral philosophy to 'present its principles . . . one and all *in concreto*', and on this as affording some protection against 'misunderstanding due to abstraction'.
[57] See Chapter 1, §1.3.

of shared cognitive concern. It is owing to a commitment to the independence of objects from any particular point of view on them that one will be
moved to respond in certain ways to this disagreement. If there is no commitment to the independence of objects, then anything should go, and the
mere fact of the disagreement should not move one to do anything. But if
the capacity to appreciate the basic requirements on cognitive conduct is
'given' in a way analogous to the way in which the capacity to appreciate
moral requirement is 'given' – namely, given along with the coming into
use of one's cognitive capacities at all – then there can be no absence of a
commitment to the independence of objects. So, as long as we are in the
sphere of the cognitively quick, and not the cognitively dead, there should
be some commitment to the independence of objects. But there must also
be a commitment to *getting* it right (the commitment to one's own cognitive agency). The fact of disagreement between *these* people, on *this* issue,
gives them a reason to do certain things – beginning, perhaps, with trying
to understand the source of the disagreement, to assess its genuine cognitive significance, reconsider the possible cognitive compatibility of the two
claims and so on. The motivational aspect of healthy understanding is a
matter of one's being impressed by these commitments; we might call it
'respect for truth'.

In order to draw out this point along the lines of the Kantian model of
moral virtue that I have been sketching, we need to see if we can accommodate a slightly different set of points as well. On this model, lack of virtue
is a susceptibility to having one's attention drawn along lines that interfere
with one's appreciation of moral requirement. Here, we would be considering an analogous susceptibility to having one's attention drawn along lines
that interfere with one's appreciation of general cognitive requirements.
Examples of this would include being culpably inattentive to evidence that
challenges your view about how things are. You may not be intentionally deceiving anyone, including yourself: the roots of your inattentiveness
might just be a certain laziness that answers to no particular interest in
things being a certain way. Or, you may indeed have an interest in things
being a certain way, which leads you to overlook countervailing evidence
because doing so suits your own purposes. (The failures will always have
the mark of arbitrariness, even if not always wilfulness.) Of course, we all
put our cognitive capacities to use for our own purposes, and these purposes will require us to direct our attention along certain lines. But there
is a purpose that is internal to any exercise of cognitive capacities at all –
knowing – and to adopt this end freely is to respect truth, which itself calls
for developing the strength to submit to it. Respect for truth is therefore a

proper part of the resource at issue. And this, finally, is what makes healthy understanding a natural perfection like no other.[58]

5.5 Conclusion

The relatively little amount of philosophical and scholarly attention that has been directed at the three maxims of healthy understanding has, for the most part, taken them to result from a special epistemic application of the categorical imperative (see Chapter 4). This assumption accords in spirit with some of the prevailing trends in contemporary virtue episte-mology, wherein epistemology is to be admitted as a branch of ethics, and the epistemic virtues as a subset of the moral virtues. That it might pos-sibly go the other way around scarcely figures as a possibility worthy of consideration. But none of this is obvious from a Kantian perspective, par-ticularly if we take seriously Kant's claims that reason must be regarded as a unitary cognitive capacity, albeit one admitting of distinct theoretical and practical employments. If we accept this, then it should follow that the self-determination of a creature that is rational by nature and by calling (even if always only imperfectly so) will be realised in appropriate development of its cognitive capacities.

Therefore, what conceivably makes healthy understanding 'the least' that is to be required of anyone is that it is the most basic realisation of our rational nature. Taking note of this, we should expect there to be *general* principles governing the exercise of our cognitive capacities – requirements that hold regardless of whether theoretical or practical knowing is at stake. This is precisely what Kant tells us in the *Anthropology*: he notes that reason directs the use of cognitive capacities in theoretical and practical employ-ments alike (Anth 7:227), and then proceeds with an account of the three maxims (Anth 7:228), giving us every indication that they are precisely those general principles of good use. The three maxims concern *general* epistemic commitments, and healthy understanding is cognitive character

---

[58] Cf. Lu-Adler (2017) on the 'Imperative of Judgment': 'for any thought that can be true or false, do not hold it as true unless you are certain about its truth'. Lu-Adler calls this the Imperative of Judgment, and argues that our standing under it makes us what we are, as epistemic agents – concluding that 'the pith of the Imperative of Judgment is not simply to avoid error, but to exercise our epistemic *agency* properly'. This is not the same thing as respect for truth, although both Lu-Adler and I are concerned, in this vein, about normative requirements on judgment. I would say, though, that Lu-Adler's imperative makes the wrong demands on us, in more or less the same way that Chignell (2007) worried about Kant's claim that 'all judgments require reflection': for it seems to me that I exercise my cognitive agency perfectly well *for my purposes* if I take it to be the case that there is enough milk in the fridge for breakfast tomorrow, even though I am not 'certain' about the truth of this (I do not go and double-check, or whatever).

that is formed by these commitments. If healthy understanding is basic cognitive virtue, moral virtue might then be the strength of specifically practical cognitive capacities. My aim in the remaining chapters is to elaborate upon, and further defend, this way of thinking about the cognitive basis of moral virtue.

CHAPTER 6

Virtue as a Skill

6.1 Introduction

My aim in this chapter is to examine Kant's consideration of the idea that moral virtue may be a certain sort of skill (*Fertigkeit*). This aspect of Kant's discussion of virtue has been thoroughly neglected by commentators. I will argue that he endorses the skill model of virtue, albeit in a highly qualified way. Indeed, if the relevant passages are read cursorily, they might even seem to offer a straight denouncement. Yet while Kant accepts the model, he – not surprisingly – understands it in his own terms. Now, intuitively, a skill is a practical intelligence that is concretely embedded as a disposition for action. Thus, by getting to grips with Kant's endorsement of the skill model of virtue, we stand to learn something about the *intelligence* of virtue by his lights. We also stand to learn something about how reflection can be infused in action. Therefore, a careful and judicious account of what Kant accepts in the skill model of virtue will put us in position to challenge standing assumptions about 'the Kantian' conception of practical thinking, and with that, attendant notions of reflection and its place in moral life.

Let me begin with a presentation of these standing assumptions, before offering a précis of the chapter. Many of the relevant assumptions are nicely encapsulated by Talbot Brewer (2011), who articulates what is widely accepted as the Kantian picture of practical thinking as a foil against which to appreciate the merits of an Aristotelian one. This picture has, Brewer points out, informed modern ethical thought well beyond the boundaries of Kantian ethics, but it is nevertheless Kantian in essence, owing to its reliance on an indubitably Kantian distinction between theoretical and practical reason and its commitment to the idea that the function of practical thinking is to discern justificatory links between generically describable features of one's circumstances and generically describable actions – a commitment borne out in the once again indubitably Kantian idea that a rational being acts under maxims, or subjective principles of action. I do not dispute the Kantian provenance of either the distinction between theoretical and practical reasoning or the idea that maxims play some constitutive role in rational agency. I do have doubts that either of these central Kantian ideas is often very well understood, but I am not going to press that case in regards to the distinction between theoretical and practical reason at all here, and will only weigh in indirectly on the role of maxims in rational agency. My case will be indirect because I will not say much about maxims as such; instead, I am interested in the related issue of what it is for a rational being to be appropriately reflective in action. Very roughly, my thinking is that Kant's recognition that moral virtue is a certain sort of skill entails that reflection need not be conceived as requiring a deliberate stepping back from action to consider, explicitly, the maxim under which one proposes to act, and (in the case of the virtuous) to endorse only those maxims which are deemed as having the appropriate provenance.

Brewer's account of the modern – and putatively essentially Kantian – picture of practical thinking presents it as a 'discrete and occasional process rather than as a continuous activity' (Brewer 2011, 120).[1] This accords with the emphasis that modern moral theory places on the deliberation procedure: the overt working out of what to do.[2] Practical thinking on this picture is episodic, encapsulated within neat temporal boundaries marked out by thinking of another kind. The other kind of thinking is 'theoretical', in the Kantian sense: it is engaged with determining or registering how things are, and it can be distinguished from practical thinking, regarded as the thinking involved in working out of what to do in light of how things are. On this picture, theoretical thinking provides an evaluatively neutral take on one's circumstances, and thereby furnishes premises for practical thinking. Paradigmatically, the conclusion of practical thinking is intentional action, but strictly speaking it is only the formation of an intention (119).[3]

On this putatively Kantian picture, practical thinking begins when one considers certain generically describable features of one's circumstances,

---

[1] Barbara Herman (1993, 2007) has done much to push back against this idea in particular – or, at any rate, a version of this claim that presents moral deliberation as a kind of 'intrusion' on one's putatively extra-moral affairs: modern moral philosophers peddle in tales that 'have me on my way in morally neutral territory when something "outside" my narrative happens. Morality intrudes' (Herman 1993, 180). Cf. Brewer on 'the starkly catastrophic terrain of the moral theorist's thought experiment' (2011, 117).

[2] To show that the model of practical thinking is quite widespread, Brewer argues that it is even adopted by particularists such as Jonathan Dancy (Brewer 2011, 121).

[3] By Kant's lights, the conclusion of practical thinking would have to be the activity of willing, which involves mustering all of the resources within one's power – but which may not be sufficient to pull the act off, as it were.

themselves registering through thinking that is theoretical in nature, as providing one with reason to do this or that. This, of course, opens up questions about what it is to see some purely descriptive fact about one's situation as providing reasons for action. But to complain that this is rendered mysterious by the model is, surely at least in part, to dispute the tenability of the distinction between theoretical and practical thinking on which it relies – a complaint that may well be on Brewer's broader agenda to lodge. Brewer, however, is perhaps more interested in challenging the conception of the intention that is supposed to be the result of practical thinking so conceived. Any intention 'to perform a brave action or to write a good book' can only yield determinate actions if one has some understanding of what counts as bravery or literary excellence, and some appreciation of their value – which, naturally, requires a 'further stretch of thinking' that can only be practical in nature (120). The standard picture cannot accommodate the form of practical thinking that is perhaps most familiar to us, and which figures in the activities that we widely regard as intrinsically valuable – and hence, in those activities that intuitively contribute much to what we normally think of as the value of a human life. Some examples of such activities include cultivating meaningful relationships, doing philosophy, engaging in athletic competition. The reason that they cannot be accommodated within the putatively Kantian picture of practical thinking is that we, of necessity, engage in them without first having a clear, and clearly action-guiding, sense of the point and value of what we are up to. Rather, our appreciation of the value of these activities is cultivated through engaging in the activities themselves. This thus doesn't fit the model where we act, clear-sightedly, on a principle to do A in circumstances C for some end E, for neither our appreciation of the end for the sake of which we act, nor what in our circumstances is relevant in light of such an end, nor finally our appreciation of the activity itself that we are engaged in, is clearly in view in the way in which that model seems to require.

Brewer argues that these intuitively intrinsically valuable activities have a 'cross-temporal unity', and for this reason he dubs them 'dialectical activities' (129): there is a back and forth, when we engage in them, between a larger thought concerning the point and value of what one is up to and the particular engagement in the activity itself. A young child in daycare may have a keen interest in making friends, but perhaps not an especially clear or deep appreciation of the value of friendship, or even of what counts as friendship (witness the readiness to proclaim, 'I won't be your friend anymore!'); or, to draw on one of Brewer's examples, an undergraduate might get excited about philosophy and pursue it avidly, 'but without a full understanding of what the activity calls for . . . since a developed sense of what counts as good philosophy is itself a high philosophical achievement' (124). What makes these activities 'dialectical' is the mutually supporting relation between the quality of one's engagement in the activity and the determinacy of one's conception of the nature, the point and the value of what one is up to. It works in both directions: one's engagement in the activity itself contributes to 'one's deepening sense of [its] intrinsic value' (126), and this deepening sense of its value yields an increase in the determinacy of one's conception of what one is up to – what counts as good friendship, good philosophy and so on – which promotes or 'carries forward' (to use Brewer's expression, passim) the activities themselves.[4]

I do not take issue with Brewer's claims about the impoverishment of what is presented as the Kantian picture of practical thinking; I only take issue with the idea that it must be admitted as the Kantian picture in the first place.[5] When we fill out Kant's claim that virtue is a certain sort of skill, the result, as I aim to show, is something like Brewer's dialectical activities. If my case about this is sound, then it militates against the acceptance of what Brewer has articulated as the *echt* Kantian model of practical thinking. Here is how I proceed. In the next section, we will consider the passage that most clearly indicates Kant's qualified endorsement of the skill model of virtue (§6.2). To interpret Brewer's claim, we need to turn to Kant's remarks on skill in two similar passages from the *Anthropology* and the *Metaphysics of Morals*; these will help us to work out how Kant distinguishes various types of skill, and in turn to identify the mode of skill that plausibly provides him with a model for conceiving of moral virtue as a skill, albeit under some further qualification (§6.3). We next compare the operative conception of skill against Brewer's dialectical activities (§6.4), before examining the closer historical context of Kant's remarks about virtue as

---

4 Brewer's point is that practical thinking at least 'sometimes' takes the form of dialectical activities; this means that 'excellence in practical thinking cannot consist solely in discerning and acting on justificatory links between non-evaluative facts about one's circumstances and non-evaluative specifications of proposed actions. It sometimes requires a continuous effort to bring into view the best and highest conception of one's own unfolding activity. This focal object will straddle the supposed divide between the circumstances of choice and the action being chosen. The task will be to grasp what one is doing in such a way as to lift it, with each moment, closer to the ideal form in whose light it is understood' (2011, 130). Much of what we do, and much of what we do that is ethically significant, Brewer concludes, involves practical thinking that takes this dialectical form.
5 Brewer, I think, might accept this. Brewer (2011) develops some points from Brewer (2002), but the earlier paper offers what he suggests could be taken as a modification of the Kantian picture from within the Kantian picture. This suggests that he doesn't take the unattractive picture of practical thinking labelled 'Kantian' in Brewer (2011) to necessarily be the correct, or most philosophically sound, interpretation of Kant's own views.

skill: namely, Moses Mendelssohn's discussion of virtue as skill in his 1761 'Rhapsody or Additions to the Letters on Sentiments'.[6] What I will bring out is the sense in which skills, for Mendelssohn, are unreflective. It is this assumption, I contend, that Kant rejects. Kant's qualified endorsement of the skill model of virtue rests on his recognition that certain skills have reflection embedded in them; this is why his endorsement of the point suggests new avenues for thinking about the role of reflection in practical thought, and so in turn in moral life, from a Kantian point of view (§6.5). Therefore, the distinguishing difference – that which makes moral virtue unlike any other skill – does not lie in the idea that normal skills are 'unreflective' in some way that moral virtue is not; rather, I argue, it lies in the role that obligatory ends play in the cultivation of moral virtue by Kant's lights. In that context, I will begin to fill in some of the specific details of the Kantian conception of virtue as a skill – although I leave the working out of most of its philosophical and textual implications for Chapter 7.

6.2 The Focal Passage

Kant registers his qualified endorsement of the idea that moral virtue could be conceived as a certain sort of skill in two passages in the *Metaphysics of Morals*. Here is the first appearance of the claim:

> But virtue is not to be explained and valued merely as a *skill* [*Fertigkeit*][7] and (as the prize essay of Cochius, the court-chaplain, puts it) a longstanding *habit* [*Gewohnheit*] of morally good actions acquired through practice. For if this skill is not the effect of principles that are reflected upon [überlegter], firm, and continually purified, then it is like any other mechanism of technically practical reason and is neither equipped for all situations, nor sufficiently secure for the change that new enticements could bring about. (MS 6:383–4)

---

[6] I am indebted to an audience member at a conference (Nature and Culture in German Romanticism and Idealism, held at the University of Sydney and the University of New South Wales in March 2014, where I presented an early version of some of this material) for pointing out to me that Kant's qualified endorsement of the skill model of virtue was likely some kind of nod to Mendelssohn; unfortunately, I did not learn her name. I am also grateful to Ursula Goldenbaum for guidance on Mendelssohn.

[7] Any translation of *Fertigkeit* in this context is bound to be somewhat problematic. In the CEWIK translation, Gregor renders it 'aptitude'; but reference to the OED cautions against this, inasmuch as 'aptitude' tends to carry the sense of purely natural agility – a gift of nature rather than something acquired through what one does. For this reason, I follow Louden, who renders the term 'skill' in his CEWIK translation of the *Anthropology*; this better carries the sense of an agility that is acquired through what one does. Moreover, the OED traces the etymology of 'skill' to the Old Norse (and later, Middle English) word for reason, regarded as a capacity for *discrimination*, which aligns with the basic point that I shall argue Kant is making.

I label this the **Cochius passage**.[8] On the face of it, the passage gives
the impression that while most skills are based in habit, moral virtue differs
in that is the result of reflection. There is something right about this first
impression, but it is also too crude. First, if we run with it without stopping
to understand what it is for a skill to be based in habit, then we will not
understand what Kant is saying when he grants that moral virtue is a skill
(albeit in some qualified sense), for we will have said that virtue is not like
a skill in what has been presented as an essential characteristic of it, namely
its basis in habit. Moreover, if a person is good, surely there must be some
sense in which he is reliably or habitually so. If Kant recognised this, then
he would not mean to deny that virtue is habitual; he would instead mean
to qualify the sense in which it is so. He implies here that the habit on which
moral virtue is based is a certain readiness for active engagement of one's
own capacities: specifically, he gestures towards some continually renewed
commitment to principles, and continually refined grasp of them. Now,
this is what gives the impression that moral virtue is reflective in some way
that ordinary skill is not. And the conclusion to the passage reinforces this
impression, for the distinction that Kant seems to have drawn is between
skills that are stimulus-driven – and thereby engaged unreflectively, given
only the appropriate stimulus – and skills that are engaged through some
active grasp of principles.

Kant returns to the topic of skill later in the *Metaphysics of Morals*, again
suggesting that moral virtue may be admitted as a certain sort of skill; this
passage – read in conjunction with a similar one from the *Anthropology* –
yields a more nuanced picture. Skills necessarily have some roots in habit
and practice, but certain types of skill are cultivated through some kind of
reflection – and these, I will argue, are the skills that provide Kant with the
relevant model for moral virtue as a skill.

6.3   Kant on Skill

The companion passages on skill each conclude with hints about the qualification under which moral virtue can be admitted as a skill. For now, I
will quote each passage just short of its conclusion to this effect, since I
first want to come to grips with what Kant takes skill to be, and what sort
of skill provides Kant with the model for understanding moral virtue as a
skill, before I begin to fuss with the qualification under which moral virtue

[8] After its reference to the court-chaplain, Leonhard Cochius, whose essay *Untersuchung über die Nei-gungen* won the Berlin Academy essay prize for 1767.

can be admitted as a skill (and thus, in turn, what conceivably makes it a skill unlike any other).

One of these passages – the one from the *Anthropology* – is additionally problematic because it seems to deny outright that moral virtue can be conceived as any sort of skill. Let's look at it first, hereby dubbed **Skill 1**:

> *Facility* [*Leichtigkeit*] in doing something (*promptitudo*) must not be confused with *skill* [*Fertigkeit*] in such actions (*habitus*). The former signifies a certain degree of mechanical capacity: 'I can if I want to', and designates a subjective *possibility*. The latter [*Fertigkeit*] signifies a subjective-practical *necessity*, that is *habit* [*Gewohnheit*], and so designates a certain degree of will, acquired through the frequently repeated use of one's faculty: 'I choose this, because duty commands it'. Therefore one cannot explain *virtue* as *skill* in free lawful actions, for then it would be a mere mechanism of applying power. (Anth 7:147)

It might seem as if much rests on the distinction between facility and skill – *Leichtigkeit* and *Fertigkeit*, which I will track now in German. Indeed, it might even seem as if the point of drawing this distinction is to deny that moral virtue is a *Fertigkeit* so as to allow that it might be some kind of *Leichtigkeit*. This would certainly not be the correct conclusion to draw, but one can see how the passage encourages it – since it *also* makes a point of denying that virtue can be explained as a skill. But what Kant says is that virtue cannot be conceived as 'a mere mechanism for applying power', which should rule out its figuring as a *Leichtigkeit*, glossed as a 'mechanical capacity'. Nevertheless, the distinction between *Leichtigkeit* and *Fertigkeit* is hard to make out: for, while Kant suggests that the difference turns on the 'certain degree of will' that is involved in the exercise of skill, he also presents the engagement of *Leichtigkeit* under the motto 'I can if I want to' – which would seem to imply that these capacities are engaged, too, only with an exercise of choice, and so apparently with a 'certain degree of will'. Furthermore, why shouldn't the gloss of *Leichtigkeit* as a 'mechanical capacity' pertain to *Fertigkeit*, given the latter's basis in habit?

Ordinary usage suggests that the distinction between *Leichtigkeit* and *Fertigkeit* in this passage may be a bit of a distraction: intuitively, it seems that a skilful action will be one performed with facility, or some kind of ease – and so with *Leichtigkeit*.[9] But I think that Kant's distinction between *Leichtigkeit* and *Fertigkeit* may bear upon how different capabilities develop. Some – like the capacity to smell – develop mechanically,

---

[9] This is the conclusion that Mellin (1799, 576) reaches on this passage; see also Adelung (1811), s.v. *Fertigkeit*: 'das Vermögen, gewisse Handlungen mit Leichtigkeit zu verrichten'.

through a normal process of growth. I do not mean any special olfactory discernment, such as a sommelier might have; I mean just the capacity to enjoy deliverances of sensation of smell. This, moreover, accords with Kant's characterisation of a *Leichtigkeit*, as it is a mechanical capacity (given a certain stimulus, it registers a certain sensation of smell), and one that I can put to use if I want to (I can choose to sniff or to hold my nose). But the capacity itself is acquired without any 'degree of will': I just have it, as a given natural endowment. Now consider, say, the special olfactory skill of a sommelier, which surely can only be acquired by making some kind of deliberate effort. I have to set myself the end of cultivating my olfactory discernment along the relevant lines; and so, to acquire this skill, I need 'a certain degree of will'. The acquisition of this skill will be easier for some, harder for others, depending at least in part on what one has to work with by way of given olfactory endowment – the mechanical capacity acquired through a normal process of growth. But the cultivation of the skill will require that one *care* to be discerning in the relevant way. This proposal accounts for Kant's claim that a *Fertigkeit*, but not a *Leichtigkeit*, involves 'a certain degree of will'.

Whether or not this is what Kant has in mind in Skill 1 is not at all clear; and it is made less so by the fact that the companion passage on skill from the *Metaphysics of Morals* finds Kant taking skill to be nothing other than a certain type of facility for action – and, moreover, following standard usage in doing so.[10] The companion passage, which I dub **Skill 2**, is of interest to our account, however, since it distinguishes two classes of skill – only one of which could conceivably provide Kant with a model for admitting moral virtue as a skill:

> *Skill* (*habitus*) is a facility for action and a subjective perfection of choice. But not every such *facility* is a *free* skill (*habitus libertatis*); for if it is a *habit* (*assuetudo*), that is, a uniformity in action that has become a *necessity* through frequent repetition, it is not one that proceeds from freedom, and therefore also not a moral skill.

> *Fertigkeit* (*habitus*) ist eine Leichtigkeit zu handeln und eine subjective Vollkommenheit der *Willkür*. – Nicht jede solche *Leichtigkeit* aber ist eine *freie* Fertigkeit (*habitus libertatis*); denn wenn sie *Angewohnheit* (*assuetudo*), d.i. durch öfters wiederholte Handlung zur *Nothwendigkeit* gewordene Gleichförmigkeit, derselben ist, so ist sie keine aus der Freiheit hervorgehende, mithin auch nicht moralische Fertigkeit. (MS 6:407)

---

[10] See previous footnote.

Here, Kant distinguishes between skills that are free in some sense and skills that are not. The passage also indicates that free skills provide the model for conceiving of virtue as a skill – for, unfree skills surely cannot. To work this out correctly, we first need to understand more clearly what Kant takes skill as such to be. And to do that, I will begin by examining what is plausibly an unfree skill.

Consider the motor skills that a baby book would mention as develop-mental markers, such as the capacity to stand upright or to pick up objects the size of a raisin. Such capacity is cultivated through repeated effort, and presumably on that ground counts as a skill. The infant might have some natural impulse to explore the world around her, and will be impelled to do this by touching and grasping. (The brute impulse at issue may well just be to touch and grasp at things; it may only conceivably figure as an impulse to *explore* once a certain amount of touching and grasping reveals to the child that there is a world to find out about.) She won't initially be coordinated enough to pick anything up; but eventually she will be able to grasp something like the corner of a blanket, and still later something like a raisin. If she struggles to grasp something, she will keep trying with moves that are like the moves that have already proved adequate for other sorts of objects; failing, she may make adjustments – perhaps at random, but she will be able to appreciate when one works, since she will be hold-ing that raisin. Prior engagement in activity of the relevant sort is what the skill is based on. Human babies presumably have the inborn interests that makes the cultivation of such skills possible. So, when Kant says that skills as such involve 'a certain degree of will', I take him to mean a degree of will compatible with *arbitrium brutum* just as well as with *arbitrium liberum*, since the cultivation of skill involves a type of directed effort that human babies and many non-rational animals are perfectly well capable of. (To clarify: the cultivation of skill does not necessarily involve *taking* an inter-est in the skill itself; this would require the self-consciousness characteristic of a rational will, and hence reflection-c. But there is a sense in which a normal human infant has an instinctual interest to grasp and so on; and it is partly due to this that the relevant motor skills can be acquired.)

What makes these examples of 'unfree' skills? Unfree skills, Kant says, rest on necessitating habit (*Angewohnheit*):[11] there is a 'uniformity of action' – a certain determinate way of going on, given certain stimuli – that has become 'a *necessity*' owing to the repetition. His point, I take it,

---

[11] A distinction between *Angewohnheit* and *Gewohnheit* (both rendered 'habit' in English translations) that can be traced in Kant's usage is relevant here; see Chapter 1, §1.5.2, 42.

is that such skills are not open to reflection, or not normally so. Once the child is able to stand, she constantly makes minute adjustments that keep her from falling over. There is no real possibility of her doing otherwise; and yet, at the same time, while the cultivation of this capacity to stand arose in part due to her having an inborn interest in standing, she has no determinate thought about standing as such, nor does she register any explicit attention to the countless little adjustments that are constantly making it possible. And this is not, or not simply, because she is an infant: standing adults don't typically consider these little adjustments either. The skill is not normally open to reflection.[12]

Kant glosses skill as a 'subjective perfection of choice' in Skill 2; and earlier in the *Metaphysics of Morals*, he explains the relevant sort of perfection as the 'harmony of a thing's properties with an *end*' (6:386).[13] When I shift my body weight in response to a change in the slope of the surface on which I am biking, I am acting on a certain cue: reliably taking perfectly adequate means, in response to this cue, to a certain end (continuing straight ahead, say). These are means that I have brought to the ready through some kind of effort, and so they constitute (at least partly) a certain skill. What I am not doing in this sort of case, however, is considering how I should respond to what I am thus conditioned to register as a cue, or even whether I should respond. That is the necessitation that is characteristic of what Kant deems unfree skills. And it is precisely this that we must set into contrast with the notion of a 'free skill' – a *freie Fertigkeit*. Someone exercising a 'free' skill must have something against which to assess the promptings of habit: that is what makes the skill freely deployed and, as I will explain, in some sense reflective.[14]

Consider now a skilled tennis player: she does not respond uncritically to stimuli, but engages in some kind of thought about how to go on, given a certain stimulus. This thinking makes reference, we might suppose, to her conception of a good game. A scrappy player doesn't care how she wins; she just wants to win. A skilled player wants to play a good game, wants to win well. So when we think of a skilled player, we think of someone who

---

[12] One might aim to manifest a certain standard in one's standing, for example when taking the basic standing pose, *Tadasana*, in hatha yoga; but then this is not plausibly an unfree skill in Kant's sense. I was reminded of this example by Bloomfield (2000), who cites B.K.S. Iyengar (1979).

[13] Also quoted in Chapter 5, §5.4.1.

[14] Mellin (1799) s.v. *Fertigkeit* seems to take it that Kant's notion of a 'free skill' is already his notion of moral skill, or moral virtue as a skill. But there is no obvious basis for assuming this: first, it assumes that there is no difference between a baby's motor skills, on the one hand, and skilful tennis, or exegesis, or argument, or listening to others etc., on the other; and second, it would leave us without any principled *basis* for coming to terms with Kant's qualified admission that moral virtue is a certain sort of skill.

does not simply determine how to go on with reference to the rules of the game, but whose practical thinking makes reference to a standard in the sense of a broader ideal that she aims to realise in the game. (Likewise, in the two passages on skill, Kant rejects a model of virtue in which someone cares to act as duty requires, but is indifferent as to how.)

Perhaps the most basic difference between free and unfree skill is that the exercise of the latter is based on necessitating habit: its exercise does not require one to consider what is relevant, in one's circumstances, to the question of how one should go on. By contrast, free skills are fundamentally skills of judgment or discernment. Their exercise involves deploying resources in a particular way in light of one's appreciation of what is relevant, in the circumstances, to the broader practical commitment governing the skill. In the tennis example, the broader practical commitment is to play a good game. The discernment that is integral to a free skill is, moreover, not separable from the cultivation of the available resources. For someone who is skilled in this way is not necessitated by habit, but rather can critically query what habit might in the first instance poise her to do.[15] She must therefore have something else to which to refer her thoughts; and this, I am suggesting, is a broader practical commitment to some ideal, as a standard for the sort of activity in question. Crucially, what one could have in mind here could vary considerably in determinacy. The sort of thought that Serena Williams could have will be very different from the thoughts of someone whose well-placed shots are somewhat a matter of luck. The relatively unskilled person operates on an accordingly more vague, and thereby impoverished, conception of what she is up to. She might have watched a lot of tennis on television, so that her conception of a good game – even her *feel* for a good game – far outstrips her capacity to play one. But this is precisely the extent to which this bigger picture is merely theoretical, as it is unable to engage her moves on the court.[16]

---

[15] Montero (2013) provides examples of how this might work in dance: a dancer might be consciously attentive to certain aspects of her performance – aiming to bring it closer to an ideal – and thereby, in the particular direction of attention, aiming that it go in some way that it wouldn't otherwise go if she were just churning away on habit.

[16] Morganna Lambeth pressed me to be clearer about the role of the broader practical commitment in a free skill: what, really, might someone like Serena Williams have in mind here? To speak of a conception of playing well, or (alternatively, for the moral case) of living well by valuing humanity, only invokes a placeholder. But it is a necessary placeholder. For, if a skill doesn't incorporate a broader practical commitment, some conception of the point and value of what one is up to, then it is hard to see how it could be anything other than a mechanical response to the promptings of habit, i.e. an unfree skill. The skill model teaches us that the *determinacy* of this commitment – the extent to which one is thinking something concretely meaningful when one aspires to play a good game, or to live well by valuing humanity – admits of degree. (I will elaborate on this feature of the

The conclusion that I just reached was that the determinacy of one's broader practical commitment – that to which one refers when one queries the promptings of habit, and thus that on the basis of which one is capable of being discerning about how to go on in the first place – depends on the resources that one has to deploy in its interest. The broader practical commitment to play a good game only keeps pace, as far as its determinacy goes, with the degree to which one has cultivated the resources to actually play one. However, it seems that there is a relation of dependence working in the other direction as well. The brute resources that enable one to play a good game – the particular skills of dexterity, speed and strength – are cultivated by putting them to use in a way that is itself the concrete manifestation of one's commitment to play a good game, however rich or impoverished, precise or inchoate, this commitment may be. The brute resources are cultivated only with a deepening appreciation of the governing standard, or the broader practical commitment. And what stands at the interchange between the two is a capacity to judge, to appreciate one's circumstances in light of both.

I have identified three elements of a free skill: a broader practical commitment, certain brute resources and discernment. These, I have been suggesting, all develop coevally with one another as elements of an integrated package: they are mutually supporting, or conditioning. The cultivation of the one keeps some kind of pace with the cultivation of the other two. Free skill emerges as a kind of practical knowledge that admits of degree, and which might very often be indefinitely perfectible. Presumably, it is in regard to this last point that free skills can be distinguished from other kinds of cultivated know-how, like knowing how to brush one's teeth.[17] Next, I

---

model more later in this chapter, and in Chapter 7.) The skill model also teaches us that intelligent practice is what normally contributes to this determinacy; that is why we cannot spell out in general terms what this determinacy consists in for any given case.

[17] It may well be that the line between free skills and cultivated know-how is not hard and fast. What about making tea, for example? This may depend somewhat on how seriously you take your tea. With cases like toothbrushing, the circumstances are unchallenging: the situation does not change – every morning and every night one must do it – although poor health and aging may give one reason to add steps to the regimen. But once one works out what one needs to do, there are relatively few further questions about how to go on. The skills that I have been considering are not like this. Even someone who exercises a skill based on necessitating habit, like in the cycling example, is responding to challenging circumstances: there is a question about how to go on, although it is one that is (in this sort of skill) addressed unreflectively, simply by responding as conditioned to the right cues. Circumstances change all the time: here, I must stop; now, I can go; here, I slow down; now, I speed up. But what are we viewing as the circumstances of cycling: are we just talking about being able to direct one's riding as one wishes, or about navigating safely in traffic? Intuitively, the former (the basic capacity to ride) seems like an unfree skill more or less akin to walking or grasping, whereas the latter (navigating safely in traffic as a cyclist) seems more like a free skill. At

want to compare this account of skill against the dialectical activities that Brewer suggests cannot be accommodated within a Kantian account of practical thinking.

6.4 Free Skills, Reflection and Dialectical Activities

The first thing that we need to try to bring out is the sense in which free skills are reflective. In Chapter 1, I canvassed Kant's remarks on reflection quite widely, and found that reflection most basically involves comparing a given mental state against some broader whole, and endorsing or rejecting the given mental state depending on whether it is conceivably the issue, or expression, of that broader whole. According to the first-pass interpretation of Kant's claim that 'all judgments require reflection' in the context of applied general logic, the given mental state is one's taking things to be a certain way (i.e. a given 'connection' of representations), which is endorsed or rejected depending on whether it is conceivably the issue of 'laws of understanding and of reason' (and variants along these lines; see Table 2), and thus whether the given view on how things are is one that anyone is open to take, at least in principle. In Chapter 2, I argued that the requirement to reflect-n at issue is reformulated in terms of the three maxims of healthy understanding, so that reflection is embedded in *knowing how* to make good or 'purposive' use of one's cognitive capacities; it therefore need not involve any sort of 'stepping back' on the occasion of each and every episode of one's taking things to be a certain way, as the initial interpretation of reflection-n may seem to imply. Then, in Chapter 5, we considered Kant's claim that the power of judgment is a 'particular talent which wants not to be taught, but only practised' (A133/B172; see also Anth 7:199). As a talent, the power of judgment is a given cognitive endowment; but it requires cultivation, and it is cultivated only as it is put to use in the cognitive engagement with particulars. For while one's understanding as the 'faculty of rules' can be equipped through instruction, the capacity to put these rules to use in judgment can only be cultivated through the independent exercise of judgment itself. This is not to claim that sound judgment can (or should) be acquired absent any kind of guidance from others: the cultivation of the power of judgment can only take place through participation in a shared practice of judgment, as the three maxims attest. But

---

any rate, circumstances for the cyclist are continually challenging in a way that they are not for the tooth-brusher, even though the challenges may not always require the cyclist (at least where only an unfree skill is deployed) to be discerning about what is salient in the moment.

the result is that healthy understanding, on this picture, should be a certain sort of free skill, one that is formed by the general epistemic commitments at issue in the three maxims. Healthy understanding, as a free skill, brings to the ready the cognitive resources needed to make purposive use of one's cognitive capacities. And indeed, Kant suggests precisely this when he claims that healthy understanding 'contains the capacity and the skill [Fertigkeit] to comprehend *truth*' (Anth 7:197).[18]

Healthy understanding, I am suggesting, is a certain sort of free skill. If that is right, then we should expect to find in it a mutually conditioning development of the relevant resources and the determinacy of the broader practical commitment (which is, in this case, to make good use of one's cognitive capacities), so that one becomes ever more discerning in the relevant ways. However, we can go only so far with this line of thought, as long as we are considering just the *general* epistemic commitments at issue in healthy understanding: intuitively, to get to talk about cultivated resources of *discernment*, we would need to accommodate domain-relative requirements on thought. But that is precisely the sort of move we are poised to make if we recognise moral virtue to be a specification of basic cognitive virtue, and accept the results of the previous chapter: that basic cognitive virtue for Kant just is healthy understanding. Kant envisions distinct domain-relative requirements for theoretical and practical thinking. So, moral virtue will be a free skill of specifically practical cognitive capacities. I will elaborate on this point, and how to distinguish virtue from ordinary free skills, in §6.6.

For now, let me briefly point out how the account of free skills that I have sketched on Kant's behalf lines up with the dialectical activities that Brewer mentions. Both involve what I referred to as a broader practical commitment, or what Brewer refers to as 'the best and highest conception of one's own unfolding activity' (Brewer 2011, 130) – some kind of governing standard, or ideal, of the activity in which one is engaged. Both accounts take it that the determinacy of one's grip on this standard admits of degree, and becomes sharper and deeper and more practically determinate with one's developing capacity to engage in the activity itself. With this increase in determinacy comes a keener appreciation of what is relevant, in one's circumstances, to acting in a way that instances or realises one's commitment to the standard or value in question. But Brewer contends that 'the Kantian'

---

[18] Kant is on record referring to healthy understanding as a skill (*Fertigkeit*) at LB (24:21); this was quoted in Chapter 2, §2.3. Recall, too, Kant's claim that the third maxim can only be attained after one has achieved a certain readiness or 'skill' (*Fertigkeit*) with the first two (KU 5:295), also from Chapter 2, §2.4.1.

conception of practical thinking cannot accommodate our engagement in such activities.[19]

Brewer concludes with a gesture towards the role of reflection in the putatively Kantian model of practical thinking: 'For the Kantian, the moral quality of our practical reasoning is entirely a matter of the content and provenance of the maxims on which we act. The practical thinking that matters, morally speaking, begins from a morally innocent description of our circumstances and culminates in a verdict about what to do in those circumstances' (2011, 144). The Kantian reflective agent, according to the standard story, is skilled at identifying the principles on which he proposes to act (the content of the maxims) and assessing their source (whether they issue from a purely practical interest in morality). On the standard story, the Kantian reflective agent is forever poised *to step back* from the immediacy of action to do all of this. On the Aristotelian model that Brewer favours, sound engagement in a dialectical activity calls for no such stepping back: to the extent that one's engagement in the activity is sound, one's focus is on 'the best and highest conception of one's own unfolding activity', where the task at hand is 'to grasp what one is doing in such a way as to lift it, with each moment, closer to the ideal form in whose light it is understood' (130). This, he stresses, is not a matter of fixing one's thought on an abstraction: the focus on the standard 'does not ordinarily protrude as a separate introspectible concomitant of the activity that it accompanies and guides', but instead 'ordinarily takes the form of rapt or concentrated attention on what one is doing' (130).

But this nice phenomenological point is perfectly well available in the Kantian account of free skills that I have sketched here. Indeed, if I am right that this account of free skill provides the model under which Kant admits moral virtue as a skill – albeit under some further qualification, which I will

[19] Brewer sketches how an attempt might be made to fit dialectical activities into the (putatively) Kantian model of practical thinking: essentially, it involves taking one's engagement in dialectical activities to involve a series of isolated episodes of practical thinking, 'launched by intentions or plans that specify a state of affairs to be produced, and continuous course corrections . . . made with an eye to the efficient production of that state of affairs' (2011, 125; see also the variant proposal at 127). His reply to these proposals is first to remind us that dialectical activities typically involve some only gradually dawning grasp of the highest standard of the activity in question, a grasp which is in itself an accomplishment acquired only through intelligent and practised engagement in the activity itself; and second to further remind us that if dialectical activities are conceived as involving repeated exercises of episodic practical thinking, as the putatively Kantian model would seem to require, each episode yielding a new intention of some kind – perhaps more specified than the previous – then the intention must nevertheless have as its object an action regarded in an evaluatively neutral light, which makes it hard to appreciate how these separate episodes of practical thinking are engagement in one and the same activity (2011, 127–8). My response to all of this is to deny that this gets the Kantian conception of practical thinking right.

spell out in §6.6 – then taking Kant at his word about this might suggest an alternative to the popular conception of practical reflection as a certain stepping back from action itself. Free skills, if I am right, embed reflection directly into the activity itself.

6.5 Kant contra Mendelssohn on Virtue as a Skill

Now that we have considered Kant's general conception of skill, we can take up the question of moral virtue as a skill. This is, of course, an idea that goes back to the ancients,[20] but the local spur to Kant's remarks on the topic was, in all likelihood, Moses Mendelssohn's account of skill and its 'fruitful implications' for ethics (1997, 165 [1771, 83]).[21] The skill model of virtue, Mendelssohn seems to think, allows virtue-based ethics to meet the following objection: that the virtuous person must take a certain interest in his own character in order to acquire this character at all. What, then, is to block the conclusion that the virtuous person acts for the sake of cultivating this character in everything that he does?[22] Mendelssohn offers an account of skill that is aimed to meet this objection. In his view, skills (*Fertigkeiten*) are capacities to perform certain actions that are perfected through habit and practice: as one becomes skilled, one no longer has to think about the concepts and principles that must be applied to one's circumstances in order to produce a certain result.[23] The skilled pianist no longer needs to think about how to hit the right notes in the right order. Rather, 'through constant practice he brings things to the point where he can play the most splendid music almost without thinking about it [fast ohne daran zu denken]' (163 [82]). Mendelssohn leaves this vague: he is explicit neither about the qualification at work in that claim, nor about the mode of thought that (he seems to allow) will remain in skilled action. But the general point is quite clear: through habit and practice, the skilled person has overcome the need to think explicitly about the rules – and their application – that make a certain action possible. What is left is only rapt attention in the activity itself.

[20] See Annas (1995) for one account of this; and see Annas (2011) for her independent development of the skill model of virtue.

[21] Further references to Mendelssohn will have the pagination of the 1997 English translation followed by the pagination of the 1771 edition of the text in square brackets. Merritt (forthcoming) offers a more in-depth reading of these passages in Mendelssohn, and their historical context; one upshot is that Mendelssohn does not *unambiguously* celebrate unreflective automatism in his account of skill.

[22] For a modern articulation of the worry, see Williams (1981).

[23] Mendelssohn maintains that skilful actions are necessarily preformed *quickly*: 'A skill [Fertigkeit] consists in a capacity to perform a certain action so speedily that we no longer remain conscious of all that we are doing in the process' (162 [78–9]).

Since the skilled person is no longer conscious of the rules, he cannot be thinking of himself as acting in the light of them, or otherwise applying them to his independently given circumstances. Rather, there is just a complete immersion in the activity, something along the lines of what has recently been dubbed 'flow'.[24] The upshot is that the attention of the skilled person is not directed towards himself and his capacity to engage in the activity at hand. Spelling out those fruitful implications for ethics, Mendelssohn concludes:

> He must continue practicing until, in the course of this exercise, he is no longer conscious of his rules, in other words, until his principles have turned into inclinations and his virtue appears to be more natural instinct than reason. Then he has attained the heroic greatness which is far beyond the battle of common passions,[25] and he exercises the most admirable virtue without vanity. If an individual's principles are on his lips in every good action performed by him, then virtue has not yet become second nature to him and he has still failed to take an important step towards ethical perfection. (166 [89])

Mendelssohn takes up the ancient idea of virtue as a skill because, on his analysis, it allows us to understand how the virtuous person acts without vanity – without, in other words, directing the wrong sort of attention to himself. I think that Kant might endorse this motivation: that is, I think that Kant might find the skill model of virtue to offer just such resources. However, it is quite clear that Kant rejects the account of skill that Mendelssohn puts on offer – or, at the very least, takes Mendelssohn to have failed to provide the right account of the relevant sort of skill, the one that could provide a basis for a tenable skill model of moral virtue.[26]

Mendelssohn claims that the concepts that guide the activity 'have become obscure' (164 [83]) for the skilled person. This is, above all, what

---

[24] Hubert Dreyfus, for example, takes 'flow' to be unreflective along something like Mendelssohn's lines. This view has not gone unchallenged: see the debate between him and John McDowell in Schear (2013), Montero (2013) and Fridland (2014).

[25] Mendelssohn's remark in this clause (that virtue must go 'beyond the battle of common passions') is indicative of the Stoic influence on his ethical thought, as it suggests that something like Stoic apathy is necessary (although not sufficient) for virtue; and in fact, Kant endorses this idea as well (see MS 6:407–9). It lies outside of the scope of my work here to take up the interesting questions this raises about the possibly very different inheritances of Stoic ethics and moral psychology that we might find in Mendelssohn and Kant, respectively. However, I return to Kant's view of apathy as a necessary condition for virtue in Chapter 7.

[26] Mendelssohn treats the musician's skill on the same par as the typesetter's (163 [82–3]), whereas intuitively there is a clear difference. The typesetter knows how to set type, but the know-how in question does not seem to be indefinitely perfectible as a musician's skill would seem to be. Knowing how to set type is more like knowing how to brush one's teeth than it is like knowing how to play the piano well.

Kant rejects in the Cochius passage – not simply the idea that moral virtue may be a certain sort of skill. For what he explicitly says there is that moral skill must be 'the effect of principles that are reflected-upon, firm, and continually purified [eine Wirkung überlegter, fester, und immer mehr geläuterter Grundsätze]' (MS 6:383). Moral skill cannot arise as mere effects of habit and practice, along the lines of Mendelssohn's account, where habit and practice serve to render one's grasp of principles obscure, freeing one from any need to think about them. If moral skill were just the result of habit and practice, à la Mendelssohn, then, Kant claims, it would be nothing other than a 'mechanism of technically practical reason', and – for that – 'neither equipped for all situations, nor sufficiently secure for the changes that new enticements could bring about' (MS 6:384). I will return to this idea that a moral skill should somehow be 'equipped for all situations'; first, I want to consider Kant's claim that a moral skill should be the effect of reflected-upon principles, *überlegte Grundsätze*.

A similar claim is made in the conclusion of Skill 1, which I quote now:

> [O]ne cannot explain *virtue* as *skill* in free lawful actions, for then it would be a mere mechanism of applying power. Rather virtue is *moral strength* in adherence to one's duty, which should never become habit [Gewohnheit] but should always emerge entirely new and original from one's way of thinking [Denkungsart]. (Anth 7:147)

Here, Kant puts up more of an appearance of resisting the skill model of virtue than he does in either Cochius or Skill 2, but what he is rejecting is, again, simply that an account of skill along Mendelssohn's lines could possibly furnish a model for moral virtue. The reason that Kant seems to reject the skill model of virtue altogether here is just his emphasis on the idea that moral virtue calls for a continual engagement of original thought. But the Cochius passage tells us to interpret this conclusion through the skill model. Thus, what the virtuous person does again and again – habitually, if you like – is exercise discernment about her situation. And that is why thinking does not cease – principles do not become obscure – in free skill as Kant conceives it. The grasp of principles, at least inasmuch as this constitutes one's broader practical commitment, becomes keener and more determinate in the skilled person – and this is what equips her with a greater responsiveness to the relevant facts. This, I submit, is what Kant means when he says (in Cochius) that if moral virtue is to be conceived as a skill, it must be one that is the result of principles that are 'reflected upon, firm, and continually purified'.[27]

---

[27] There are a couple of other places in the *Metaphysics of Morals* where Kant presents virtue as a skill. One passage concerns the role of sympathy in virtue, which I will discuss in Chapter 7. Another

To back up this claim, let me draw upon the interpretation of reflection that I offered in Part I of the book. What is particularly at issue is not reflection-c – that tacit grasp of oneself as the source of a point of view – but reflection-n, where a given mental state is compared against a greater whole, and accepted or rejected in light of its compatibility with one's commitment to that greater whole. When we conceive of reflection-n in this way, it can seem as if the normative guidance runs only in one direction. The given mental state can be conceived as a kind of response to one's circumstances, and one reflects 'on' this response to one's circumstances – accepts or rejects it – in light of some broader practical commitment – and it is this broader practical commitment, something framed in terms of principles or rules, that calls all the shots. But the skill model suggests that the guidance might run in both directions. The broader practical commitment governs what figures (or should figure) as salient for one in action, yet it is only rendered determinate through practice – only, that is, through the concrete engagement of one's attention and resources in the activity itself. So, there is a certain way in which the broader practical commitment is informed, or at any rate becomes practically determinate, from skilful engagement in one's circumstances *in concreto*.

In this section, I have argued that the Cochius passage contains Kant's rejection of Mendelssohn's account of skill. What Kant rejects is not the idea that moral virtue might be a skill, but rather the automatism that Mendelssohn takes skill essentially to involve. Kant, I have argued, takes there to be an important distinction between skills based on necessitating habit and what he calls 'free' skills; and free skills involve a certain consciousness of principles. That allows him to accept the skill model of virtue without accepting the automatism that Mendelssohn takes it to entail.

can be found in a section of definitions in the Introduction to the entire *Metaphysics of Morals*. In this passage, Kant defines human choice (*menschliche Willkür*) as choice that *can be affected* but not *determined* by impulses [Antriebe]'. He says that it follows from this that human choice considered in itself '(apart from an acquired skill [Fertigkeit] of reason) is not pure but can still be determined to actions by pure will' (MS 6:214). The distinction he draws here is between human choice as such (i.e. uncultivated) and human choice cultivated *as an acquired skill of reason* (i.e. virtue).

Finally, in the Vigilantius record of Kant's lectures on ethics, we again find virtue invoked as a kind of skill: 'It is true that one can find enjoyment in virtue and in the contemplation of it, but only when and for the reason that one has become skilled to carry out one's duties [nur dann und nur deshalb, insofern es uns schon zur Fertigkeit geworden, Pflicht zu erfüllen], so that it becomes easy to follow the prescriptions of reason; from this one attains a contentment about one's actions and about the strengthening of one's will for the prescriptions of reason; and one regards the future with cheerful courage' (MV 27:490–1). Here, Kant is rehashing his debate with Schiller over the 'aesthetic constitution of virtue' (see Rel 6:23–4n), and elaborating on how indeed by his lights the temperament of virtue is properly 'joyous', not dejected and downtrodden; for more on the Vigilantius passage in this context, see Merritt (2017c).

Moreover, Kant's acceptance of the skill model of virtue might also call into question the 'stepping back' model of reflection. If I am right, the basic lesson that Kant draws from the general idea of (free) skill is that the determinacy of one's broader practical commitment only keeps pace with the extent to which one has brought to the ready the brute resources and the discernment required to act in a way that honours or instances this commitment. There is little or no role, in such a picture, for a representation of the law *in abstracto*. One's consciousness of rules takes shape as the appreciation of possible ways forward: this is what it is to grasp a practical principle *in concreto*. And so, there is no obvious need to step back from the exigencies of action in order to compare the more determinate principle on which one proposes to act against a formal law. There is only the quality of one's engagement in the action or activity itself. Commitment to the moral law, in other words, *need* involve no explicit thoughts about the law as such, nor even about the principles on which one proposes to act, and the ideally reflective person need not be conceived, in the familiar way, as the one who is always poised to 'step back'.

Kant rejects Mendelssohn's view that skilful action is possible only when the rules that govern the action become obscure, receding into the dark shadows of the agent's consciousness. What Kant is calling into question, if I am right, is just what it is to be conscious of rules in action. For the model of free skills suggests that skilful activity may embed a certain consciousness of rules, without requiring any abstract representation of rules. Thus, by Kant's lights, the distinguishing difference – that which makes moral virtue a skill like no other – does not lie in some idea that normal skills are unreflective whereas moral skill is not. Free skills are reflective, and that is precisely why they provide Kant with a model for conceiving of moral virtue as a skill.

6.6   Virtue as a Skill

So far, I have been working to articulate the basis on which Kant can accept that moral virtue is a skill, but in order to work out Kant's positive view of moral skill, it is necessary to appreciate how that general model gets 'filled in' for the case of moral virtue. I leave most of the filling in for Chapter 7, where we will see in greater detail how the skill model plays out in Kant's account of virtue in the *Metaphysics of Morals* – as well as how it allows us to make better sense of puzzling passages than interpretations which do not admit Kant's qualified endorsement of the skill model of virtue. What I want to clarify here is the distinguishing difference: moral virtue is a certain sort of free skill, but nevertheless a free skill like no other. How do we understand this?

According to the Cochius passage, moral skill is not 'like any other mechanism of technically practical reason': does this mean that any ordinary skill – whether free or unfree – is a stimulus-driven aptitude? I have been arguing that *free* skills cannot be like this: if they are embodied capacities of judgment, then they cannot be a matter of responding blindly or mechanically to stimuli. Thus, on my interpretation, there is not a single distinction between moral virtue and all other skills (which would then be conceived as mechanisms of technically practical reason). Rather, within the notion of skill, there is a distinction between skills that are robustly stimulus-driven and therefore based on necessitating habit, and the free skills that have at their heart a ready discernment that makes them essentially modes of judgment. Kant is prepared to accept that moral virtue may be a type of free skill and, moreover, that the intelligence of free skill is not entirely driven by habit. A person so skilled must have something to which to refer her thoughts about what to do, given the promptings of habit. That is why such skills might in principle be equipped for situations that do not fall neatly into the patterns of prior past experience.

But we need to take a closer look at the conclusion of the Cochius passage, and the two passages on skill, in order to set out, in an initial way, what Kant's positive conception of moral virtue as skill would be. The Cochius passage, we saw, claims that moral virtue can be conceived as a skill that is based on reflected-upon principles (*überlegte Grundsätze*). Kant's point here, I have been arguing, is that moral virtue cannot be modelled on the 'unfree' mode of skill that is based on necessitating habit. For any conception of virtue modelled on such skills, Kant concludes, would neither be

> equipped for all situations, nor sufficiently secure for the change that new enticements could bring about.

> auf alle Fälle gerüstet, noch vor der Veränderung, die neue Anlockungen bewirken können, hinreichend gesichert. (MS 6:384)

What does this tell us about moral virtue as a skill? One thing that it might appear to claim is that moral skill is exercised on the circumstances of the subject's own inner life. For Kant appears to claim here that 'new enticements' – misleading attractions of some kind – amount to changes in one's circumstances: changes that the morally skilled person is equipped to handle. Virtue then looks to be a kind of skilful self-management, so that one sticks to one's principles in the face of what is presumably, at least in principle, an inexhaustible fount of enticements drawing one away. The conclusion to Skill 2 also appears to support the conclusion that virtue is essentially a kind of skilful self-management. I quote the conclusion of that passage now:

> Hence one cannot *define* virtue as skill [Fertigkeit] in free action in conformity with law unless it is added 'to determine oneself through the representation of the law in action', and then this skill is not a property of choice, but rather of will, which is a faculty of desire that, in adopting a rule, is at once universally legislative. Only such a skill can be counted as virtue. (MS 6:407)

Here, Kant seems to spell out exactly what you need to add to the idea of skill to get moral virtue: it is a readiness to act in a certain way that is driven by one's resolve to act simply from one's recognition of what the moral law requires. Virtue would then seem to be a certain skill in getting oneself to act from the genuinely moral motive. Let me call this the *self-management interpretation* of the skill model of virtue.

We should reject the self-management interpretation. To see why, consider how it would have to work. The discernment of this skill would consist in an unflinching sharp-sightedness about one's own motives: but this interpretive conclusion is cast into doubt by Kant's repeated insistence that one can never determine, of any prima facie dutiful action, such as helping another person or speaking truthfully, whether one acts simply from one's recognition of moral requirement ('*from* duty') or from some 'covert impulse of self-love'.[28] If we are incapable of being discerning in the way in which the self-management interpretation of the skill model of virtue would require us to be, presumably it cannot be the right way to follow through on Kant's qualified endorsement of the skill model of virtue.

Now, some interpreters respond that all Kant is saying in those passages is that no agent can be *certain* of her motives in such cases, which allows for taking a reflective person to be someone who *tries* to figure this out. But there are different ways to think about what it is to consider one's own motives for some action. Sometimes, it is thought that we do this through introspection, conceived as a special kind of perception trained on mental goings-on – and indeed, that this is what Kant means by 'reflection' in the ordinary sense of moral reflection.[29] If we try to work through the skill model of virtue on these premises, we will suppose that a person

---

[28] As Kant memorably puts it at G (4:407); see also MS (6:392–3, 447). He makes this sort of point often (see also Introduction, §0.2, note 8).
[29] See Grenberg (2005, e.g. 62, 67, 99, 101), especially in response to O'Neill, for this approach.

who is developing virtue gets better at this introspection over time. Maybe one day she 'catches' herself about to speak the truth from some covert impulse of self-love – what then? Assuming she is skilled according to the self-management interpretation, she manages to dampen that impulse, and somehow gets herself to act from a genuinely moral motive. The mystery around how any of this might work suggests the need for another interpretation of Kant's concluding remarks in these passages about virtue as a skill.

I have been developing an interpretation of Kant's notion of reflection that provides an alternative to the idea that reflection is a kind of inner sense, understood as a perception trained on inner goings-on. According to this interpretation, reflection is a matter of taking the appropriate interest in one's own capacity to think about how things are and what is worth doing. We take this interest adverbially, I have suggested: that is, by considering the objective questions about how things are and what is worth doing in the right spirit. Reflection is not introspective in the sense just sketched. Further, our account of free skills as embodied modes of practical intelligence adds something to this account of what it is to be reflective. It teaches us that a person can be reflective simply by considering whether she is appreciating her situation correctly, whether she is paying attention to *what matters* in light of the broader practical commitment governing the skill. We are reflective, in the first instance, by considering what we are paying attention to and why. Quite plausibly, this is how we set about considering what we take to be a reason for doing what, and thus how we might consider our motives for any given action.

Of course, this needn't mean that a reflective person is never introspective. Given facts about our own mental states can tell us something about what our motivations are, or might be. And we generally have good reason to pay attention to our own feelings and desires – not only when they give us pause, but also when we find ourselves carried along by them. Suppose I am in a situation that appears to call for uttering an uncomfortable and surprising truth, and I find myself cheered along by an image of myself acting nobly and high-mindedly in saying it. To act from such considerations would surely be to direct the wrong sort of attention to myself – even if the truth is important, and even if I am the one who ought to say it, now, to these people. Part of what it might mean for a deeply flawed person to be reflective, in this instance, would be to recognise that she has been fantasising, and failing to pay attention to what matters if she cares to act well. *Does* this need to be said, right here, to these people? The reflective person has a standing interest in what she is paying attention to, and why – which prepares her to correct course accordingly. There is nothing essentially introspective about reflection, so conceived.

What, finally, is the distinguishing difference that makes moral virtue a free skill like no other? Recall that a free skill generally is a 'facility for action and a subjective perfection of choice' (MS 6:407 (Skill 2)). The relevant notion of perfection, again, is teleological: perfection is 'the harmony of a thing's properties with an *end*' (6:386). Skill is a readiness to carry on in a way that is conducive to a certain end. The ends governing standard-issue free skills are *discretionary*, in the sense that it is up to the subject whether to adopt them or not – one is at leave to accept or reject them at will.[30] In a tennis match, how the ball is coming over the net and whatever movements my opponent is making are salient as I gear up to return the shot. What I do next will not only form my answer to the particular challenge these circumstances pose, but will be how I make manifest my commitment to play a good game. (If, that is, I care to play a good game: I might care to win at any cost. And then my skill, if I have any, will be of a different sort.) But in the conclusion to Skill 2, Kant implies that moral skill is a perfection *of the will*, or practical reason.[31] Practical reason, by his lights, is a source of substantive ends: its constitutive principle, the moral law, makes claims about what we categorically ought to care about (humanity in oneself and in others). Therefore, moral virtue *as a skill*, as an acquired perfection of practical reason, can only be a harmony of a person's 'properties' – a person's temperament and frame of mind – with *morally obligatory ends*. The virtuous person is disposed to be appropriately attentive to those facts about her situation that give her inexorable reason to do this or that in light of a fully determinate commitment to the value of humanity. That, in roughest overview, is the account of virtue that I will attribute to Kant at greater length in Chapter 7.

Crucially, the qualification at work in Kant's endorsement of the skill model of virtue is twofold. First, Kant emphasises – against the implications of Mendelssohn's account – that only *free* skills provide an appropriately reflective model by which to understand moral virtue as a skill. And free skills, in contrast to unfree skills, are indefinitely perfectible. Second, while ordinary free skills are fitnesses for discretionary ends, virtue (as a skill) is

---

[30] Standard-issue free skills are governed by the adoption of 'arbitrary' ends, as Kant suggests at EE (20:200n): they are skills of technically practical reason. Here, Kant suggests that prudence is a skill of roughly the same sort, even though the end that governs it – one's own happiness – cannot be thought of as discretionary or arbitrary. The similarity of such skills consists in the fact that their ends have a source other than pure reason; this would suffice to distinguish them from moral skill, or virtue.

[31] See also MS (6:214) – the bit quoted in note 27 of this chapter.

a fitness for morally obligatory ends.[32] Therefore, if moral virtue is a free skill so specified, the upshot must be that one's appreciation of the value of persons is indefinitely perfectible. Thus, when Kant tells us that '[v]irtue is always *in progress* and yet always starts *from the beginning*' (6:409), he may not be having the drearily puritanical, and vaguely narcissistic, thought we might immediately suppose him to be having. He may simply be saying that virtue is a skill.

---

[32] A familiar objection to the skill model of virtue is that skills admit of intentional misuse – e.g. medical skill can be used either to kill a patient or to make him healthy – and virtue does not. It should be clear that this objection is not applicable to the Kantian version of the skill model of virtue as I have sketched it here.

CHAPTER 7

The Cognitive Basis of Moral Virtue

7.1 Introduction

In Part II of this book, I have been pursuing two lines of thought about the Kantian conception of virtue. One led to the *specification thesis*: all virtue is cognitive virtue, and moral virtue can be admitted as a certain specification of the basic and *general* cognitive virtue that goes by the name of 'healthy human understanding' (Chapter 5). The other led to the *skill thesis*: moral virtue is a certain sort of 'free' skill – one governed by the adoption of morally obligatory, rather than discretionary, ends (Chapter 6). So far, I have pursued these lines of thought largely independently of one another; one of my aims in this chapter is to show how they are joined in a coherent and compelling account of moral virtue.

The key to the connection between these two theses lies in the importance both place on the concrete engagement of thought. Recall that healthy human understanding is nothing other than common human understanding that is *correct*, and common human understanding is nothing other than the capacity to judge *in concreto*. So, if all virtue either is, or involves, general cognitive virtue by Kant's lights, and general cognitive virtue is healthy understanding, then virtue is essentially realised and developed through the concrete engagement of thought. Skills, likewise, are modes of practical intelligence *in concreto*.

However, the two theses need to be traced to the full sweep of Kant's account of virtue in the *Tugendlehre* (Doctrine of Virtue[1]) of the *Metaphysics of Morals*: so far, I have drawn only on select aspects of the *Tugendlehre* in making a case for each thesis.[2] However, a more comprehensive reading

---

[1] I will use the German term '*Tugendlehre*' simply because it is more concise.
[2] When I argued for the specification thesis, I drew attention to the special role assigned to the cultivation of cognitive capacities under the general heading of duties of virtue that one owes to oneself: this is just one detail of one half of Kant's account of virtue in the *Tugendlehre* – there are the duties that we owe to others as well. Likewise, my account of the skill thesis was based on select passages from the *Tugendlehre*, read in conjunction with parallel passages from the *Anthropology*.

of the *Tugendlehre* introduces further complications. For here we will find Kant most often speaking of virtue as a certain moral strength – *fortitudo moralis* (MS 6:380), or 'a moral strength of the will' (MS 6:405). This gives us a third element to accommodate in the account of the Kantian conception of virtue. Altogether, then, we have three claims:

(a) moral virtue is a specification of general cognitive virtue
(b) moral virtue is a certain sort of free skill
(c) moral virtue is a certain sort of 'strength'

When Kant presents virtue as strength, he indicates that he is drawing out the implications of Latin *virtus* (MS 6:380; see also 6:390); and if the strength of virtue is analogous to physical strength, we might suppose that it is a certain kind of force. However, Kant also makes something of the etymology of the German word for virtue, *Tugend*, claiming its connection with the verb *taugen*, to be fit for (MS 6:390). Talk of 'fitness' invokes teleological considerations that put us again in the neighbourhood of the skill model. Ordinary free skills are cultivated fitnesses for discretionary ends; moral virtue, as a free skill, is a cultivated fitness for a morally obligatory end – an end that it is not up to us to adopt or not (it is non-discretionary) and yet (like any end) that can only be freely adopted. Kant claims, as we saw, that the cultivation of virtue is made possible through the adoption of morally obligatory ends: one's own perfection and the happiness of others. This is what yields a twofold division into duties of virtue that one owes to oneself and duties of virtue that one owes to others; they are united, Kant intimates, in the idea of making 'the human being as such' one's end (MS 6:395). The source of any morally obligatory end can only be our rational nature; and thus virtue, by Kant's lights, is a perfection, or completion, of our rational nature. It is with this in mind that Kant deploys one further trope for speaking of virtue, presenting it as a certain kind of *health* (MS 6:384, 405, 409; cf. 419). Intuitively, health is a kind of strength. Bodily health is, at any rate: it is the power to overcome assaults on the body from without, sustaining life. So, the 'strength' of virtue is not an arbitrary force, but something more like a fitness for ends – since living a life of a certain kind must be an end, if anything is. The strength of virtue is something like a fitness to live a life that is a proper expression of our rational nature. What we find, then, is a family of ideas that bring out different aspects of Kant's conception of virtue.

That said, we need to be careful with (c), virtue as 'strength'. Strength admits of degree; and if we are inclined to suppose that moral virtue is composed of separable cognitive and motivational components, we may be inclined to conceive of the characteristic 'strength' of virtue as the ability to overcome obstacles to an independent appreciation of moral requirement. On this view, the strength – and so the moral motivation – admits of degree, while the recognition of moral requirement is assumed not to.[3] However, closer examination of the textual context of Kant's remarks about virtue as strength will show these assumptions to be misplaced (§7.2). Kant's claims about virtue as strength (c) accord with the idea that virtue is a skill (b), and an acquired perfection of specifically practical cognitive capacities (a).

I will go on to show how this model of virtue is in evidence in the full sweep of the *Tugendlehre* – i.e. in duties of virtue to oneself and to others alike (§7.3). After clarifying a point about the conception of practical knowledge at issue (§7.4), I will conclude by outlining how the Kantian model of virtue that I have been arguing for rebuts the widespread assumptions about the Kantian reflective ideal with which I began this book (§7.5).

7.2   Virtue as 'Strength'

My aim in this section is to show how Kant's claims about virtue as strength (c) accord with the idea that virtue is a skill (b), conceived as an acquired perfection of specifically practical cognitive capacities (a). We will consider a series of passages in which Kant distinguishes the strength of virtue (*Tugend*) from the weakness of 'mere lack of virtue' (*Untugend*).[4] As we will see, both *Tugend* and *Untugend* involve a commitment to morality: on this basis, Kant distinguishes both of them from vice. But they differ in the determinacy of this commitment, I argue. This can be understood along the same lines as the determinacy of any commitment that I may have to play a fine match of tennis: given my lack of skill, there is not much that I can be thinking here, and certainly not much that can engage my moves on the court. The determinacy of the broader practical commitment of a skill admits of degree – specifically, a degree of *strength* – inasmuch as this determinacy is what makes it concretely action-guiding. Likewise, while *Tugend* and *Untugend* both involve a commitment to morality, in *Untugend* this commitment is weak and indeterminate, and the resources that one has

---

[3] For a version of such a view, consider Baxley (2010, 83), who claims that for Kant, 'morality is epistemically easy but executively difficult', since it is easy to know 'what are duties are' and yet difficult to act from this knowledge. For the difficult part, on such a view, we need the special strength of virtue.

[4] It will be more concise to work with the German terms when considering the distinction in question. So, hereafter: *Tugend* and *Untugend* for 'virtue' and 'mere lack of virtue', respectively.

to act in a way that honours it are accordingly unskilled. This account will yield an interpretation of (c) that does not presuppose, or otherwise require, assumptions about separable cognitive and motivational aspects of virtue. Virtue is strength of the will, or practical reason: for Kant, this means that only a notional distinction can be drawn between cognitive and motivational aspects of virtue.

When Kant invokes the idea of virtue as strength, he immediately notes that it 'does not exhaust' the concept of virtue:

> for such strength could also belong to a *holy* (superhuman) being, in whom no hindering impulses work contrary to the law of its will and who would thus gladly do everything in conformity with the law. (MS 6:405)

His express point is that virtue is the strength of a *human* will (6:405). To some extent, the point is terminological: moral virtue is a strictly human attribute by Kant's lights, a perfection of practical reason in a human being, a rational animal that is subject to sensuous inclination. A holy will is not subject to sensuous inclination, so it has no 'hindering impulses' to deal with; and yet, Kant contends, it should possess the same 'strength' of will that is proper to human virtue. In the neighbourhood of this remark, Kant identifies virtue with practical wisdom (*praktische Weisheit*, MS 6:405). With this in mind, we can read this remark about the strength of virtue by the lights of a similar remark from the *Critique of Practical Reason*, where Kant says that wisdom and holiness are 'identical in their ground and objectively' (5:11n).[5] Their 'identical ground' can only be practical reason: the virtuous person and the holy will are governed by the same principle, the moral law. There is no difference in the 'objective' content of their commitment to morality.[6] This is why Kant rejects the idea that the holy will lacks strength. Kant's rejection of this idea indicates that, by his lights, the 'strength' at issue is not that of a special force for overcoming hindering impulses.

The idea that the virtuous and the holy have the same strength should give us pause about modelling the strength of virtue too closely on the

---

[5] The term 'wisdom' is ambiguous, since we speak both of human and of divine wisdom: this ambiguity is reflected in Kant's own usage, where 'wisdom' can be either human or divine (compare e.g. KrV A569/B397 with A328/B385). In the second *Critique*, Kant charges the Stoics with exploiting this ambiguity – they would have done better to develop their view strictly in terms of virtue, *human* perfection. For, their ideal of the sage is supposed to have transcended human nature, having made himself no longer susceptible to sources of incentive that would impel one to act contrary to law (KpV 5:86, 5:127n); the result, Kant complains, is a distinctly rationalist moral enthusiasm (*Schwärmerei*) (5:86).

[6] We can postulate a 'subjective' difference, however. I will return to this point at the end of §7.3.

strength of muscles.[7] By my lights, the strength that they share can only be the strength of practical reason – the strength of a cognitive capacity – however exactly this idea should be unpacked. There are passages that will seem recalcitrant to this proposal, of course. For example, a bit prior to the passage just quoted, we find:

> *Virtue* is the strength of the maxims of a human being in fulfilling his duty. – Any strength is recognised only through the obstacles that it can overcome [überwältigen]; and in the case of virtue these are the natural inclinations [Naturneigungen], which can come into conflict with the moral resolve [Vorsatz]. (MS 6:394)

But the passage will only seem recalcitrant if we assume that the 'moral resolve' is some kind of separate power that a human being needs in order to muscle through the natural inclinations and make good on her recognition of moral requirement. The skill model shows us how to avoid this assumption. The 'moral resolve' that Kant speaks of here is the 'broader practical commitment' at work in any free skill: in virtue, it is a commitment to morality. According to the skill model, the determinacy of the broader practical commitment is the extent to which one can have a concretely action-guiding thought by means of it. The greater the determinacy of this commitment, the stronger it is. This is a practical-cognitive strength (or weakness).

The relevance of skill to Kant's claims about the strength of virtue comes out more clearly in a set of passages where Kant distinguishes *Untugend*, as moral weakness, from *Tugend*, as moral strength. The first such passage is a remark appended to the Cochius passage, where (as we saw in Chapter 6) Kant gives his qualified endorsement of the skill model of virtue:

> Virtue = +a is set against the *negative lack of virtue* [*Untugend*] (moral weakness) = o as its *logical opposite* [als *logisches Gegentheil*] (*contradictorie oppositum*); but virtue is set against vice = −a as its *real opposite* [als *Widerspiel*] (*contrarie s. realiter oppositum*); and it is not merely unnecessary but also improper to ask whether a somewhat greater strength of soul might belong to great *crimes* than to great *virtues*. For by 'strength of soul' we mean the strength of resolve [die Stärke des Vorsatzes] of a human being as a being endowed with freedom, hence insofar as he is in control of himself [seiner selbst mächtig] (in his senses) and so in the state of *health* proper to a human being. But great crimes are paroxysms, the sight of which makes one whose soul is healthy shudder. (MS 6:384)

---

[7] Notice that I put this in terms of muscular, rather than physical, strength: physical strength includes health, and here the analogy is more fruitful.

Kant is here allowing for lack of virtue (*Untugend* = o) as a moral condition distinct from both virtue (+a) and vice (−a). Intuitively, the difference between virtue and vice should lie in the active commitment: only the virtuous person has a broader practical commitment to morality. This intuition is backed up in the remark about great crimes, which Kant likens to a sudden outburst of disease, as in a seizure. This leads Kant to consider the question whether vice could be a strength of soul, only under a different (non-moral) commitment. The answer turns on how the analogy with health and disease is cashed out. A paroxysm is violent: its force does not come from you, in your nature as a creature of a certain kind; rather, it acts on you, compromising this nature. Moral health will then consist in having the commitments that are proper to the nature of a rational being. On Kant's view, this is generally the commitment to the 'human being as such', on which the fulfilment of all duties of virtue depends (MS 6:395).

There are two further passages in the same vein, which will bring out more clearly that *Untugend* shares with *Tugend* a broader practical commitment to morality, differing only in the determinacy of this commitment. One such passage comes just after Kant explains that ethical duties (i.e. duties of virtue) are of '*wide* obligation' (MS 6:390):[8]

> Imperfect duties are . . . alone *duties of virtue*. The fulfilment of them is *merit* [*Verdienst*] (*meritum*) = +a; but their violation is not in itself *culpability*[9] (*demeritum*) = −a, but rather mere moral *lack of worth* [*Unwerth*] = o, **unless the subject should make it his principle not to comply with such duties**. It is only the strength of one's resolve [*Vorsatz*], in the first case, that is properly called *virtue* (*virtus*); one's weakness, in the second case, is not so much *vice* (*vitium*) as rather mere *lack of virtue* [*Untugend*] (*defectus moralis*). (MS 6:390; my bold)

It would seem that to violate an imperfect duty of virtue, one must have failed to adopt the morally obligatory ends on which it is based. However, Kant says here that the violation of these duties does not necessarily mean that one has made it one's principle not to comply with them, and so to be governed by some other end. Mere *Untugend* remains a possibility, in which one has adopted the morally obligatory ends in question. Of course,

---

[8] The status of duties of virtue as 'wide' was explained in Chapter 5: ethical duties are to cultivate the particular mindedness, or *Denkungsart*, that follows from the free adoption of morally obligatory ends, of which Kant names two (self-perfection and the happiness of others). Ethical duties are of wide obligation because they do not prescribe particular actions, but only a certain mindedness, which itself allows for a degree of latitude (a *Spielraum*, as Kant puts it here; MS 6:390) of choice in making good on these commitments.

[9] The German here is *Verschuldung*, which typically means 'indebtedness', but Gregor's translation, which I follow here, is supported by Kant's Latin gloss, *demeritum*.

mere *Untugend* lacks something present in *Tugend*: one is weakness, and the other is strength. But how should we understand this? It is worth noting that it is right around here that Kant invokes his view of the etymological roots of *Tugend* in *taugen*, 'to be fit for', so that mere lack of virtue (*Untugend*) is linked to the idea of not being fit for anything ('*zu nichts taugen*') (6:390). The difference is thus to be conceived in terms of the fitness for this end. And since skill is a fitness for an end, and Kant has just indicated his qualified endorsement of the skill model of virtue (6:383–4), we can look to that model to fill in the blanks here. *Untugend* and *Tugend* share a commitment to morality, but *Untugend* is missing the resources needed to act in a way that positively honours or instances this commitment. The resources are not yet, or not adequately, *cultivated*. This commitment, in the case of *Untugend*, is correspondingly vague and indeterminate: it therefore fails to guide action.

The final passage in this vein is an interlude in which Kant claims that virtue requires 'mastery over oneself'. This is also where Kant talks about affect and passion in the *Metaphysics of* Morals;[10] it is thus a passage that I have already relied upon, in Chapter 1, in order to work out how affect and passion are distinguished as different sorts of reflective failure by Kant's lights. I return to it now, equipped with an account of Kant's endorsement of the skill model of virtue from Chapter 6. In this passage, Kant presents affect as a certain

> weakness in the use of one's understanding combined with the strength of the movement of the mind [Stärke der Gemüthsbewegung]

and he says that this is

> only a lack of virtue [Untugend] and, as it were, something childish and weak, which can even coexist with the best will; and it even has one good thing about it, that this storm soon ceases. (MS 6:408)

Kant indicates that susceptibility to affect is a mark of *Untugend*, which he strikingly claims can 'coexist with the best will'. Although it is sometimes assumed by commentators that Kant identifies the notion of a good will with virtue, that cannot follow in light of this remark.[11] Rather, the remark confirms what I have been saying throughout this section: namely, that *Untugend* and *Tugend* alike involve a commitment to morality – this is

[10] This interlude is a clear nod to the Stoics; but, as noted previously, I will not make a dedicated case for that claim here.
[11] Wood (2008) argues against this identification at length; my work here turns out to corroborate his claim.

the 'good will' at issue. The difference, I will argue, is that *Untugend* is an unskilled commitment to morality, and virtue a skilled one. That is foreshadowing; let's first look at how Kant continues, distinguishing affect from passion:

> A propensity to affect . . . does not enter into kinship with vice as readily as passion does. For *passion* is sensible *desire* that has become lasting inclination . . . The calm with which one gives oneself up to it permits reflection [Überlegung] and allows the mind to form principles on it; thus if inclination lights upon something contrary to law, brooding upon it, rooting it deeply, and thereby taking up something evil (as premeditated [vorsätzlich]) into its maxim, then it is *properly* evil, that is, a true vice. (MS 6:408)

Vice involves some alternate governing commitment, presumably to one's own happiness – or what Kant conceives of as culpable self-love, as opposed to the rational self-love that is limited by one's commitment to morality (*vernünftige Selbstliebe*, KpV 5:73). Passion is the handmaiden to vice, as affect cannot be, because passion (not affect) involves undertaking practical commitments. Hence, Kant says here that passion 'permits reflection': it involves reflection-c, as set out in Chapter 1. The passionate person undertakes practical commitments, and may be quite keenly attentive to what, in her situation, answers to those commitments. So, she must have the at least tacit grip on herself as the source of a point of view on how things are and what is worth doing that is constitutively required for thought. But the passionate person undertakes practical commitments *unreflectively*, in the sense that she fails to reflect-n, or to do so adequately: she fails to take the appropriate interest in the soundness of her own cognitive capacities.

Now, it is in this passage that Kant explains that

> [t]he true strength of virtue is *the mind at peace* with a reflected-upon and firm resolution to put the law of virtue into practice. That is the state of *health* in moral life (6:409)

The 'resolution to put the law of morality into practice' is what I have been referring to as the broader practical commitment in the Kantian skill model. When is it strong? Kant's answer here is that its strength depends on a kind of apathy – '*the mind at peace*' – which is its freedom from affect and passion.[12] As we know from Chapter 1, affect and passion are both forms of blindness: they leave us failing to attend to what we ought to attend to, inasmuch as we are to be in possession of our cognitive capacities (reflecting-c, which is momentarily lost in affect) and apt to employ

---

[12] For Kant, apathy doesn't mean a 'subjective indifference with respect to objects of choice' (6:408). See also Baxley (2010, 71–6) on the role of apathy in Kantian virtue.

them well (reflecting-n, which is lost through passion and prejudice). Thus, Kant suggests here that a 'mind at peace' is prerequisite for being appropriately discerning, i.e. attending to what matters in the particulars for the end of 'putting the law of virtue into practice'. According to my account of the skill model, a person's commitment to morality can only be concretely action-guiding and truly practical to the extent that this discernment is cultivated – along with the other resources needed to act in a way that honours or instances the broader practical commitment.[13] Hence, the 'true strength of virtue' must be a specific mark of healthy understanding, because the moral law is grasped *in concreto* in the recognition of how particular facts about one's situation give one reasons to do and not do certain things. A commitment to morality can be 'reflected-upon and firm' through the development of skill, and so through an intelligent and fully motivated clear-sightedness about particulars. And so Kant is able to insist that learnedness does not necessarily have any advantage over common human reason as far as the acuity of moral discernment goes.[14]

Armed with the skill model of virtue, we can make good sense of Kant's otherwise puzzling claim that *Untugend* is 'compatible with the best will'. When *Untugend* is present together with 'the best will', there must be a commitment to morality, and thus to making the 'human being as such one's end' (as per MS 6:395). And so it might be said that the good-willed *Untugender* and the genuine *Tugender* share the same moral commitment, and share an understanding of the good. But whatever we might specify about the content of this shared understanding can only be mere words: formulaic, and practically indeterminate. The quality of their knowledge, in other words, cannot possibly be the same. For the virtuous person knows *full well* how to go on in light of this commitment, while the *Untugender* does not. The *Untugender* doesn't fully, or fully adequately, appreciate the value of humanity – for, the determinacy of such knowledge, and so its ability to be concretely action-guiding, admits of degree.[15]

---

[13] More on the cultivation of these 'brute resources' in §7.3.   [14] As I noted in Chapter 2.

[15] We might wonder what these conclusions, and my interpretation in this book more generally, would imply about Kant's views on weakness of will. Kant does not in fact provide any dedicated account of weakness of will, although some commentators assume one can be derived through straight exegesis (e.g. Broadie and Pybus 1982). Hill (2012) – rightly, by my lights – acknowledges that only a reconstruction is possible; he also points out that any knowledge that may be at stake in *knowing the better and doing the worse* can only be vague and indeterminate, and likens this indeterminacy to the uncertain implications of a law with a lot of loopholes (2012, 121). By suggesting that practical knowledge admits of degrees of adequacy, understood in terms of determinacy, his proposal may be consonant with my account of *Untugend*. Overall, my own arguments in this book suggest that we should not expect Kant to countenance clear-eyed weakness of will, but careful study of the matter lies outside of the scope of my work here.

7.3 The Skill Model in the *Tugendlehre*

According to the skill model, moral virtue and lack of virtue share a commitment to morality, but differ in the determinacy of this commitment, and so in the extent to which this commitment is concretely action-guiding. Moreover, the determinacy of this commitment only keeps pace with the extent to which one has cultivated the raw resources to act in a way that honours or instances this commitment. Much should turn, in cashing out this model, on what these resources are, and what it is to cultivate them. Kant points to what these raw resources might be in the *Tugendlehre*: 'There are certain moral endowments such that anyone lacking them could have no duty to acquire them', since it is owing to them that any human being 'can be put under obligation [verpflichtet]' in the first place (MS 6:399).[16] They are all '*subjective* conditions of receptiveness to the concept of duty': they are not themselves the basis of moral discriminations, but are rather ways of being *affected* by one's recognition of moral requirement. Under this heading, Kant considers: moral feeling, conscience, love of neighbour and self-respect (MS 6:399–403).[17] What I want to consider in this section is how the cultivation of these resources yields the basic outlines of Kant's account of the various duties of virtue in the main text of the *Tugendlehre*. Deploying the skill model, I will first consider duties of virtue to others, then duties to oneself.

7.3.1 Duties of Virtue to Others

Kant's account of duties of virtue to others begins with the 'wide' ethical duties that he denominates 'duties of love to others' (MS §§23–35, 6:448–58), followed by contrasting vices of hatred (MS §36, 6:458–61). Then, with a section break, Kant takes up duties of virtue that arise from the respect that anyone is due as a person, regardless of his merit (MS §§37–45, 6:462–9). Call these duties of recognition respect. It is necessary to distinguish between the capacity to recognise *here is a person* (not a thing) from *recognition respect*.[18] First, the mere recognition that *here is a person* is arguably

---

[16] This general point was noted in Chapter 5; here, I will be looking in more detail at the specific moral endowments at issue, and how they figure in the skill model of virtue.

[17] In the initial list, Kant specifies that he means *self*-respect for the last item (6:399). The subsequent discussion treats each item under its own heading, which in this case is 'respect [Achtung]' alone, but the actual discussion concerns self-respect, as initially indicated, rather than respect for others.

[18] The origin of this term is Darwall (1977, 2008). However, Darwall (2008) treats respect for the moral law as a type of recognition respect; this is confusing, since Kant indicates that all respect is ultimately respect for the moral law – suggesting that recognition respect should be a type of respect

not in itself a thought about what to do, although it might be said that
if one *does* genuinely recognise a person as a person, then one has corre-
sponding thoughts, at least implicitly, about what one must and must not
do. The latter is what Kant attempts to codify in his account of the duties
of recognition respect. However, there is some sense in which the vicious
and virtuous alike must recognise persons as persons. Although Kant never
says so outright, the capacity to recognise persons as persons (rather than
as things) must be something so basic that it would come online at least as
soon as one is capable of practical thought at all – and so, if we accept the
Kantian doctrine on this, with that first dim grasp of the categorical imperative. For, surely, there is some sense in which the torturer recognises his
victim *as a person*, specifically a human person, even as he seeks to degrade
that person by exploiting his characteristically human susceptibility to certain forms of suffering, both physical and psychological. If he could not
recognise persons as persons, or at least his victim as a person, he would
be a psychopath rather than a paragon of vice. Although the example may
be extreme, it indicates that there may be some distinction to be drawn
between recognising a person as a person, on the one hand, and fulfilling
duties of recognition respect, on the other.

Kant separates duties of recognition respect from duties of *love*. To
meet duties of recognition respect is not, in itself, to have positive virtue,
Kant claims: meeting these duties is compatible with mere lack of virtue,
Untugend (MS §41, 6:464). Since everyone is owed recognition respect
regardless of merit, the fulfilment of duties of recognition respect is not
especially context-sensitive, and should not require any remarkable discernment. That is one way of thinking about why Kant takes the fulfilment of
these duties to be compatible with mere *Untugend*. Yet, by the lights of
the skill model, it should follow that the person with mere *Untugend* will
have the same governing practical commitment as the person who fulfils
duties of love and thereby has positive virtue – at least, if this commitment
is regarded at a sufficient level of abstraction. The difference between the
two will consist in the cultivation of the resources needed to act in such
a way as to honour or instance this commitment. The commitment they
share, in this instance, is the happiness of others. The person with mere
lack of virtue has an accordingly impoverished and vague conception of
this commitment, because she doesn't yet have the resources at the ready
to act in such a way as to honour or instance it.

for the moral law, rather than the other way around. In my usage here, 'recognition respect' refers
to respect *for persons* simply as persons (regardless of merit).

The raw resource to be cultivated for duties of virtue to others is presumably what Kant calls 'love of human beings' (MS 6:401–2). By this, he has in mind natural sympathy – not exactly in the Humean sense of a psychological mechanism by which sentiment is transferred, more or less automatically, from one person to another, but rather natural beneficence as an inclination, and so presumably a readiness to be appropriately moved by this communication of sentiment. After he introduces this, Kant looks ahead to the duties of virtue to others, and remarks:

> *Beneficence*[19] is a duty. If someone practices it often and succeeds in realising his beneficent intention, he eventually comes actually to love the person he has helped. So the saying 'you ought to *love* your neighbour as yourself' does not mean that you should love him immediately (at first) and then (afterwards) by means of this love do good to him. Rather it means: *do good* to your fellow human beings and this beneficence will produce in you love of human beings (as a skill [Fertigkeit] of the inclination to beneficence)![20] (MS 6:402)

Here, Kant points explicitly to the notion of skill. What he means, presumably, is that the natural inclination to sympathy, when duly cultivated through the practice of beneficence itself, becomes skilful. What does that mean? The simple answer is that the natural inclination becomes an intelligent receptivity to the needs and desires of others, so that I recognise facts about these needs and desires *as providing me with reasons* for doing certain things. Later, Kant points to a 'duty of *humanity*', which consists in the cultivation of sympathy. *What* gets cultivated seems to be Humean-style sympathy, a natural propensity for the communication of feeling: 'the *receptivity*, given by nature itself, to the feeling of joy and sadness in common with others (*humanitas aesthetica*)' (MS 6:456). In light of the earlier remarks about 'love of human beings', Kant seems to take it that Humean communicative sympathy naturally gives way to some propensity to act on the feelings thus communicated. However, the cultivation of sympathy is a duty of virtue inasmuch as it figures as 'a *means* for the promotion of active

---

[19] Kant stresses *beneficience* here because he is nodding to his earlier argument that the *perfection* of others cannot be a morally obligatory end, and hence nor can the *moral perfection* of others (MS 6:385–6). He indicates right before this remark that *hatred* of human beings 'is always *hateful* [*häßlich*], even when it consists only in completely turning away from human beings (separatist misanthropy) and not active hostility' (MS 6:402). He then distinguishes this from hating vice in human beings, but remarks that the latter 'is neither a duty nor contrary to duty', presumably in light of the fact that the morally obligatory end governing duties of virtue to others is for their *happiness*, not their virtue.

[20] The exclamation mark is Kant's, and is not preserved in Gregor's CEWIK translation.

and rational benevolence' (MS 6:456; my emphasis).[21] Such sympathy is 'grounded on practical reason' (6:456), since one cultivates it with an eye to honouring one's commitment to the happiness of others: it is the *'capacity [Vermögen]* and the *will* to *share in others' feelings (humanitas practica)'* (MS 6:456). Thus, it is the cultivated resource of duties of love to others.

If we try to think about what it is for the natural inclination to sympathy to become *skilled*, it must be that it becomes more responsive in concrete and finely grained ways. One way in which this may happen, presumably, is through our close relationships with *particular* other people – people whom we know well, and in whose well-being and happiness we naturally take a visceral interest. When Kant says that the duties of virtue are of 'wide' obligation, he adds that they leave 'a playroom [Spielraum] (*latitudo*) for free choice in following (complying with) the law', which allows 'permission to limit one maxim of duty by another (e.g. love of one's neighbour in general by love of one's parents) by which in fact the field for the practice of duty is widened' (MS 6:390). This remark has something surprising about it, since it casts a certain *limitation* of one's attention to one's parents' happiness as a way in which the practice of duty becomes somehow more *expansive*. Although Kant does not much elaborate, this seems like it must have something to do with the fact that many people, at least, will be capable of having a more concretely determinate appreciation of their own parents' needs and desires, as well as of their reason-giving force, than of the needs and desires of anyone they know less well and to whom they are less intimately indebted.[22]

7.3.2   Duties of Virtue to Oneself

To consider how the skill model plays out on the other side, for duties of virtue to oneself, let me return to Kant's list of the given endowments – the raw resources – by which we stand to be moved by the recognition of moral requirement. They are: moral feeling, conscience, love of neighbour and

---

[21] Kant says here that it is indeed a 'particular, but yet only conditional [bedingte] duty' (MS 6:456): conditional *upon what*, exactly? Kant says that the duty acknowledges not the nature of a rational being as such, but the nature of 'an animal endowed with reason' (6:456). Presumably, he means that it is conditional on the fact, as he said earlier, that 'a human being can have duties only to human beings', and (as he elaborates) to actually and presently existing human beings, i.e. persons who can be 'given as an object of experience' (MS 6:442). So, while this condition holds for all of *our* duties of virtue, certain of these duties can only come to light if we take account of the human condition: that, I take it, is his point in designating the duty as 'conditional'.

[22] Much of what I am saying in this paragraph draws from Herman's work on the notion of a 'deliberative field' (Herman 1993, 2007).

self-respect (MS 6:399–403). Love of neighbour has just been considered, as one would expect, with regard to duties of virtue to others. That leaves three on the list: moral feeling, conscience and respect. Respect, in this context, Kant presents as *self*-respect in particular; and he does not indicate, as he does with the other items on the list, that it stands to be *cultivated*. Perhaps this is not surprising. On both sides of the *Tugendlehre*, Kant distinguishes duties that are based on recognition respect, the fulfilment of which is in itself compatible with mere lack of virtue or *Untugend*.[23] These duties of recognition respect are *perfect*: they do not call for any kind of context-specific discernment. Kant divides the perfect duties of self-respect into what one owes oneself 'as an animal being' (e.g. do not commit suicide) and what one owes oneself 'as a moral being' (e.g. do not lie).[24] Failure to fulfil them counts as vice, whereas simply meeting them is compatible with mere lack of virtue (*Untugend*).[25] This means that fulfilling these duties is an expression of one's commitment to one's own humanity, but not yet in itself a skilled one. This is presumably why self-respect stands out as the sole given endowment on the list that does not call for active cultivation: the perfect duties of respect, as such, only ward against one's own (moral) degradation.

The two other items on the list are conscience and moral feeling, and I will be looking at these – particularly moral feeling – more closely. At this point, though, a word about the expository structure of the account of duties of virtue to oneself is in order. After the account of the perfect duties of self-respect, we come to an interlude in which Kant discusses conscience (*Tugendlehre* §13, MS 6:437–40) and then proclaims the '**first command** of all duties to oneself', which is his version of the Delphic command *know yourself* (*Tugendlehre* §§14–15, MS 6:441–2). What we make of Kant's Delphic command lies at the heart of the agenda of this book: it has everything to do with what we make of the Kantian reflective ideal, in the end. So,

---

[23] As I explained at the start of this section.
[24] In the first category, we find prohibitions against suicide, defiling oneself through lust and stupefying oneself by drunkenness and gluttony (MS *Tugendlehre* §§5–8, 6:421–8), and in the second prohibitions against lying, avarice and servility (MS *Tugendlehre* §§9–12, 6:429–37).
[25] Kant does not quite say this explicitly for the perfect duties of self-respect. He rather links them to one's 'moral *self-preservation*', distinguishing this from the 'positive duties' of self-perfection (6:419). He then associates the perfect duties of self-respect with 'moral **health**', claiming that the wide duties of self-perfection belong instead to one's 'moral *prosperity*' (6:419). This is confusing, since every other time Kant invokes the metaphor of health in the Doctrine of Virtue, it seems to be offered as a way of conceiving of virtue on the whole. At any rate, I am drawing here on what Kant says about the duties arising from respect due to others: I take it that the compatibility of the fulfilment of such duties with *Untugend* should likewise hold for duties of self-respect.

I will build up to it slowly, starting with the discussion of conscience that immediately precedes it.

When Kant discusses conscience, he picks up on the fact that he had earlier identified it as among the given endowments. Conscience is not acquired; we have it in us 'originally': it is part and parcel of the reflective nature of the rational mind, specifically in its practical employment (MS 6:400).[26] In the 'most extreme depravity', Kant claims, one can only bring oneself 'to *heed* it no longer', but one can never stop '*hearing*' it (MS 6:438). To *cultivate* conscience is to become more heedful of it, 'to sharpen one's attention' to it (MS 6:401). But what exactly does one hear? And what exactly is the difference between hearing it and heeding it? In the later discussion of conscience, Kant points to the 'internal *imputation* of a *deed*, as a case falling under a law (*in meritum aut demeritum*)', noting that this is an act of judgment (MS 6:438).[27] I assume that this internal imputation cannot itself be conscience, since the ability to exercise judgment can only come online through active efforts of various kinds: it is not a given endowment, a fact about human nature, in quite the same way that conscience is supposed to be. Conscience itself must be the manner in which this imputation strikes us. The internal imputation takes the form: *I did such a thing* – I really mocked that guy; I wasn't just teasing. Conscience is being impressed by such a judgment. Kant says that we will always 'hear' our conscience. In effect, this means that even the most depraved among us will still think, *it matters what I do*. But conscience does not issue discursive claims; rather, for Kant, it is a mode of moral feeling, and so a receptivity to moral requirement. So, it is a matter of being *impressed* by these imputations.

This brings us to the Delphic command, which Kant touts as the '**first command** of all duties to oneself: the 'moral self-knowledge [moralische Selbsterkenntniß]' that it calls for is supposed to be 'the beginning of all human wisdom' (MS 6:441). I will approach the passage on the Delphic command by way of the remaining item on the list of given endowments at issue: namely, moral feeling.

The particular conception of moral feeling that Kant notes in this list of natural endowments is 'the susceptibility to feel pleasure or displeasure

---

[26] This is a place where, for present purposes, I am simply admitting a core claim that is arguably established in the *Critique of Practical Reason*, namely that the categorical imperative is constitutive of practical cognition (much as the principles of pure understanding are constitutive of theoretical cognition). For Kant, this means that we have a tacit grasp of this principle just as soon as we come into the practical use of our reason; that is roughly why conscience is a given endowment by his lights.

[27] It belongs to *Urtheilskraft*, he says.

merely from being aware that our actions are consistent with or contrary to the law of duty' (MS 6:399). When cultivated, this presumably leads eventually to the 'contentment' with oneself (*Zufriedenheit, Selbstzufriedenheit*) to which Kant points in order to endorse a version of the ancient idea that virtue is its own reward (MS 6:377; see also KpV 5:117–18). At this point, though, we are considering the raw resource, not yet its cultivation. Let us look, then, at how Kant elaborates on the conception of moral feeling at issue:

> Every determination of choice proceeds *from* the representation of a possible action through the feeling of pleasure or displeasure, taking an interest in the action or its effect, *to the deed*. The state of *feeling* [*ästhetische* Zustand] here (the affection of inner sense) is either *pathological* or *moral*. – The former is that feeling which precedes the representation of the law, the latter the feeling that can only follow upon it. (MS 6:399)

I want to focus first on the claim that the affection of inner sense can be either pathological or moral. In Chapter 3, I drew upon Kant's claim from the Transcendental Deduction that 'every act of attention' gives us an example of the self-affection of inner sense (B156n). Here, Kant supposes that any determination of choice involves considering a possible action, and that attending to this possibility is likewise a case of the affection of inner sense – i.e. of one's being affected by one's own thought. Kant also notes in the passage from the Deduction that the self-affection of inner sense proceeds 'in accordance with the combination that it [the understanding] thinks' (B157n). Now, *here* Kant distinguishes between pathological and moral self-affection. Thus, one might represent a possible action (have a thought about what to do), and this thought will affect one with pleasure or displeasure; but the distinction between pathological and moral self-affection turns on whether the thought of what to do, and with it the self-affection, precedes or follows one's recognition of moral requirement. If the affection is pathological, then the pleasure or displeasure will presumably answer to one's commitment to one's own happiness in Kant's view: for this is the principle under which one conceives of the action; it is the rule of the 'combination that [the understanding] thinks' (to slot this into the remark from the Deduction). But if the affection is moral, then the pleasure or displeasure will answer to one's commitment to morality – and that will be the principle under which one conceives the action and is thereby affected by one's own thought.

What I am trying to do here is see how the skill model is deployed in the *Tugendlehre*. According to this model, the determinacy of a broader practical commitment to morality can only keep pace with the extent to which one has cultivated the raw resources needed to act in a way that concretely honours or instances this commitment. What, then, might it be to cultivate moral feeling in this way? The answer, I think, lies in the idea from the Deduction that every act of attention provides an example of self-affection, where (again) 'the understanding always determines inner sense in accordance with a combination that it thinks' (B157n). For action, the 'combination' is a matter of seeing facts about one's situation as providing one with reasons to do this or that. A particular fact is a reason in particular circumstances, given one's broader practical commitments, to φ. The reason that one actually has, and can recognise, is a function of some such relation. Now, again, Kant here presents moral feeling as 'the susceptibility to feel pleasure or displeasure merely from being aware that our actions are consistent with or contrary to the law of duty' (MS 6:399). To *cultivate* this should be something like what it is to cultivate conscience: it involves taking these feelings to *matter*. Presumably, then, one can only cultivate conscience by taking an interest in one's acquired moral condition.

This brings us finally to the Delphic command. Let us keep in mind the idea that every act of attention provides us with an example of the self-affection in the inner sense. Here is the passage:

> *Know* (scrutinise, fathom) *yourself*, not in terms of your natural perfection (your fitness or unfitness for all sorts of discretionary or even commanded ends), but rather in terms of your moral perfection in relation to your duty – your heart – whether it is good or evil, whether the sources of your actions are pure or impure, and [in terms of] what can be imputed to you either as belonging originally to the *substance* [*Substanz*] of a human being or as derived (acquired or developed) and belonging to your moral *condition*. (MS 6:441)

The moral self-knowledge to which Kant points here is impossible: for, it is well known, as is repeated throughout Kant's moral writings, that we can never know of any action that accords with duty whether it was performed from the motive of duty, which is to say *directly from one's recognition of moral requirement*.[28] Some commentators suppose that what Kant is saying here is that we ought to *try* to answer this question, and moreover that introspection – trying to identify what was going on in our heads when, what we felt and so on – provides viable means for answering this question as best we can.[29] However, the requirement seems to me to be that one

---

[28] See e.g. G (4:407); see also MS (6:392–3, 447), Rel (6:20). Kant makes this sort of point often, as I have previously noted.

[29] For example, Grenberg (2005).

take an interest in one's acquired moral condition, which is not necessarily an introspective affair in the standard sense. After all, we can never tell whether our hearts are good or evil, whether the sources of our actions are pure or impure. There is no determinate answer that we can provide to *those* questions.

What we know from the Transcendental Deduction and related passages in the *Anthropology* considered in Chapter 3 is that I know myself, as an intelligence, only as I appear and not as I am in myself. I know myself only as I appear through the deliverances of inner sense. Now, if every act of attention provides an example of the self-affection of inner sense, then I appear to myself in the concrete engagement of my own thought: namely, in the very facts of what I pay attention to and why. And this is presumably also the only way in which I can know myself as a moral agent, an intelligence engaged with the question of what to do. There is no other way for me to take an interest in my own moral agency than by considering what figures in my attention as providing me with reasons for doing this or that. These reasons, as long as moral duty is at issue, will all stem from the objective and unconditioned value of persons – but always only *actual* persons, the empirically given ones to whom alone I can have duties (see MS 6:442). Therefore, the Delphic command is not a call to be introspective as this is commonly understood. It is a call to be reflective as *Kant* understands it, which is to take an interest in the soundness of one's own cognitive capacities – specifically, one's practical cognitive capacity, which is nothing other than one's ability to know what is worth doing and why.

On the 'adverbial' account of the normative requirement to reflect that I have offered in this book, this requirement is met by exercising one's cognitive capacities in the right way, or in the right spirit. It need not be a matter of 'stepping back' on the occasion of taking things to be a certain way, considering the source of this taking things to be a certain way and deciding whether – so assessed – one is thereby entitled to make a cognitive claim. The reflection can be embedded in the act of judgment itself: this is an idea that I have sought to elaborate further through the skill model of virtue. By these lights, the idea that we ought to be reflective should not be interpreted as saying that we ought to be especially introspective, where introspection is modelled on sense perception, and thus is a matter of registering the goings on of one's own mind, or the special impressions etched by the activity of thought itself. Rather, we might say, reflection-n is the self-concerned aspect of judgment – but this does not make it essentially a matter of 'looking inward'. This account of reflection-n can seem starkly at odds with the Pietist strains of Kantian morality, and perhaps particularly with the Delphic command. My account of the Delphic command is, of course, aimed to assuage these concerns, by questioning the default appearance of the passage and others like it. I want to conclude, though, by noting that there is a sense in which I can take account of perfectly ordinary views about the importance of introspection in a conscientious moral life.

To do that, we need to return to Kant's curious remarks about the holy will noted in §7.2: i.e. Kant's suggestion that the same strength of will belongs to a holy will as belongs to a virtuous human being (MS 6:405). A holy will is a perfectly rational being: *perfectly* rational, the story goes, because it is unembodied. There is nothing to obstruct its operation according to its own internal principles. It lacks sensuous inclination, and thus is not subject to non-moral incentives. Virtue, by contrast, is a *human* ideal, by Kant's lights. Virtue is a perfection of the will, of practical reason – but an *acquired* perfection, not one that is enjoyed simply because there are 'no hindering impulses [that] work contrary to the law of its will' (6:405). Although virtue is an ideal, it is not one that amounts to a change in given human psychology. In us, sensuous desires work themselves up into inclinations, habitual desires: this is just a fact about how the human mind works. And this fact, paired with the reflective nature of the rational mind, entails that a human being is irremediably subject to non-moral incentives. So, it is strange, on the face of it, that Kant would suggest that the same strength should characterise both the holy will and the ideal of human virtue: for the holy will has no non-moral incentives to overcome. I have accounted for the apparent strangeness of this by explaining the strength of virtue by the lights of the concept of skill.

Since Kant takes the moral law to be constitutive of reason in its practical capacity, it follows, on his view, that a person has some grasp of this law – however dim – just as soon as she comes into the use of her reason. This is part of the 'predisposition to the good' that is, in this special sense, given in human (rational) nature. With this, there are three grades of the 'natural propensity to evil' (Rel 6:29–30): they stem from the fact of our embodiment, which leaves us irremediably subject to non-moral incentives to act. There is no way of being on the path to moral virtue without a commitment to morality; there is also, in Kant's view, no way of knowing whether one is indeed on this path. We cannot know this because there is no *given* fact of the matter: the requisite 'revolution' in one's 'way of thinking' (*Denkungsart*), where one no longer subordinates the moral law to the principle of self-love, but now commits oneself to morality, is not an introspectible event. But the commitment to morality is not achieved through any kind of incantation, or simply by deciding that one shall so commit oneself. It is achieved through works; and from our point of view, it can only take hold gradually, its strength acquired through *practice* in virtue.[30]

The strength of virtue is acquired through effort, and it is continually engaged. On my view, Kant says that the holy will should have the same strength because this strength is essentially cognitive: it is the readiness of one's commitment to morality, and the content of this commitment can be spelled out through the moral law. So, there is a sense, again, in which the content of the commitment is the same if it is regarded simply objectively, according to its internal principle. But a holy will does not gradually acquire a skill; a holy will does not – it seems – have to learn. Although anything we might say about the holy will is essentially speculative – an inference about an unembodied rational agent drawn from what we know of what it is to be an embodied rational agent – it seems that there should be a difference between the holy will and the virtuous person as regards the *content* of their respective commitments to morality, as long as this commitment is regarded 'subjectively', or from what is possible given the point of view of the sort of creature in question. The point can be illustrated with a familiar example.

Suppose a virtuous person is a teacher, and has to mark a bunch of essays online. The teacher knows that he is susceptible to implicit bias. There is hardly anything profoundly introspective about this knowledge: he knows it in part from having read articles about the issue and in part from having considered his own feelings and attitudes during previous sessions of marking essays. He cares about being fair, and he acts accordingly, perhaps electing to identify each paper by the author's student number, rather than by name. Considerations like this plausibly figure in the content of a human being's commitment to morality, but have no place in that of a holy will. The 'strength' is the same, inasmuch as both holiness and virtue are conceived by Kant as a perfection of practical reason; but the content of the commitment to morality will differ for each, because in the one case this perfection is given, and in the other case it is acquired. The fact that it is acquired through effort – through the development of skill – simply means that there are things that need to be kept specially in mind from our point of view.

---

[30] I am referring, of course, to the culmination of *Religion* I. For an excellent discussion of these issues, and for a somewhat different version of the point that the commitment to morality is strengthened, gradually, through practice, see Sussman (2005).

7.4 Practical Knowledge and the Independence of Objects

A worry that someone might raise about my specification thesis, and the ensuing account of the cognitive basis of moral virtue, is that it mischaracterises *practical* reason. On my story, general cognitive virtue is acquired through the adoption of two basic epistemic commitments: one is a commitment to one's own cognitive agency, the other is a commitment to the independence of any object of knowledge from the contingencies of any particular point of view on it (see Chapter 2, §2.4.1). The first commitment clearly figures in Kant's account of moral pedagogy, because it is operative in any developed exercise of practical reason; I have argued for this claim elsewhere (Merritt 2011b). But a commitment to the independence of objects might seem to have no place in a Kantian account of practical knowledge.

When Kant distinguishes theoretical from practical rational cognition in the first *Critique*'s Preface, he says that each relates in a distinct way to its object – theoretical cognition merely determines its object (which must be given to it through sensibility), whereas practical cognition does not merely determine its object, but also makes it actual, *wirklich* (Bix-x). In the second *Critique*, Kant says that the sole objects of the cognition of practical reason are the good and the evil: the good as what is to be realised, the evil as what is to be avoided in action according to a rational principle (KpV 5:57–60). So, it can seem as if an epistemic commitment to the independence of objects has no place, is an utter non-starter, as far as practical cognition is concerned, since Kant's whole point in drawing the distinction is to say that the object of practical cognition comes into being, is made actual, in the cognition itself. In the second *Critique*, Kant reinforces these claims when he says that the principles of practical knowledge 'do not have to wait for intuitions in order to receive meaning; and this happens for the noteworthy reason that they themselves produce the reality of that to which they refer (the disposition of the will), which is not the business of theoretical concepts' (KpV 5:66). He says here that the moral disposition of the will is the good to be brought about, or realised, through what we do. So, the idea seems to be roughly this: practical thinking is expressed in action, and action that emanates from the right source counts as *cognition* because it makes actual what any rational being is bound to value – autonomy. Thus, practical cognition does not seem to call for a commitment to the independence of objects – at least, not if an object is something that obtains anyway, independently of any particular exercise of cognitive capacities. For the object of practical reason, Kant seems to be saying, can only be realised in action itself: thus it doesn't obtain, apparently, independently of the exercise of the cognitive capacity.

However, there is another set of considerations that preserves the spirit of the epistemic commitment to the independence of objects – it preserves, at least, the idea that practical thinking owes fidelity to something that obtains quite independently of anything anyone does or doesn't do, and thus independently of any particular exercise of practical reason. These considerations stem from the *respect* that persons are due *simply as persons*, regardless of merit. This is the respect that, after Darwall (1977, 2008), we can call 'recognition respect', and distinguish from the 'esteem respect' that is wrung from us when we recognise in someone else better moral character than we are aware of in ourselves.[31] I have already noted how recognition respect figures in the *Tugendlehre* (see §7.3.1).[32] Recognition respect is basic regard for the objective and unconditioned value of humanity in particular, empirically available persons.[33] It is the acknowledgement, or practical estimation, of a value that obtains regardless of anything anyone does or doesn't do, and thus a value that obtains independently of any particular exercise of practical reason (although not, for Kant, independently of practical reason as such). So, the spirit of the epistemic commitment to the independence of objects is preserved for practical cognition, even though other persons are not the object of practical reason, not themselves the good that is to be realised in what one does. The spirit of this commitment is preserved because the value of any actual, empirically given person obtains anyway, independently of anything anyone does or doesn't do. I take this to be analogous to the way in which phenomenal objects exist independently of any particular exercise of theoretical reason (although not, again on Kant's view, independently of theoretical reason as such[34]).[35]

---

[31] As in the 'humble common man' vignette from the second *Critique* (KpV 5:76–7).

[32] But it should be noted that it scarcely figures in the earlier *Groundwork* or *Critique of Practical Reason*. Darwall (2008) discusses this point.

[33] In the Doctrine of Virtue, Kant maintains that we can have duties only to empirically available human beings or persons that can 'be given as an object of experience' (MS 6:442). The express point of the remark is to deny that we have duties to God or to angels ('*superhuman*' beings), or to non-persons (inanimate nature, non-human animals). However, it shows how recognition respect differs from respect for the moral law, at least inasmuch as the latter is typically construed as regard for abstract principle.

[34] This last proviso in both cases is simply Kant's transcendental idealism broadly construed, i.e. as the particular way in which reason and reality remain ultimately inseparable by his lights.

[35] My argument in this and the previous paragraph recapitulates the core proposal of Merritt (2017a).

7.5 Self-Determination through Understanding

Let me conclude with a summary of how the arguments of this book take us a good distance from the caricature of the Kantian reflective ideal with which we began. The caricature is forever poised to step back from the exigencies of judgment and action, to consider the source of his taking things to be a certain way or worth doing, and whether this source renders the given view sound or unsound, to be accepted or rejected. There are undeniable traces of this picture in the account of reflection that Kant provides in the context of applied general logic, where he repeatedly claims that 'all judgments require reflection'. I argued, however, that Kant ultimately understands the normative requirement to reflect in terms of the maxims of healthy understanding. Once we see this, we can recognise that the requirement is to be met by putting one's cognitive capacities to use *in the right way*, or *in the right spirit*: reflection can be adverbial, and it is not essentially episodic. This already takes us some distance from the hyper-deliberate caricature of the Kantian reflective ideal.

The caricature is also precious and moralistic. Some concerns about preciousness linger in the account of reflection-n through the three maxims. For the upshot of the three maxims is a requirement to take an issue in one's own cognitive agency, and so the interpretation of the normative requirement to reflect through the three maxims might leave a lingering trace of a persistent anxiety in the reflective person about his own character. However, this concern can be addressed by stressing the implications of the adverbial conception of the requirement: if reflection-n is making use of one's cognitive capacities in the right way, or in the right spirit, then what drives the development of cognitive and moral character is an essentially outward-directed interest in knowing. This is the notion of healthy understanding that, as I argued in Chapter 5, is fundamental cognitive virtue by Kant's lights. This argument led me to the specification thesis: moral virtue is a specification of the *general* cognitive virtue that Kant calls 'healthy human understanding'.

In Chapter 6, I drew attention to Kant's qualified endorsement of the skill model of virtue, and began to work out its implications. I suggested that the local stimulus of Kant's consideration of the skill model of virtue came from Mendelssohn, who saw in the model a certain promise for addressing the problem of preciousness, or a certain persistent anxiety about one's own character. By Mendelssohn's lights, the promise lies in the *automatism* of skill: a skilled person, in his view, no longer thinks about what he is doing and loses himself in the 'flow'. But Kant rejects

Mendelssohn's automatism about skill. For Kant, there is a way of preserving the importance of being reflective while avoiding the concerns about preciousness: the answer lies in distinguishing between unfree and free skills, recognising how the latter have reflection built into them and taking only free skills to provide a model for conceiving of virtue as a skill.

When I began working on this book, I had expected to find separate sets of theoretical and practical cognitive virtues. What I found instead was a conception of *general* cognitive virtue (healthy understanding) that can be specified, in the practical case, as *moral* virtue. There is, in other words, no special theoretical cognitive virtue, or set of theoretical cognitive virtues. The reason for this is that the cultivation of virtue follows from the adoption of rationally obligatory ends. There is nothing that anyone categorically ought to care about, as far as knowledge of nature is concerned. But in Kant's view, we categorically ought to care about the cultivation of our cognitive capacities: this is part of what accounts for the status of healthy understanding as cognitive *virtue*. And likewise, on his view, we categorically ought to care about 'the human being as such': we have no leave to be indifferent about the relevant facts concerning the existence of persons, as we have leave to be indifferent about astronomy or the Greek War of Independence. There are, of course, cultivated skills of inquiry in various domains: but these are developed at one's discretion, which is why they are not virtues.[36] None of this speaks directly against the moralism of the caricature; and it must be acknowledged that, for Kant, the source of all genuine value is the moral law. But the *Tugendlehre* does reveal that Kant works with a conception of ethics (in the strict sense, as a doctrine of virtue) as the fulfilment of human nature, and so is concerned with the complete package of what we are, according to both natural and moral perfections.

Crucially, the idea that all virtue is fundamentally cognitive virtue by Kant's lights pushes back against the idea that the Kantian reflective ideal is 'always in control' in some objectionable way. This charge is often linked with a certain way of interpreting Korsgaard on reflective endorsement. Korsgaard says that it is owing to the reflective nature of the rational mind that we need reasons for belief and for action; and she suggests that we address this need through reflective endorsement. It is not clear whether the need is supposed to be addressed by giving ourselves reasons that we would

---

[36] In the Delphic command passage, Kant glosses natural perfection as one's 'fitness or unfitness for all sorts of discretionary or even commanded ends' (MS 6:441). This remark tacitly notes the special place of healthy understanding among possible natural perfections: it is fitness for a commanded end, whereas your standard-issue free skill – including e.g. skills of inquiry in field biology – is a fitness for a discretionary end.

not otherwise have or by recognising the reasons that we have anyway. She is often interpreted along the former lines, as I noted in Chapter 1, which would make her a voluntarist about reflective endorsement. Whether or not this is the correct interpretation of Korsgaard, it is often supposed that voluntarism about reflection is part and parcel of the Kantian legacy.

By contrast, the guiding thread of this book is that Kant conceives of reflection in resolutely cognitivist terms. It is in the interest of knowing, and that alone, that we ought to be reflective. The motto of the Kantian reflective ideal is *self-determination through understanding*. There is an element of submission to this, of owing fidelity to what obtains independently of any particular exercise of cognitive capacities. This includes fidelity to a value that obtains independently of anything anyone does or doesn't do, cares about or doesn't care about. The submission, moreover, is not to any indifferent fact about what is the case. We owe fidelity, chiefly, to what is most worth caring about in the complete order of things. For Kant, this can only be actual human beings.

References

Adelung, Johann Christoph. 1811. *Grammatisch-kritisches Wörterbuch der hochdeutschen Mundart.* http://lexika.digitale-sammlungen.de/adelung/online/angebot (accessed 24 March 2015).

Allison, Henry. 2001. *Kant's Theory of Taste: A Reading of the Critique of Aesthetic Judgment.* Cambridge: Cambridge University Press.

Ameriks, Karl. 2006. 'A Common-Sense Kant?' In *Kant and the Historical Turn: Philosophy as Critical Interpretation,* 108–33. New York, NY: Oxford University Press.

Annas, Julia. 1995. 'Virtue as a Skill.' *International Journal of Philosophical Studies* 3 (2): 227–43.

Annas, Julia. 2001. 'The Structure of Virtue.' In *Intellectual Virtue: Perspectives from Ethics and Epistemology,* edited by Michael DePaul and Linda Zagzebski, 15–33. Oxford: Oxford University Press.

Annas, Julia. 2011. *Intelligent Virtue.* Oxford: Oxford University Press.

Anscombe, G. E. M. 1958. 'Modern Moral Philosophy.' *Philosophy* 33 (124): 1–19.

Aristotle. 1984. *The Complete Works of Aristotle: The Revised Oxford Translation,* edited by Jonathan Barnes. Princeton, NJ: Princeton University Press.

Bacin, Stefano. 2010. 'The Doctrine of Method of Pure Practical Reason.' In *Kant's Critique of Practical Reason: A Critical Guide,* edited by Andrew Reath and Jens Timmerman. Cambridge: Cambridge University Press.

Baehr, Jason. 2011. *The Inquiring Mind: On Intellectual Virtues and Virtue Epistemology.* Oxford: Oxford University Press.

Battaly, Heather. 2014. 'Intellectual Virtues.' In *The Handbook of Virtue Ethics,* edited by Stan van Hooft, 177–87. Durham: Acumen.

Baxley, Anne Margaret. 2010. *Kant's Theory of Virtue: The Value of Autocracy.* Cambridge: Cambridge University Press.

Betzler, Monika, ed. 2008. *Kant's Ethics of Virtue.* Berlin and New York, NY: DeGruyter.

Bloomfield, Paul. 2000. 'Virtue Epistemology and the Epistemology of Virtue.' *Philosophy and Phenomenological Research* 60 (1): 23–43.

Boswell, Terry. 1988. 'On the Textual Authenticity of Kant's Logic.' *History and Philosophy of Logic* 9 (2): 193–203.

Brandt, Reinhard. 1999. *Kritischer Kommentar zu Kants Anthropologie in pragmatischer Hinsicht (1798).* Hamburg: Felix Meiner Verlag.

209

Brandt, Reinhard. 2003. 'The Vocation of the Human Being.' In *Essays on Kant's Anthropology*, edited by Brian Jacobs and Patrick Kain, 85–104. Cambridge: Cambridge University Press.

Brewer, Talbot. 2000. *The Bounds of Choice: Unchosen Virtues, Unchosen Commitments*. New York, NY and London: Routledge.

Brewer, Talbot. 2002. 'Maxims and Virtues.' *Philosophical Review* 111 (4): 539–72.

Brewer, Talbot. 2011. 'Two Pictures of Practical Thinking.' In *Perfecting Virtue: New Essays on Kantian Ethics and Virtue Ethics*, edited by Lawrence Jost and Julian Wuerth, 116–46. Cambridge and New York, NY: Cambridge University Press.

Broadie, Alexander and Elizabeth M. Pybus. 1982. 'Kant and Weakness of Will.' *Kant-Studien* 73 (4): 406–12.

Cambiano, Giuseppe. 2012. 'The Desire to Know: Metaphysics A1.' In *Aristotle's Metaphysics Alpha: Symposium Aristotelicum*, edited by Carlos Steel and Oliver Primavesi, 1–47. Oxford: Oxford University Press.

Carlisle, Clare. 2014. *On Habit*. Abingdon: Routledge.

Chignell, Andrew. 2007. 'Belief in Kant.' *The Philosophical Review* 116 (3): 323–60.

Ciafardone, Raffael, ed. 1990. *Die Philosophie der deutschen Aufklärung: Texte und Darstellung*. German edition prepared by Nobert Hinske and Reiner Specht. Stuttgart: Reclam.

Clarke, Bridget. 2010. 'Virtue and Disagreement.' *Ethical Theory and Moral Practice* 13 (3): 273–91.

Cohen, Alix, ed. 2014a. *Kant on Emotion and Value*. Basingstoke and New York, NY: Palgrave Macmillan.

Cohen, Alix. 2014b. 'Kant on the Ethics of Belief.' *Proceedings of the Aristotelian Society* 114 (3): 317–34.

Collins, Arthur W. 1999. *Possible Experience: Understanding Kant's Critique of Pure Reason*. Berkeley, CA, Los Angeles, CA and London: University of California Press.

Cooper, John. 1998. 'The Unity of Virtue.' *Social Philosophy and Policy* 15 (1): 233–74.

Darwall, Stephen. 1977. 'Two Kinds of Respect.' *Ethics* 88 (1): 36–49.

Darwall, Stephen. 2008. 'Kant on Respect, Dignity, and the Duty of Respect.' In *Kant's Ethics of Virtue*, edited by Monika Betzler, 175–200. Berlin: de Gruyter.

de Boer, Karin. 2011. 'Transformations of Transcendental Philosophy: Wolff, Kant, and Hegel.' *Bulletin of the Hegel Society of Great Britain* 32 (1–2): 50–79.

Deligiorgi, Katerina. 2002. 'Universalisability, Publicity, and Communication: Kant's Conception of Reason.' *European Journal of Philosophy* 10(2): 143–59.

Denis, Lara. 2000. 'Kant's Cold Sage and the Sublimity of Apathy.' *Kantian Review* 4 (1): 48–73.

Descartes, René. 1985. *The Philosophical Writings of Descartes*. Translated by John Cottingham, Robert Stoothoff and Dugald Murdoch. Cambridge: Cambridge University Press.

Driver, Julia. 2003. 'The Conflation of Moral and Epistemic Virtue.' *Metaphilosophy* 34 (30): 367–83.

Dyck, Corey W. 2016. 'Spontaneity before the Critical Turn: Crusius, Tetens, and the Pre-Critical Kant on the Spontaneity of the Mind.' *Journal of the History of Philosophy* 54 (4): 625–48.

Elizondo, E. Sonny. 2013. 'Reason in Its Practical Application.' *Philosophers' Imprint* 13 (21): 1–17.

Engstrom, Stephen. 2009. *The Form of Practical Knowledge: A Study of the Categorical Imperative*. Cambridge, MA: Harvard University Press.

Fridland, Ellen. 2014. 'They've Lost Control: Reflections on Skill.' *Synthese* 191 (12): 2729–50.

Frierson, Patrick. 2003. *Freedom and Anthropology in Kant's Moral Philosophy*. Cambridge: Cambridge University Press.

Frierson, Patrick. 2014. *Kant's Empirical Psychology*. Cambridge: Cambridge University Press.

Formosa, Paul. 2011. 'A Life without Affects and Passions: Kant on the Duty of Apathy.' *Parrhesia* 13: 96–111.

Gardner, Sebastian. 2006. 'The Primacy of Practical Reason.' In *A Companion to Kant*, edited by Graham Bird, 259–74. Malden, MA: Blackwell Publishing.

Geiger, Ido. 2015. 'How Do We Acquire Moral Knowledge? Is Knowing Our Duty Ever Passive? – Two Questions for Martin Sticker.' *British Journal for the History of Philosophy* 25 (5): 990–7.

Gelfert, Axel. 2006. 'Kant on Testimony.' *British Journal for the History of Philosophy* 14 (4): 627–52.

Grenberg, Jeanine. 2005. *Kant and the Ethics of Humility: A Story of Dependence, Corruption, and Virtue*. Cambridge: Cambridge University Press.

Grenberg, Jeanine. 2013. *Kant's Defence of Common Moral Experience: A Phenomenological Account*. Cambridge: Cambridge University Press.

Guyer, Paul. 2011. 'Kantian Perfectionism.' In *Perfecting Virtue: New Essays on Kantian Ethics and Virtue Ethics*, edited by Lawrence Jost and Julian Wuerth, 194–214. Cambridge: Cambridge University Press.

Hare, John. 2011. 'Kant, the Passions, and the Structure of Moral Motivation.' *Faith and Philosophy* 28 (1): 54–70.

Harrower, Elizabeth. 2012 [1966]. *The Watch Tower*. Melbourne: Text Publishing Australia.

Harrower, Elizabeth. 2014. *In Certain Circles*. Melbourne: Text Publishing Australia.

Heidemann, Dietmar H. 2012. 'The "I Think" Must Be Able to Accompany All My Representations: Unconscious Representations and Self-consciousness in Kant'. In *Kant's Philosophy of the Unconscious*, edited by Piero Giordanetti, Riccardo Pozzo, and Marco Sgarbi, 37–60. Berlin: de Gruyter.

Herman, Barbara. 1993. *The Practice of Moral Judgment*. Cambridge, MA: Harvard University Press.

Herman, Barbara. 2007. *Moral Literacy*. Cambridge, MA: Harvard University Press.

Hill, Thomas E., Jr. 2012. 'Kant on Weakness of Will.' In *Virtue, Rules, and Justice: Kantian Aspirations*, 107–28. Oxford: Oxford University Press.

Iyengar, B. K. S. 1979. *Light on Yoga*, rev. ed. New York, NY: Schocken Books.

Jost, Lawrence and Julian Wuerth, eds. 2011. *Perfecting Virtue: New Essays on Kantian Ethics and Virtue Ethics*. Cambridge and New York, NY: Cambridge University Press.

Keller, Pierre. 1998. *Kant and the Demands of Self-Consciousness*. Cambridge: Cambridge University Press.

Kennett, Jeanette. 2015. 'What is Required for Motivation by Principle?' In *Motivational Internalism*, edited by Gunnar Björnsson, Caj Strandberg, Ragnar Francén Olinder, John Eriksson and Fredrik Björklund, 108–29. New York, NY: Oxford University Press.

Kitcher, Patricia. 2003. 'What is a Maxim?' *Philosophical Topics* 31 (1–2): 215–43.

Kitcher, Patricia. 2011. *Kant's Thinker*. New York, NY: Oxford University Press.

Kitcher, Patricia. 2012. 'Kant's Unconscious "Given".' In *Kant's Philosophy of the Unconscious*, edited by Piero Giordanetti, Riccardo Pozzo and Marco Sgarbi, 5–36. Berlin: de Gruyter.

Kleingeld, Pauline. 2007. 'Kant's Second Thoughts about Race.' *Philosophical Quarterly* 57 (229): 573–92.

Klemme, Heiner F. 2014. 'Is the Categorical Imperative the Highest Principle of *Both* Pure Practical *and* Theoretical Reason?' *Kantian Review* 19 (1): 119–126.

Kohl, Markus. 2015. 'Kant on Freedom of Empirical Thought.' *Journal of the History of Philosophy* 53 (2): 301–26.

Korsgaard, Christine. 1996. *The Sources of Normativity*. Cambridge: Cambridge University Press.

Korsgaard, Christine. 2008. *The Constitution of Agency: Essays on Practical Reason and Moral Psychology*. New York, NY: Oxford University Press.

Korsgaard, Christine. 2009. *Self-Constitution: Agency, Identity, and Integrity*. New York, NY: Oxford University Press.

Kuehn, Manfred. 1987. *Scottish Common Sense in Germany, 1768–1800: A Contribution to the History of Critical Philosophy*. Kingston, ON and Montreal, QB: McGill-Queen's University Press.

Kuehn, Manfred. 2009. 'Reason as a Species Characteristic.' In *Kant's Idea for a Universal History with a Cosmopolitan Aim: A Critical Guide*, edited by Amélie O. Rorty and James Schmidt, 68–93. New York, NY: Cambridge University Press.

Larmore, Charles. 2008. *The Autonomy of Morality*. Cambridge: Cambridge University Press.

Leibniz, G.W. 1981. *New Essays on Human Understanding*. Translated and edited by Peter Remnant and Jonathan Bennett. Cambridge: Cambridge University Press.

Leibniz, G.W. 1989. *Philosophical Essays*. Translated and edited by Roger Ariew and Daniel Garber. Indianapolis, IN: Hackett Publishing.

Liedtke, Max. 1966. 'Der Begriff der Reflexion bei Kant.' *Archiv für Geschichte der Philosophie* 48 (1–3): 207–16.

Longuenesse, Béatrice. 1998. *Kant and the Capacity to Judge: Sensibility and Discursivity in the Transcendental Analytic of the Critique of Pure Reason.* Translated by Charles T. Wolfe. Princeton, NJ: Princeton University Press.

Louden, Robert B. 2011. *Kant's Human Being: Essays on His Theory of Human Nature.* New York, NY: Oxford University Press.

Lu-Adler, Huaping. 2015. 'Constructing a Demonstration of Logical Rules, or How to Use Kant's Logic Corpus.' In *Reading Kant's Lectures*, edited by Robert Clewis, 137–58. Berlin and New York, NY: de Gruyter.

Lu-Adler, Huaping. 2017. 'Kant and the Normativity of Logic.' *European Journal of Philosophy* 25 (2): 207–30.

Mahon, James Edwin. 2009. 'The Truth about Kant on Lies.' In *The Philosophy of Deception*, edited by Clancy Martin, 201–22. Oxford: Oxford University Press.

Makkreel, Rudolf. 2014. 'Self-Cognition and Self-Assessment.' In *Kant's Lectures on Anthropology: A Critical Guide*, edited by Alix Cohen, 18–37. Cambridge: Cambridge University Press.

McAndrew, Mathew. 2014. 'Healthy Understanding and *Urtheilskraft*: The Development of the Power of Judgment in Kant's Early Faculty Psychology.' *Kant-Studien* 105 (3): 394–405.

McDowell, John. 1979. 'Virtue and Reason.' *The Monist* 62 (3): 331–350. Reprinted in McDowell (1998, 50–73).

McDowell, John. 1994. *Mind and World.* Cambridge, MA: Harvard University Press.

McDowell, John. 1998. *Mind, Value, and Reality.* Cambridge, MA: Harvard University Press.

McDowell, John. 2009. *Having the World in View: Essays on Kant, Hegel, and Sellars.* Cambridge, MA: Harvard University Press.

Meier, Georg Friedrich. 1752. *Auszug aus der Vernunftlehre.* Halle: Gebauer.

Meier, Georg Friedrich. 2016 [1752]. *Excerpt from the Doctrine of Reason.* Translated by Aaron Bunch in collaboration with Axel Gelfert and Riccardo Pozzo. London: Bloomsbury.

Mellin, G.S.A. 1799. *Encyclopädisches Wörterbuch der Kritischen Philosophie*, Vol. 2, Part 2. Jena and Leipzig: F. Frommann.

Mendelssohn, Moses. 1771. *Philosophische Schriften. Zweiter Teil.* Berlin: Christian Friedrich Voß.

Mendelssohn, Moses. 1997. *Philosophical Writings.* Translated by Daniel O. Dahlstrom. Cambridge: Cambridge University Press.

Merritt, Melissa McBay. 2009. 'Reflection, Enlightenment, and the Significance of Spontaneity in Kant.' *British Journal for the History of Philosophy* 17 (5): 981–1010.

Merritt, Melissa McBay. 2011a. 'Kant's Argument for the Apperception Principle.' *European Journal of Philosophy* 19 (1): 59–84.

Merritt, Melissa McBay. 2011b. 'Kant on Enlightened Moral Pedagogy.' *Southern Journal of Philosophy* 49 (3): 227–53.

Merritt, Melissa McBay. 2015. 'Varieties of Reflection in Kant's Logic.' *British Journal for the History of Philosophy* 23 (3): 478–501.

Merritt, Melissa McBay. 2017a. 'Practical Reason and Respect for Persons.' *Kantian Review* 22: 53–79.

Merritt, Melissa McBay. 2017b. 'Respect, Love, and Individuals: Murdoch as a Guide to Kantian Ethics.' *European Journal of Philosophy*. DOI: 10.1111/ejop.12280.

Merritt, Melissa McBay. 2017c. 'Sublimity and Joy: Kant on the Aesthetic Constitution of Virtue.' In *The Palgrave Kant Handbook*, edited by Matthew C. Altman, 447–67. London: Palgrave Macmillan.

Merritt, Melissa McBay. Forthcoming. 'Mendelssohn and Kant on Virtue as a Skill.' In *Routledge Handbook of Skill and Expertise*, edited by Ellen Fridland and Carlotta Pavese. Abingdon: Routledge.

Merritt, Melissa and Markos Valaris. 2017. 'Attention and Synthesis in Kant's Conception of Experience.' *Philosophical Quarterly* 67 (268): 571–92.

Mikelsen, Kjartan Koch. 2010. 'Testimony and Kant's Idea of Public Reason.' *Res Publica* 16 (1): 23–40.

Mikkelsen, Jon M., ed. and trans. 2013. *Kant and the Concept of Race: Late Eighteenth Century Writings*. Albany, NY: State University of New York Press.

Mole, Christopher. 2011. *Attention is Cognitive Unison: An Essay in Philosophical Psychology*. New York, NY: Oxford University Press.

Mole, Christopher, Declan Smithies and Wayne Wu, eds. 2011. *Attention: Philosophical and Psychological Essays*. New York, NY: Oxford University Press.

Montero, Barbara. 2013. 'A Dancer Reflects.' In *Mind, Reason, and Being-in-the-World: The McDowell-Dreyfus Debate*, edited by Joseph K. Schear, 303–19. Abingdon: Routledge.

Montmarquet, James. 1987. 'Epistemic Virtue.' *Mind* 96 (384): 482–97.

Montmarquet, James. 1993. *Epistemic Virtue and Doxastic Responsibility*. Lanham, MD: Rowman and Littlefield.

Mudd, Sasha. 2016. 'Rethinking the Priority of Practical Reason in Kant.' *European Journal of Philosophy* 24 (1): 78–102.

Munzel, G. Felicitas. 1999. *Kant's Conception of Moral Character*. Chicago, IL and London: University of Chicago Press.

Murdoch, Iris. 1971. *The Sovereignty of Good*. Abingdon: Routledge.

Naragon, Steve. 2006. 'Kant in the Classroom: Materials to Aid the Study of Kant's Lectures.' Available from www.manchester.edu/kant/ [accessed 7 December 2017].

O'Neill, Onora. 1989. *Constructions of Reason: Explorations of Kant's Practical Philosophy*. Cambridge: Cambridge University Press.

O'Neill, Onora. 1996. *Towards Justice and Virtue: A Constructive Account of Practical Reasoning*. Cambridge: Cambridge University Press.

O'Neill, Onora. 1998. 'Kant's Virtues.' In *How Should One Live?*, edited by Roger Crisp, 77–97. Oxford: Oxford University Press.

Pozzo, Riccardo. 2005. 'Prejudices and Horizons: G.F. Meier's *Vernunftlehre* and Its Relation to Kant.' *Journal of the History of Philosophy* 43 (2): 185–202.

Roberts, Robert C. and W. Jay Wood. 2007. *Intellectual Virtues: An Essay in Regulative Epistemology*. Oxford: Oxford University Press.

Roessler, Johannes. 2011. 'Perceptual Attention and the Space of Reasons.' In *Attention: Philosophical and Psychological Essays*, edited by Christopher Mole, Declan Smithies and Wayne Wu, 274–91. New York, NY: Oxford University Press.

Sandel, Adam Adatto. 2014. *The Place of Prejudice: A Case for Reasoning Within the World*. Cambridge, MA: Harvard University Press.

Schear, Joseph K., ed. 2013. *Mind, Reason, and Being-in-the-World: The McDowell-Dreyfus Debate*. Abingdon and New York, NY: Routledge.

Schmidt, James, ed. 1996. *What is Enlightenment?: Eighteenth-Century Answers and Twentieth-Century Questions*. Berkeley, CA: University of California Press.

Schneiders, Werner. 1983. *Aufklärung und Vorurteilskritik: Studien zur Geschichte der Vorurteilstheorie*. Stuttgart-Bad Cannstatt: frommann-holzboog.

Sherman, Nancy. 1997. *Making a Necessity of Virtue: Aristotle and Kant on Virtue*. Cambridge: Cambridge University Press.

Smit, Houston. 1999. 'The Role of Reflection in Kant's *Critique of Pure Reason*.' *Pacific Philosophical Quarterly* 80 (2): 203–23.

Sosa, Ernest. 1991. *Knowledge and Perspective: Selected Essays in Epistemology*. Cambridge: Cambridge University Press.

Sosa, Ernest. 2015. *Judgment and Agency*. New York, NY: Oxford University Press.

Stevenson, Leslie. 2011. 'Freedom of Judgment in Descartes, Spinoza, Hume, and Kant.' In *Inspirations from Kant: Essays*, 95–117. New York, NY: Oxford University Press.

Sticker, Martin. 2015. 'The Moral-Psychology of the Common Agent – A Reply to Ido Geiger.' *British Journal for the History of Philosophy* 25 (5): 976–89.

Strawson, Galen. 2003. 'Mental Ballistics *or* the Involuntariness of Spontaneity.' *Proceedings of the Aristotelian Society* 103 (3): 227–56.

Sussman, David. 2005. 'Perversity of the Heart.' *The Philosophical Review* 114 (2): 153–77.

Tolley, Clinton. 2006. 'Kant on the Nature of Logical Laws.' *Philosophical Topics* 34 (1/2): 371–407.

Tolley, Clinton. 2012. 'The Generality of Kant's Transcendental Logic.' *Journal of the History of Philosophy* 50 (3): 417–46.

Valaris, Markos. 2008. 'Inner Sense, Self-Affection, and Temporal Consciousness in Kant's *Critique of Pure Reason*.' *Philosophers' Imprint* 8 (4): 1–18.

Waterlow, Sarah. 1982. *Nature, Change, and Agency in Aristotle's Physics: A Philosophical Study*. Oxford and New York, NY: Oxford University Press.

Watkins, Eric, ed. and trans. 2009. *Kant's Critique of Pure Reason: Background Source Materials*. Cambridge: Cambridge University Press.

Waxman, Wayne. 1991. *Kant's Model of the Mind*. New York, NY: Oxford University Press.

Williams, Bernard. 1973. 'Ethical Consistency.' In *Problems of the Self: Philosophical Papers 1956–1972*, 166–86. Cambridge: Cambridge University Press.

Williams, Bernard. 1981. 'Utilitarianism and Moral Self-Indulgence.' In *Moral Luck: Philosophical Papers 1973–1980*, 40–53. Cambridge: Cambridge University Press.

Wood, Allen. 2003. 'Kant and the Problem of Human Nature.' In *Essays on Kant's Anthropology*, edited by Brian Jacobs and Patrick Kain, 38–59. Cambridge: Cambridge University Press.

Wood, Allen. 2008. *Kantian Ethics*. Cambridge: Cambridge University Press.

Young, J. Michael. 1992. 'Translator's Introduction.' In *Immanuel Kant: Lectures on Logic*, translated and edited by J. Michael Young, xv–xxxii. Cambridge: Cambridge University Press.

Zangwill, Nick. 2012. 'Rationality and Moral Realism.' *Ratio* 25 (3): 345–64.

Zagzebski, Linda. 1996. *Virtues of the Mind: An Inquiry into the Nature of Virtue and the Ethical Foundations of Knowledge*. Cambridge: Cambridge University Press.

Zagzebski, Linda. 2012. *Epistemic Authority: A Theory of Trust, Authority, and Autonomy in Belief*. New York, NY: Oxford University Press.

Index

abstraction. *See also* attention
  and attention, 84–5, 92
  distinguished from distraction, 84
affect (*Affect*), 20, 154
  as a mode of reflective failure, 21, 38, 46
  distinguished from passion (*Leidenschaft*),
    20–1
affection, sensible, 92, 93, 98
agency
  cognitive, 10, 30, 44, 48, 72, 77, 81, 82, 86, 91,
    94, 100, 106, 107
  relation between moral and cognitive, 120
Annas, Julia, 129, 174
Anthropology from a Pragmatic Point of View, 19,
  27, 34–5, 39, 55, 73–4, 82, 131–6, 141,
  165
apperception, 15, 48, 99
  pure, 27, 105, 106
Aristotle, 6, 31, 101, 126
attention, 82, 83–4, 86–9, 156
  and reflection, 107
  Anthropology account, 84–5, 91–4, 95–8
  as a topic for applied logic, 91
  as self-affection, 93, 199
  requisite for experience, 82, 95, 99

Brewer, Talbot, 4, 159–62, 172–3

categorical imperative, 152
  Formula of Universal Law, 119
character, 54, 128, 131–6
  cognitive, 139. *See also* virtue, cognitive
Chignell, Andrew, 3, 157
cogito (Kantian), 15, 16, 48, 94, 105
Cohen, Alix, 119–20
communicability, 74
  and the second maxim of healthy
    understanding, 56, 57, 70, 72
communication, 74, 75, 90, 108
comparison, 25, 34, 35, 46, 47, 71
  distinguished from reflection, 35, 36

conscience, 193, 197, 198–200
consistency
  and reflection, 37, 42–3, 45–6
  and the third maxim of healthy
    understanding, 71
contentment (*Zufriedenheit, Selbstzufriedenheit*),
  199
Critique of Practical Reason, 115, 116, 139
Critique of Pure Reason, 22, 90, 115, 117, 142–3
  Amphiboly of the Concepts of Reflection, 29,
    30, 44, 69
  Analytic of Concepts, 102–3
  Analytic of Principles, 60, 63
  Transcendental Deduction, 93, 106
Critique of the Power of Judgment, 55, 73, 117, 123,
  144

Denkungsart ('way of thinking'), 54, 56, 69, 77,
  131, 132, 135
  epistemic, 139–44
Descartes, René, 103
discrimination (*Scharfsinnigkeit*), 139–44
distraction (*Zerstreuung*), 82, 85
Driver, Julia, 128, 129

egoism
  logical. *See* prejudices of logical egoism
Elizondo, E. Sonny, 118, 119, 121
Engstrom, Stephen, 118
enlightenment (*Aufklärung*), 1, 56, 105, 107, 110,
  150
enthusiasm
  Schwärmerei vs *Enthusiasmus*, 68
experience, 103
  as empirical cognition, 82, 92

Frierson, Patrick, 19, 26, 30, 38

Garve, Christian, 67
good, concept of, 139
Grenberg, Jeanine, 5, 6

217

bye!

Richard